Bernard Pyne Grenfell, J. P. Mahaffy, King of Egypt Ptolemy II
Philadelphus

Revenue Laws of Ptolemy Philadelphus

Bernard Pyne Grenfell, J. P. Mahaffy, King of Egypt Ptolemy II Philadelphus

Revenue Laws of Ptolemy Philadelphus

ISBN/EAN: 9783337187101

Printed in Europe, USA, Canada, Australia, Japan

Cover: Foto ©Suzi / pixelio.de

More available books at **www.hansebooks.com**

REVENUE LAWS

OF

PTOLEMY PHILADELPHUS

*EDITED FROM A GREEK PAPYRUS IN THE BODLEIAN LIBRARY, WITH
A TRANSLATION, COMMENTARY, AND APPENDICES*

BY

B. P. GRENFELL, M.A.

FELLOW OF QUEEN'S COLLEGE, OXFORD; CRAVEN FELLOW

AND AN INTRODUCTION

BY THE

REV. J. P. MAHAFFY, D.D., Hon. D.C.L.

FELLOW OF TRINITY COLLEGE, DUBLIN
HONORARY FELLOW OF QUEEN'S COLLEGE, OXFORD

WITH THIRTEEN PLATES

Oxford

AT THE CLARENDON PRESS

1896

London

HENRY FROWDE

Oxford University Press Warehouse
Amen Corner, E.C.

New York

MACMILLAN & CO., 66 FIFTH AVENUE

TO

W. M. FLINDERS PETRIE

PREFACE.

THE Revenue Papyrus consists of two rolls, of which the first containing columns 1–72 was obtained by Prof. Flinders Petrie in the winter of 1893-4; the second, containing the other columns and originally perhaps wrapped round the first roll, if not actually forming a part of it, was obtained by myself in the winter of 1894–5.

The first roll measures 44 feet long; the second, of which only fragments exist, must at one time have measured not less than 15 feet. The height of the papyrus cannot, owing to its fragmentary condition, be precisely determined, but was in the case of columns 59–72 about 9½ inches, in that of the rest 3½ inches more. The papyrus is thus by far the largest Greek papyrus known, and as it is in several places dated 'in the twenty-seventh year' of Philadelphus, or 259/8 B.C., it is also nearly the oldest.

Both the external and the internal evidence point to its *provenance* having been the Fayoum, a remarkable fact, since the countless Greek papyri which have been found in that province have, with the exception of the Gurob papyri and a few others, all belonged to a much later date.

The papyrus is written by a number of scribes, but to

determine exactly how many is a difficult problem. I think that I can distinguish twelve, in addition to one or more correctors. The choice of the columns to be reproduced in facsimile has been made with the view of exhibiting both the variety of the hand-writings and those columns of which the contents are most important.

With regard to the text I have endeavoured to present as faithful a transcription of the original as is convenient to modern readers. I have therefore divided the words, and caused the initial letters of the proper names and the headings of sections written in large spaced letters to be printed in capitals. But in other respects the text is printed just as it is in the original. Blunders or mistakes in spelling are left uncorrected, criticism being reserved for the commentary; and I have not thought it worth while to disfigure the pages by the constant insertion of *sic*. Any blunder in the text which is liable to misconception is explained in the Commentary, as are the few abbreviations and symbols which occur. Nor have I inserted stops, breathings or accents, which, in publishing a papyrus of such antiquity, seem to me a needless anachronism. There is the less reason for inserting them in the present case, since in places which are ambiguous the reader can refer to the translation, where he will find the construction which I propose. The division-marks in the original between lines mark the beginning of new sections, and where a new section begins in the middle of a line, as occasionally happens, the division-mark is between that line and the one following.

Square brackets [ ] indicate that there is a lacuna in the papyrus, and the number of dots enclosed by the brackets signifies the approximate number of letters lost, judging by the analogy of the average number of letters which occupy the same space in the preceding and following lines. Of course certainty must decrease in proportion to the length of the lacuna, and where the ends of lines are lost, a guess—more or less probable, as it is based on the ends of lines preserved above or below, or merely on general considerations from the requirements of the sense or the average length of lines in the column—is all that is possible. Moreover letters, of course, vary considerably in size, e. g. there is hardly any scribe in the papyrus who does not occupy as much space with a τ as with οις. Nevertheless, in those cases where I have supposed the lacuna to be not greater than six or seven letters, not being the end of a line, I am ready to deny the admissibility of emendations which are clearly inconsistent with the average number of letters of normal size being what I have suggested. I have ventured to insist somewhat strongly on this point, partly because a number of emendations can. very easily be made by ignoring the dots, and partly because when a column is broken in two, or when fragments are detached from the rest of a column, as e. g. frequently happens in the first twenty-three columns, it may at first sight seem impossible to fix the number of letters lost with even the approximate certainty which is all that I wish to claim. But in most cases this is not so. When a column is broken in half, the holes and breaks which occur at regular intervals in the folds of the papyrus enable us to calculate to $\frac{1}{10}$ inch, if necessary, the position of the two halves, while as the detached fragments for the most part fell away from the rest in lumps containing several thicknesses, the determination of any one of these layers is therefore sufficient to fix precisely the position of all the others in the same series. That the position of every fragment is certain I do not wish to maintain, but I would ask my readers

to believe that both Prof. Petrie and I have spent much
time in fixing the places of the fragments, that the positions
depend for the most part on careful measurements, and that
where there was neither external nor internal evidence sufficient
to fix the position of a fragment with a near approach to
certainty, the doubt has been recorded in the notes, or no
attempt has been made to decide the exact relation of the
separate parts. Thus in columns 79–107, I have left undetermined the amount lost between the two halves into which
nearly every column is divided, although the approximate
position of nearly all the fragments making up those columns
is certain.

Dots outside square brackets indicate letters which, either
through the dark colour of the papyrus or through the oblitera-
tion of the writing, we have been unable to decipher.

Dots underneath letters signify that the reading of the
letters is doubtful, in nearly all cases owing to the mutilation
of the papyrus. But where a letter is for the most part broken
away, and yet the context makes it certain what the letter was,
wishing not to create apparent difficulties where none really
exist, I have generally printed the mutilated letter either
without a dot or inside the square bracket, and have reserved
the dots underneath letters for cases where there is a real
doubt.

Round brackets ( ) represent similar brackets in the original,
which mean that the part enclosed was to be omitted. Angular
brackets 〈 〉 mean that the letters enclosed have been erased
in the papyrus. Corrections in the original are reproduced
as faithfully as possible, the smaller type implying that the
correction was made not by the scribe himself, but by another
writer. This distinction is of considerable importance, espe-

cially in columns 38–56, where the reader will easily be able to differentiate mere corrections of blunders by the scribes themselves from the changes introduced by the διορθωτής.

The excellence of the facsimiles can hardly perhaps be appreciated to the full by any one who has not the original before him, and therefore cannot realize the difficulties with which the photographers of the Clarendon Press have had to contend. Most of the papyrus is written in large clear hands which are easy to read, and of which the facsimile is almost, or even quite, as clear as the original. But the papyrus is in many parts stained a very dark brown, sometimes almost black, and in many parts the surface of it has scaled off; and these parts, although by holding the papyrus in different lights they are generally decipherable with certainty, must of necessity be less clear in the facsimile than in the original. Nevertheless that the facsimiles are, on the whole, extremely successful will, I am sure, be admitted.

As has been implied in the foregoing remarks, there are not many passages where there is much doubt about the reading of the papyrus, when the writing is there. There are, however, a few passages. which have resisted our combined efforts, but of which the correct reading can be verified as soon as it is suggested. On the other hand, the great difficulty throughout has been to fill up the lacunae. Here it will not be out of place to explain the principles on which I have adopted or rejected conjectural readings. In printing a reconstructed text of a papyrus so mutilated as the present one, two courses were possible. One would have been to carry conjectural emendations to the furthest point, and to have stated the precise grounds on which each one was made. The other course was to draw a sharp distinction between conjectures which were based on parallel passages in the papyrus itself or elsewhere, and conjectures which, though often probable enough in themselves, were not so based, and while admitting the first class into the text, to reserve the second for the Commentary. It is the latter course, not the first, which I have adopted. And if it be a matter of regret to some that in so many places gaps have been left, which could with more or less probability have been easily filled up, the answer is this, that the place of many fragments was not found until after our text had almost reached its present condition, and that we have therefore been able to some extent to test the value of our conjectures. The result showed that where our conjectures had been based on a parallel passage in the papyrus itself, they were nearly always right, and where they had been based on a parallel passage in another papyrus, they were generally right, but that where they were based on the grounds of *a priori* probability, they were generally wrong. I have therefore not admitted into the text any conjectures which are not based on a parallel passage either in the papyrus itself or in papyri of the same period and dealing with the same subjects, except in cases where the conjecture was so obviously right that it required no confirmation, and in a few other cases, where some *a priori* conjecture was necessary in order to attach any meaning to the passage. Where a conjecture is based on a parallel passage in the papyrus itself, from considerations of space I have not as a rule stated the grounds in the Commentary, unless there was some difficulty, as the reader who wishes to verify the conjecture can do so by referring to the Index. But where a conjecture is based on a parallel passage in another papyrus, or where it is only based on *a priori* grounds, the fact is recorded in the Commentary, in which will also be found a number of conjectures not admitted into the text. In addition, more or less obvious conjectures, which for various reasons will not suit, are occasionally recorded.

A word of explanation is necessary with regard to the mounting of the papyrus, and especially of these columns which are facsimiled. The unrolling and mounting of the first roll was undertaken by Prof. Petrie himself, and the skill which he has shown in mounting so mutilated a papyrus of which the texture is excessively fine and brittle, is beyond all praise. It was clearly impossible for him to accurately fix the position of fragments which became loose as soon as the papyrus was opened, and he rightly preferred to paste the fragments down in places which were approximately correct, than to run the risk of their being lost before their precise position could be fixed. The result of this was that, especially in the earlier and most mutilated part, a number of pieces were more or less misplaced, though the correct position of all but a very few has now been determined, and in many cases marked in pencil on the papyrus. Without claiming any infallibility, I would therefore ask my readers when they notice, as they frequently will, apparent inconsistencies both in readings and in spacings between the printed text and the original, to believe that the arrangement or reading in the text has not been adopted without good reason. In one or two places I noticed, on reading through the papyrus since my return to England, that a few letters had disappeared, but fortunately the loss was of practically no consequence.

My last and most pleasant duty is to express my sincerest thanks to the many friends who have aided me in the present work, and particularly to those distinguished specialists in the history and palaeography of this period, with whom the interest in a common study has made me privileged to become acquainted.

The debt which lovers of antiquity owe to Prof. FLINDERS PETRIE for the recovery and preservation of the first roll, which alone gives to the scanty fragments of the second what value they possess, has already been stated. But it is my duty in particular to thank him for placing the work of publication in my hands, and for his frequent help in the difficult matter of arranging the detached fragments in their correct places.

With Prof. MAHAFFY I have discussed on frequent occasions all the problems both of reading and interpretation. We have read the original together, and the Translation and Commentary have been completely revised by him. Many both of the readings in the text and of the explanations are his, and whatever merits this book may possess are in the main due to the fact that I have had the constant help and criticism of a scholar whose knowledge of both the history and the papyri of this period is equalled by his brilliancy in overcoming difficulties. On nearly all points we are agreed, but as there are a few on which I have ventured to differ from him, the responsibility for error lies only with the writer of each section.

Prof. G. LUMBROSO I visited at Rome in September 1894, when our edition had not nearly reached even its present degree of completeness, and he most kindly consented to go through the whole text with me, and to him I owe a large number of most valuable criticisms and suggestions.

Recently in August 1895, in our final consultation over the text we have had the great benefit of Prof. U. WILCKEN's aid. Several of the remaining difficulties were solved by him, and he has also made many admirable suggestions and criticisms. Besides these I have specially to thank him for most generously placing at my disposal the materials of his two forthcoming great works, the Corpus of Greek ostraca and the Corpus of Ptolemaic papyri. These have proved of inestimable service in several places, especially in reaching that solution of the coinage questions which I have proposed in Appendix III.

Professor E. P. WRIGHT of Dublin has given me valuable help on special points connected with botany, and Prof. P. GARDNER has aided me on special points of numismatics. Though he is not in the least responsible for any errors in Appendix III, without his aid I should not have ventured— with a boldness of which I am fully conscious—an excursion into the difficult and technical field of Ptolemaic numismatics.

My friend and partner in the Craven Fellowship, Mr. A. S. HUNT, has lightened for me considerably the burden of revising the proofs, and while doing so has made several good suggestions.

The typography of the Clarendon Press requires no commendation; but I cannot conclude without expressing my thanks to the Delegates for publishing this book, and to the Controller and staff of that institution for the care which they have spent both in preparing the facsimiles and in printing a text so difficult as the present.

Finally, some consideration will, I hope, be shown for the shortcomings of this volume on account of the speed with which it has been produced. Neither Prof. Mahaffy nor I saw the papyrus until June 1894, and the work of publication had to be suspended from November 1894–April 1895 owing to my enforced absence in Egypt, a delay which however has amply justified itself by the recovery during the winter of the second roll. It is possible that a longer period of deliberation would have resulted in fewer difficulties in the text and greater completeness in the explanations. But I have not wished to violate the traditional example which this country has set to the rest of Europe, of placing its latest discoveries before the world with the utmost possible despatch.

Meanwhile, in the words of one of my predecessors in this field of research, *Iudicent doctiores, et si quid probabilius habuerint, proferant.*

B. P. GRENFELL.

Queen's College,
October 5, 1895.

CONTENTS

INTRODUCTION
TO THE REVENUE PAPYRUS.

————

§ 1. GENERAL DESCRIPTION.

SINCE the discovery of the collection now known as Mr. Petrie's papyri, of which the mummy cases of the Gurob cemetery were mainly composed, no greater surprise has come upon the students of Ptolemaic Egyptology than the acquisition, by the same discoverer, of another great document belonging to the third century B.C. In the year 1894 Mr. Petrie bought from a dealer in Cairo a roll which is actually 44 feet long. There was no clear evidence to be had concerning its *provenance*, but the probability that it came from the Fayoum was raised to certainty by Mr. Grenfell in 1895, since he acquired, not only at Cairo, but in the Fayoum, further very important fragments so similar in texture, handwriting, and subject, as to make it clear that they belonged to the same roll or set of rolls. Most unfortunately, Mr. Petrie's great roll had been broken near the top, probably by a stroke of the spade, at the moment of its discovery, from some fellah digging for *sebach* or for antiquities, and moreover the whole roll was in the most delicate and brittle condition. It could not be opened with safety without pasting down each fragment as it was detached from the rest, and all the skill and patience of Mr. Petrie were required to carry out so tedious an

c

operation. Even after this was done, many replacements and rearrangements were necessary, which could only be made by Mr. Grenfell after he had become perfectly intimate with the subject and style of the document. To him is due the first transcription of the document; since that time we have constantly discussed the difficulties, re-examined the original on every doubtful passage, and solved many of the problems which at first resisted his efforts. In September, 1894, Mr. Grenfell went to Rome, and consulted Prof. G. Lumbroso on several unsettled points. In our final conference over remaining difficulties, we have had the advantage of the advice, the corroboration, and in a few passages the corrections of Prof. Wilcken, who spent a week with us (August, 1895) in Oxford, and examined with us these passages with constant reference to the original, which is now one of the treasures of the Bodleian Library. We have thus had the advantage of the criticism of the two foremost specialists on Ptolemaic papyri in Europe.

As regards the present state of the text, it will readily be understood that nothing could save for us the outer parts of the roll, which had been exposed to wear and handling. The middle part of all the earlier columns was gone. It was only as the interior was reached that we found any large proportion of the writing preserved.

Fortunately the whole document was written on the *recto* side of the papyrus, with the exception of two short notes added by a corrector and specially referred to by the curious direction ΕΞΩ ΟΡΑ, *look outside*, at the point of the text (cols. 41, 43) to which each of them belongs. It was accordingly necessary to set up these columns only between panes of glass; the rest has been laid upon sheets of paper and framed. The roll as originally opened contained 72 columns of text, but the fragments since acquired, which apparently belong to a sister roll wrapped round it, bring up the total number of columns, according to Mr. Grenfell's estimate, to 107, with some undetermined fragments. I must refer the reader to his translation and commentary for the details which justify our general conclusions, and for a discussion of the many particular problems raised by this great new document. The only text which evidently bears a close analogy to it is the well-known Papyrus 62 of the Louvre collection[1]. This, as it both illustrates and is illustrated by the present documents, has been re-examined in Paris, collated, and printed by Mr. Grenfell in a more accurate form in this volume. He has also added some unpublished fragments of the Petrie papyri on cognate subjects.

§ 2. AGE OF THE DOCUMENT.

The dates extant in the document are not only of the greatest importance in fixing its precise age, but also because they suggest some important rectifications of the hitherto accepted facts of Ptolemaic history, and of the theories adopted to explain them. It was plain at first sight, to any reader of the Petrie papyri, that the various hands in the new document were all of the third century B.C. The occurrence of the year 27 in several places made it further certain that it must have been issued during the reign of the first or the second Ptolemy, for of the succeeding kings, no successor till the sixth (known as Ptolemy VII, Philometor) attained to so many years' sovranty.

The opening formula (cf. Plate I) might very well have misled us into attributing the ordinance to the first Ptolemy; for although such a formula as it now represents has never yet occurred, it could hardly, taken as it stands, signify any one else.

---

[1] Cf. *Les pap. grecs du Musée du Louvre*, Paris, 1866.

Nevertheless we were not for a moment misled by this snare. The second date (col. 24), which is also reproduced in our first plate, though very much mutilated, was clearly parallel to that occurring once in the Petrie papyri, and found also in demotic contracts; it was a formula used by the second Ptolemy, after he had associated his son (afterwards Euergetes I) in the royalty. I need not now refer to the fanciful theory of Revillout, which is wholly inconsistent with this, but which has now been so completely refuted that he himself has probably abandoned it. So far then we find ourselves on firm ground, and the date on cols. 24 and 38 is equivalent to 259–8 B.C., the twenty-seventh year of Ptolemy usually called Philadelphus [1].

But why does the first column contain a new and strange formula? The Petrie papyri show us in the king's later years (33, 36) a well-known title: ΒΑΣΙΛΕΥΟΝΤΟΣ ΠΤΟΛΕΜΑΙΟΥ ΤΟΥ ΠΤΟΛΕΜΑΙΟΥ ΣΩΤΗΡΟΣ, and this I attempted to find here, by assuming that the second ΠΤΟΛΕΜΑΙΟΥ had been lost between the scraps containing ΤΟΥ and ΣΩΤΗΡΟΣ. To this solution Mr. Grenfell was from the first opposed, as he urged that the two scraps fitted perfectly together. But I was not satisfied till Mr. Grenfell, arguing that the word ΣΩΤΗΡΟΣ had been thrust in at the end of a full line, and that even so

---

[1] As is now well known, we have no evidence that he was so called during his life, though his wife was. The king and queen jointly are called ΘΕΟΙ ΑΔΕΛΦΟΙ. Strangely enough, we have as yet found no epithet, such as Soter, by which he was recognized, till at least a century later, when he is distinguished by historians, &c. for convenience sake, by his wife's title. Thus in Manetho's letter dedicating the history to the second Ptolemy, of which Syncellus quotes the opening βασ. Πτολ. Φιλαδελφῷ σεβαστῷ κ.τ.λ. ἔρρωσό μοι βασ. φίλτατε, it was long since observed that σεβαστῷ was an evidence of spuriousness. We now know that Φιλαδελφῷ is so also, and lastly that ἔρρωσο would be an unpardonable piece of rudeness, Manetho being bound to say εὐτύχει.

there was no room therein for another ΠΤΟΛΕΜΑΙΟΥ, hit upon the true solution. He suggested that the erasures immediately under the first line, as well as the crowded and smaller characters of the word CΩΤΗΡΟC, pointed to a correction of the date. Even so, the corrector must have blundered, for he should have left ΠΤΟΛΕΜΑΙΟΥ in the second line, and there added CΩΤΗΡΟC. But on re-examining the original according to this theory, I found the remains of the old formula still faintly visible in the second line, and this was corroborated by Mr. Grenfell and Professor Wilcken. What happened was then briefly this. The corrector desired to replace the older formula by the later; but he erased too much, and then added his new word in the wrong place. Though the document was officially corrected, as is stated twice over, the corrector was fortunately guilty of the further negligence of leaving the old formula undisturbed on col. 24, thus enabling us to solve the difficulty.

There remains the highly interesting question : why should the second Ptolemy have not only changed the formula of his dates in his twenty-seventh year, but also have removed the name of his son, the crown prince, now of age and the accepted heir, to substitute for it the title of his deified father? Demotic scholars and numismatists are ready with an answer on the last point. They maintain that the first Ptolemy was not formally deified till long after his death. It is shown on apparently good evidence by Revillout and Poole that this deification took place in the twenty-fifth year of the reign [1]. Even then the *gods Soteres* were not introduced into the list of deified kings, beginning with Alexander, whose priest was eponymous magistrate at Alexandria. But as the cities of Phoenicia began to coin with the legend ΠΤΟΛΕΜΑΙΟΥ CΩΤΗΡΟC at this time, it

[1] Cf. *Coins of the Ptolemies*, p. xxxv.

is but reasonable to expect that the king would also now style himself Ptolemy, son of Ptolemy Soter.

So far the change is explicable, but how can we account for the extrusion of his son, now for some years appearing in the royal formula ? For this Krall and Wilcken, with others, have adopted the hypothesis of an unknown son of Queen Arsinoe II, born after her marriage with this Ptolemy, and associated by her influence in the royalty, to the exclusion of the elder crown prince, her stepson[1]. This supposed youth is further assumed to have died when he was nearly grown up, and so to have given occasion for a change of the formula. This complicated series of assumptions, which has been consistently opposed by Wiedemann, is highly improbable in itself, and contradicted by good evidence. In the first place it were passing strange that all our historical authorities should keep silence on such a matter. The crimes of Arsinoe in her earlier life are well known, and had she indeed compelled Philadelphus to oust his elder children for a new heir, not only would she have murdered them if she could, but we should certainly have heard of this family feud. The very well informed scholiast on Theocritus' 17th Idyll (l. 128) even states directly the contrary. He says that Arsinoe being childless—ἄτεκνος, her elder children had been murdered, and she had none by Philadelphus—adopted her step-children, and more especially Euergetes, who is called in all the formulae of his own dates, the son of Ptolemy and [of this] Arsinoe, ΘΕΩΝ ΑΔΕΛΦΩΝ. This then is the young prince who appears with his parents on the steles of Pithom and of Mendes[2], nor is

---

[1] Krall, *Sitzungsber. of Vienna Acad. for* 1884, pp. 362 sqq.; Wilcken, art. ARSINOE in Paully-Wissowa's *Encyclop.* ii. p. 1286; Ehrlich, *De Callim. Hymnis Quaest. Chronol.* (Breslau, 1894), p. 56.

[2] Wilcken was the first to call attention to these representations, as well as to

there any positive evidence for the conjecture of Wilcken, that this figure points to the newly assumed son of Arsinoe II. The lady must have been forty years old when she became Queen of Egypt, so that a new child would have been remarkable, and would from this very circumstance have excited unusual notice. His assumption into the succession would moreover not have been delayed till the king's nineteenth year, from which Revillout has found the first mention of an associated prince, and from this time on we have mention of him in years 21, 22, and 24, not to speak of the present case in 27. These facts lead us to infer that though recognized as prince royal in earlier Egyptian documents, such as the steles to which Wilcken has first called attention, Euergetes was not formally associated in the sovranty till he had reached the age of puberty, when Arsinoe, his stepmother, was growing old, and the king's health was failing.

The question, however, remains more strange, more pressing than ever—why was the crown prince's name removed from the formula starting from the year 27 (B.C. 259-8) of his father's reign? After much perplexity, I have found what seems to me the true answer to this question.

We know that the prince had been already betrothed to the infant daughter of King Magas of Cyrene, who died, according to the most probable computation of his fifty years' reign, at this very time. The queen-mother of Cyrene, Apama, who was opposed to the match, promptly sent for Demetrius the Fair, who hurried at once to occupy Cyrene. The whole narrative in Justin, our only and wretched authority, points to

one at Philae (Lepsius, *Denkmäler*, iv. 6 a), where Isis is represented suckling the young prince. He infers from the youth of this figure that it must be an infant son of Arsinoe II. But as the date of the relief is not given, it may have been set up just after her adoption of the future Euergetes, and while he was but a child.

a most rapid course of events [1]. But Demetrius commenced an intrigue with Apama, instead of waiting for the time when he could marry her heiress-daughter, Berenike, and was put to death with the knowledge, though not at the instigation of the child-princess. Thereupon, by common consent, Euergetes is called to Cyrene, and the marriage with Berenike follows, possibly as soon as the princess was of age, but in any case some years later. It has sometimes been assumed, perhaps on the suggestion of a blunder in Porphyry's fragment, which confuses this Demetrius with Demetrius II, King of Macedonia, that the usurpation of the intruder at Cyrene lasted for some years [2]. There is no evidence for this. Nay, the words of Justin imply that the whole affair only occupied a few months. If so, and if Euergetes was called by the people of Cyrene to assume the government as prince consort expectant, he doubtless assumed a title there inconsistent with his associated rank in Egypt. The Cyrenaeans would have been offended that the second in command of Egypt should assume their sovranty; in any case it would have been a direct absorption of the royalty of Cyrene into the

---

[1] Justin xxvi. 111 'Per idem tempus rex Cyrenarum Magas decedit, qui ante infirmitatem Beronicem, unicam filiam, ad finienda cum Ptolomeo fratre certamina filio eius desponderat. Sed post mortem regis mater virginis Arsinoe [of course Apama], ut invita se contractum matrimonium solveretur, misit qui ad nuptias virginis regnumque Cyrenarum Demetrium, fratrem regis Antigoni, a Macedonia arcesserent, qui et ipse ex filia Ptolomei [Soteris] procreatus est. Sed nec Demetrius moram fecit. Itaque quum secundante vento celeriter Cyrenas advolasset; fiducia pulchritudinis, qua nimis placere socrui coeperat, statim a principio superbus regiae familiae militibusque impotens erat, studiumque placendi a virgine in matrem contulerat. Quae res suspecta primo virgini, dein popularibus militibusque invisa fuit. Itaque versis omnium animis in Ptolomei filium insidiae Demetrio comparantur, cui, cum in lectum socrus concessisset, percussores inmittuntur.'

[2] Porph. *Fr.* 4, § 9 in Müller, *FHG* iii. p. 701.

crown of Egypt, whereas the dynastic rights of the popular
Berenike were to be preserved, so far as possible, intact[1]. Moreover, Euergetes must have been obliged to hurry to Cyrene,
and to remain there in charge of the disturbed and doubtful
throne. It was, I believe, against the habit of these associations
in the sovranty that the associated prince should be sent to
govern a distant province or dependency. Though the old
Pharaohs had called their eldest sons 'prince of Kush,' I cannot
find an instance where the associated crown prince of Egypt was
called prince of Cyrene, of Cyprus, or of Palestine.

My reply then to the question for which an answer is im-
peratively demanded, is simply this: In the year 27, or perhaps
28, of Philadelphus' reign, his son, the crown prince, was called
to an independent control, probably with the title of king, by
the people of Cyrene; owing to which his title as associated
prince of Egypt was abandoned, being probably contrary to
court etiquette, as it certainly would be to the susceptibilities of
the Cyrenaeans[2].

[1] Thus in the inscription of Adule, in which Euergetes enumerates all the
provinces of the empire which he inherited from his father, Cyrene is (no doubt
studiously) omitted.

[2] Strange to say, there is another consideration, overlooked hitherto, which helps
to remove the difficulty occasioned by the delay in Euergetes' marriage till he
became King of Egypt. In most other monarchies a suitable bride is found for
the crown prince as soon as he is of age; in Ptolemaic Egypt I have observed
with surprise that this is against the practice of the court, *though the reigning
Ptolemies marry as early as possible*. Philadelphus, though grown up in 290 B.C.,
does not apparently marry till his assumption of royalty, in the opinion of some
critics, not till his father is dead. Euergetes, though long grown up, seems to have
no wife till his accession. Philopator, succeeding at about the age of twenty-four,
has no wife till some years later. We hear of no wife of Euergetes II till he
succeeds in middle life and marries the widowed queen. So it is (with one
exception) down to the case of Caesarion, who would doubtless have been
married before his early death, but for this curious court tradition. A satisfactory

A few words will suffice concerning the other dates occurring in the papyrus, and appended to those earlier documents, which are cited as standing orders. The royal rescript ordering the transmutation of the EKTH from a privilege of the temples into a gift to the queen is dated in the twenty-third year of the reign. In order to discover the average yearly value, the tax produced

explanation of it I have not yet found. But the following suggestion is worth making upon this new problem. Among the later Ptolemies we hear of a daughter succeeding, because she was the only legitimate one (ἡ μόνη γνησία οἱ τῶν παίδων ἦν, Paus. i. 9, § 2), whereas there were younger children of the same parents who must have been equally entitled ⅃o succeed but for their age. I have often puzzled over this statement. It now seems to me intended to point out that the child in question was the eldest born after her father had succeeded to the throne, and that previous children born of the same mother were regarded as νόθοι when the question of the succession arose. In the corresponding passage of Strabo (xvii. 1, § 11) it is even stated ὧν μία γνησία ἡ πρεσβυτάτη, κ.τ.λ., which, I think, should certainly be emended to ἡ οὐ πρεσβυτάτη, 'who, though not the eldest, was the only legitimate heiress.' The text as it stands seems to me to have no point whatever. If this be so, there were obvious reasons why a crown prince should not marry. All the children begotten before his accession would be technically illegitimate, as not being the offspring of an actual king and queen, and the danger of having such elder children about the court was, of course, very great. Perhaps this explains the (false) declaration of the court poets that Philadelphus was marked out for sovranty while still in his mother's womb. Thus, too, we might find some reason for the apparently tyrannous act of Cleopatra III, widow of Euergetes II, who, when she was compelled by the Alexandrians to associate her eldest son (Lathyrus or Soter II) in the throne, compelled him to divorce his wife and sister Cleopatra, who had already borne him two children, and marry her younger daughter, Selene. These two children disappear from history, as if they had no right to the throne, unless, indeed, Auletes was one of them, and he is always spoken of as *illegitimate*. Without the aid of some hypothesis of this kind we cannot understand the monstrous and absurd facts retailed for us out of all logical connexion by the remaining histories of the Ptolemies. It is not improbable that Ptolemy Apion, who ruled for many years undisputedly over Cyrene, was an elder son of Euergetes II, borne to him by a Cyrenaic or Egyptian princess during his sovranty there, and whom he left behind in control, when he became King of Egypt in 146 b.c.

in the previous years (cols. 36, 37) is to be ascertained. We know from independent sources that the deification of Arsinoe Philadelphus was gradual; that she attained divine honours first at one, then at another of the Egyptian temples. The establishment of a *canephoros* or eponymous priestess in her honour, at Alexandria, which dates as far back as the year 19 of the reign, according to demotic documents, appeared to be the climax or consummation of this gradual apotheosis. We now know that, practically at least, the process was not complete till the king's twenty-third year, when she absorbed one of the great revenues of all the Egyptian gods.

§ 3. Subjects treated in the Document.

Having determined the date we approach the contents of the text. What is the subject? Clearly the taxing of the country. We know from many literary sources that the land of Egypt was in a great measure regarded (even in old Pharaonic days) as the personal property of the sovran[1], and that in no kingdom of the Hellenistic epoch was the Exchequer more carefully attended to, or the income of the king so great. The Ptolemies always appear in the history of those days as commanding enormous wealth. Even queens and princesses have such fortunes that they can raise armies, and carry on wars on their own account. There can only have been two sources of such wealth—commerce and agriculture. For it does not appear that the gold mines of Nubia afforded any considerable portion of the royal revenue; had such been the case, we should have found a much wider use of gold coinage than existed in Ptolemaic Egypt. The largest item in the exchequer was doubtless the revenue derived, not only from the taxing of

[1] Cf. the account of the matter in Genesis xlviii. 18-26.

correction: Gen. xlvii. 18-26

produce, but from its regulation. The Petrie papyri have already made us acquainted with a variety of imposts, such as salt-tax, police-tax, grazing-tax, and even occasional benevolences called *crowns* (the Roman *aurum coronarium*) presented to the king as a gift, but a gift extracted from the population by compulsion.

The present ordinance (putting aside the most mutilated columns and the fragments recently acquired by Mr. Grenfell) is concerned with only two of these sources of revenue, but we may well believe that they were two of the most important: the first is the tax upon vineyards and orchards; the second that upon oil, or rather the revenue from the monopoly exercised in the case of that indispensable article of Egyptian diet. As the revenues both from wine and from oil were farmed out to middlemen, the present Revenue Papyrus is concerned exclusively with the regulation of these contracts with the State. In both cases it is very likely that the Ptolemies merely adopted and regulated the practice of the Pharaohs; nay, in the former, they only extended a policy long since adopted by these kings[1]. There had been a time when the 'Established Church' was so dominant as to secure enormous estates and revenues from the Crown. The inventory of the property of the temples of Amon in the Harris papyrus[2], and the fact that the twentieth dynasty was one of sacerdotal kings, whose first interest was the exaltation of priestly influence, show us plainly enough that the Egyptian corporations of priests,

[1] On this point I feel some hesitation, as the regulations concerning oil (col. 49) seem to imply that the monopoly was an innovation at this very time. Otherwise there could hardly have been private oil-presses recognized as existing, without being contraband.

[2] Cf. A. Erman's *Aegypten*, p. 405 sqq.

like the mediaeval Church in Europe, had gradually absorbed a great part of the property of the State. But the reaction had set in long before the Ptolemies supervened. Successful soldiers who became kings had begun to strip the temples gradually of their estates, and there is not wanting direct evidence of the remonstrances and complaints of the sacerdotal corporations. Every successful usurper began by restoring lost revenues to the priests in order to purchase their powerful support; every established dynasty proceeded to exhibit its security by invading the privileges of this order. Thus we know that the first Ptolemy admitted the claims of the priests to large revenues in the Delta, near the Sebennytic mouth of the river—revenues, too, which they claimed as the gift of a previous usurper[1]. The present papyrus contains a step in the contrary direction; for we know from it that in the twenty-third year of the second Ptolemy the share of one-sixth of the produce of all the vineyards and orchards in Egypt, hitherto given to the gods of Egypt, and apparently delivered by the husbandmen at the nearest temple, was claimed by the queen, in consequence of her deification. The stele of Pithom and that of Mendes commemorate, it is true, vast gifts of money from this king and queen to the priests. Very probably this may have been regarded as a sort of compensation; but the change of the ecclesiastical property from revenues or charges on the land of the country into a yearly grant or *syntaxis* from the Crown must have been felt as a loss of dignity, and probably of wealth. For whenever the Crown fell into pecuniary difficulties, the syntaxis could be diminished or refused[2]. It is very likely that the national insurrections, so

---

[1] Cf. the text translated in my. *Greek Life and Thought*, &c., p. 176 sq.

[2] Thus the Roman Catholic priesthood of Ireland received for their College at Maynooth a yearly *syntaxis* of over £26,000 from the British Government up to

frequent under the later Ptolemies, were aided by priestly discontent at this subordination of their wealth to the Crown. The very command to furnish an inventory of sacred property, such as the king here issues (col. 37. 15–7), must have appeared a gross insult to these proud conservative corporations.

Such however being the case, we may be certain that the bulk of the duties to the local temples were paid not in money, but in kind, and this ancient and once universal form of tax makes the institution of tax-farmers, under a centralized government, almost a necessity. And the State, in contracting with private individuals or with joint stock companies, allows them a certain profit for the cost and trouble of collecting such taxes, and is content to take from them a fixed income. This income in the instance before us was not indeed fixed for more than one or two years, but in every recurring case it was settled by public auction, the State selling the right of collection and sale of the produce paid as tax, or even of money taxes, to the highest bidder. It is easy to see that many precautions were necessary to secure the State against loss. Then as now, dishonesty towards State charges, especially if they be felt oppressive or unjust, is regarded as hardly an offence against morality, or at most as a very venial offence, and so a very careful householder, such as the Egyptian sovran, had need to protect himself. The most obvious policy was to play off each of the parties concerned against the rest. There were three separate interests to afford scope for this diplomacy.

the year 1870, but they were quite content to take fourteen years' purchase of it then in a lump sum, which brought them in only half the yearly amount, in order to attain security in their endowment, and an escape from inquiries in Parliament and by Royal Commissions: they also feel just as much at liberty to abet the national aspirations against the Crown as the Egyptian priesthood did.

First come, naturally, the Government officials in each district, who must not be allowed to have any private pecuniary interests to conflict with their loyalty to the king. Secondly come the contractors who undertake the collection of taxes. They must be rich men, at least men who can find good security to guarantee the State against loss, and such men must on the one hand be induced to come forward by allowing them considerable profits, and hence promoting competition for the contract, whilst on the other they must not be allowed to damage the State by combining to bid low at the auction, or again by extorting from the population more than was due to the State. Thirdly, the taxpayer must be protected from oppression, and also punished for dishonesty to the State, by allowing stringent inquisition into his produce in the latter case, facilities of appeal to an umpire in the former. Such are the general lines of the legislation before us.

§ 4. Division of Subjects into Chapters.

The first chapter or division (A), cols. 1–22, so far as we can understand its mutilated text, contained the regulations governing the relations of the Government officials in each district, particularly of the ΟΙΚΟΝΟΜΟC and his deputy or ΑΝΤΙΓΡΑΦΕΥC, to the men or companies of men who undertook the farming of the revenue. It appears from col. 15 that no such official was allowed to take any such contract, either personally or through his slaves—an obvious precaution which separated at once the official from the tax-farming class. In this chapter the regulations seem to be quite general; no special tax is even once mentioned.

The second chapter (B), contained in cols. 23–37, is far more definite, and contains the orders and regulations for the transmutation of the share (ΑΠΟΜΟΙΡΑ) of one-sixth of the produce of all the vineyards and orchards of Egypt, hitherto paid to gods of Egypt, into a Government tax, payable to the deified queen Arsinoe Philadelphus. The just assessment and collection of this tax must have been very difficult ; for much of it had been paid to the local temples ; the produce of wine is always very variable : the new form of the tax must have been unpopular ; the State is therefore not satisfied with a statement under affidavit from each cultivator, but authorizes the farmer of the tax to watch the vintage, to pry into the profits, and to secure both his own advantage and that of the State. This supervision of the actual gathering of the crop is likely to entail great hardships on the cultivator, for the inspector may not attend when the time of harvest requires the crop to be saved, and may exact bribes from the peasants either for his prompt attendance or for an estimate favourable to themselves [1]. These contingencies are provided for here, as they are not in modern states which levy similar taxes, by permitting the peasants to gather grapes and make wine under protest that it cannot be delayed, and transact the payment of the tax directly with the Government officials. For the details I must refer the reader to the commentary.

Wherever this share of the gods (ΑΠΟΜΟΙΡΑ) occurs, we find coupled together vineyards and orchards (ΠΑΡΑΔΕΙCΟΙ). This is the case both in the Petrie papyri and on the Rosetta stone, as well as in other fragments of that period. All the regulations concerning the making and storing of wine from the ΑΜΠΕΛΩΝΕC are given us explicitly enough. But when we come to inquire what was the produce of the ΠΑΡΑΔΕΙCΟΙ,

---

[1] Such is the case now in Turkey, and is, or was, the case in Greece, when taxes were assessed upon standing crops, before they could be reaped.

and why they were coupled with vineyards in this tax, we come upon a serious difficulty. What is meant by the term, and is our *orchard* a proper equivalent? It was adopted by Xenophon from the Persians, among whom it meant a park with trees, even large enough for a game preserve. It is distinguished not only from a vineyard, but from a garden (ΚΗΠΟϹ) in a document among the Petrie papyri (II. p. 68). Another document in that series contrasts it with a palm-grove (ΦΟΙΝΙΚΩΝ), apparently for taxing purposes. Another specifies a pumpkin-field (ϹΙΚΥΗΡΑΤΟΝ). What then was the produce of a *paradeisos* in a country where very few kinds of fruit-trees grow? There is but one column (29) which deals with ΠΑΡΑΔΕΙϹΟΙ, without closer specification, except that here an estimate of the value is to be made in money, and the sixth paid in money, not in kind. Were it not for this provision, I should be inclined to hold that the crop of the *paradeisoi* which paid the sixth to the gods was no other than grapes. For we know that in such climates it is both grateful and convenient to grow vines as creepers on trees and trellises, and we have in the Petrie papyri (I. xxix.) one distinct mention of an ΑΝΑΔΕΝΔΡΑϹ which is exactly a case in point. As it is by this established that vines were so grown, how is it that there is no mention of the *anadendras* in the present careful legislation concerning grapes and wine? Here again the obvious answer is that such cultivation came under the title of ΠΑΡΑΔΕΙϹΟΙ, and that the fruit of these orchards consisted chiefly, if not wholly, of grapes. It seems to me exceedingly improbable that in a country noted for its very careful and varied agriculture, any number of different products should be confused under the title ΚΑΡΠΟϹ, as in col. 29. 13, without any apparent enumeration. I therefore still incline to the belief that the ΑΠΟΜΟΙΡΑ was a sacred due on wine only, probably coeval with its introduction into Egypt in ancient times, and that, as all the succeeding chapter of our papyrus relates exclusively to oil, so this does to wine. But as I have not been able to persuade either Mr. Grenfell or Prof. Wilcken that this is so, and as they do not feel the difficulty which I have here stated to be of serious weight, I shall not here press the matter further [1].

§ 5. The State Monopoly in Oil.

We now turn to the third part (C) of the papyrus, which concerns exclusively the State monopoly in oil. It was this part of the text, which is in a far better state of preservation than the rest, which led me at first to use the term Monopoly Papyrus for the whole. But seeing that the growing of wine and of orchard produce, treated in the second chapter, was not a monopoly, and that the first chapter is quite general, Mr. Grenfell thought the word too narrow, and proposed to call it the Revenue Papyrus. But this term, now adopted, is really too wide. For so far as we can see, no source of revenue is anywhere discussed in it which is not levied through middlemen, through tax-farmers, and in no case are the officials to deal directly with the peasants, unless the tax-farmer fails to perform his duties. But for its awkwardness, the *tax-farming*, and but for its pedantry, the *Telonic* Papyrus would be the most accurate designation.

The manufacture of wine was only under State control in the same way that our manufacture of beer and spirits is, for in both cases there is no limitation of the amount produced

---

[1] At the close of this Introduction the reader will find an important inscription bearing on this topic discussed. Cf. also Mr. Grenfell's note, pp. 94–6.

or the retail price demanded, but an inquiry into the actual quantity as a basis for taxation ; in both cases the excise takes care to watch and register the amount produced in each locality of manufacture, and so far to pry into private industry.

The manufacture of oil was carried on under quite different conditions, such for instance as that of tobacco is in some modern states. For here not only is all private enterprise forbidden, but the very amount of seed to be sown, the amount of oil produced, the retail price—all these are fixed with the greatest care. Importation of oil for trading purposes is strictly forbidden, and every care is taken to secure a fixed income from this source for the State. There is reason to believe that there were other productions laid under this restriction. Papyrus is said to have become extinct owing to a private monopoly[1], probably introduced to prevent the library of Pergamum from obtaining it in large quantities or on easy terms. But in the present case the State takes special care that a sufficient quantity of oil shall be produced each year. For this the oeco-nomus and the nomarchs are bound to provide, and in case of difficulty in procuring seed the State is even prepared to advance it to the cultivator, just as in Ulster, thirty years ago, landlords commonly advanced flax-seed to their tenants, in order that the crop might be sown in good time. In most Ulster leases of that day there was also a clause restricting the amount upon each farm, in the landlord's interest, lest the tenant should exhaust the land with this crop.

The first point of interest in this section is the total absence of olive oil. This in itself was no small evidence of the antiquity of the ordinance, for we know from Strabo that in his day the olive was quite at home in the Fayoum, and we

---

[1] Strabo, xvii. 1, § 15.

may presume that the large settlement of Greeks there during Philadelphus' reign soon brought this favourite tree from their old homes into this rich province. But it was only here, and in the neighbourhood of Alexandria, apparently in the specially Greek parts of Egypt, that it was even in his day cultivated.

The oils dealt with in the chapter before us are mainly of two kinds: sesame oil, and kiki, which is our castor oil, made from the croton-plant, a tall shrub, with a ferruginous glow upon its dark green leaves, which may yet be seen cultivated for the same purpose in Upper Egypt and Nubia. This latter is, however, a foetid oil, mainly used for lamps. In addition to these two, which seem to be the principal products, other kinds are mentioned, viz. colocynth oil, made from the seeds of gourds; *cnecinum*, made from the head of a thistle or artichoke; and linseed oil [1]. It is not quite certain how far the production of these lesser kinds was controlled, but the chief kinds were certainly both grown and gathered under State supervision; the oil was made in State presses; it was sold by the middlemen to the retailers in each village by auction, and was retailed at fixed prices.

[1] We read in Pliny, *N. H.* xix. 5 (26) 'Aegypto mire celebratur [raphanus] olei propter fertilitatem quod e semine eius faciunt. Hoc maxime cupiunt serere, si liceat, quoniam et quaestus plus quam e frumento, et minus tributi est nullumque ibi copiosius oleum.' This seems to be the ραφανέλαιον of Dioscorides, i. 26, and is therefore a species of oil additional to all those mentioned in our papyrus. The variety now called *oleifera* of the *Raphanus sativus* is still used in Egypt and Nubia for the purpose. Pliny speaks (xv. 7) of the sesamine, and also of the kiki, or castor oil, of which he describes the manufacture, likewise of the *cnecinum* if we adopt a discarded MS. reading now rehabilitated (I think) by our papyrus. He calls the cnecus a sort of *urtica*, a thistle, probably a species of artichoke. The various aromatic oils mentioned by him and by Dioscorides, and used both for medicines and unguents, have their parallel in the curious list I have published in the *Pet. Pap.* ii. p. [114].

The details of this legislation are amply illustrated in Mr. Grenfell's commentary, but, as might be expected, many are the difficulties which arise in the interpretation. For in all such documents, the most necessary assumptions are those which every contemporary reader took for granted as obvious, whereas we have to infer or detect them from stray and casual allusions.

In the whole of this intricate legislation, intended to secure the State from loss, the peasants from oppression, the middlemen from injustice, the restrictions are so precise, the room for profit on the part of the middlemen so small, that we are at a loss to know why men of wealth or of credit should have competed at auction for a business so onerous and so invidious.

§ 6. THE COINAGE.

The next question is one constantly suggested in this papyrus, but which has long agitated the minds of those who deal with the political economy of Ptolemaic Egypt, and especially with that of the third century B.C. It is the relation of silver to copper in the many prices which are set down sometimes in the one, sometimes in the other. On the complicated questions of the standard metal, the rate of exchange, and the ratio of weights under the Ptolemies, Mr. Grenfell has attained to a new solution which seems both simple and satisfactory, and which, if it be generally adopted, will save the world from much idle speculation. I shall not here anticipate his discoveries, but merely refer the reader particularly to this important feature in the book, Appendix III.

xxxviii *REVENUE LAWS OF PTOLEMY PHILADELPHUS.*

§ 7. THE VARIETIES OF LAND TENURE.

Another interesting question raised by the present text is that of the variety of tenure in land (cols. 24 and 36) throughout Egypt. We have first the ΙΕΡΑ ΓΗ (which Prof. Wilcken restored for us in 36. 8), apparently not subject to the ΑΠΟΜΟΙΡΑ, though it appears from the Rosetta stone that there was a tax of a ΚΕΡΑΜΙΟΝ per aroura due to the State upon its vineyards, remitted by Epiphanes. Then comes the land held in ΚΛΗΡΟΙ, or farms granted by the king to soldiers (ΚΛΗΡΟΥΧΟΙ), of which we hear so much in the Petrie papyri. There is further the land held ΕΝ ΔΩΡΕΑΙ, *in gift* from the king. For that this must be the meaning appears plainly from parallel passages in the books of Maccabees (I. x. 29 ; II. iv. 31). This tenure, then, must have been either a life tenure, as opposed to the ΚΛΗΡΟϹ, which was hereditary, or must have referred to some other limitation, such as the produce of some particular crop, or the cession of the taxes due to the king from a definite estate. Another tenure, ΕΝ ϹΥΝΤΑΞΕΙ, is mentioned (43. 12) as distinguished from ΕΝ ΔΩΡΕΑΙ, but what is remarkable, both may include the possession of a village, as well as land. This points back to those cases where the king gave a favourite or a mistress the revenue of a town as a private gift. Possibly ϹΥΝΤΑΞΙϹ means by *commutation* of the various imposts for a yearly contribution, which the people could levy among themselves and pay to the State. Seeing that the document is corrected according to the copy of Apollonius the ΔΙΟΙΚΗΤΗϹ, and that a man of this name appears in the Petrie papyri as holding this office in the Fayoum two years later, the conclusion is hardly to be avoided, that we have before us the copy of the ordinance specially intended for this province, and accordingly that the ΚΛΗΡΟΥΧΟΙ here mentioned are those whom we find in the province in the succeeding years. Hitherto we possess no definite evidence of such a class elsewhere in Egypt; the ΙΠΠΕΙC ΚΑΤΟΙΚΟΙ of the next century at Memphis or Thebes were evidently no landholders in the same sense. It is not impossible that though ΚΛΗΡΟΥΧΙΑ is here stated quite generally among the various forms of land tenure, this particular colony in the Fayoum may be intended. In any case, the documents quoted from the twenty-third year of the reign prove to us that the settlement of the Fayoum was not a sudden, but a gradual legislation.

The Petrie papyri show us the extension of dykes and draining operations, and the larger reclaiming of land, which took place in the province in the twenty-ninth and thirtieth years of the reign. But the new title, *Arsinoite* nome, is not known in the present document, where the word Η ΛΙΜΝΗ is used, and this seems also the case with the earlier Petrie papyri. There is but one fragment among them of the thirtieth year (according to Mr. Grenfell) which speaks of the nome under its new name. We may therefore refer this honour done to the queen, probably in relation to her ceding part of her property in the fish of the lake for the reclaiming of land, to the last years of her life, possibly even to an act of gratitude passed after her decease. The fact of her being deified during her life prevents our laying any stress upon the curious simplicity with which she is named. She appears either as Arsinoe Philadelphus, or still more briefly as Η ΦΙΛΑΔΕΛΦΟC. But this absence of titles is here rather a distinction than the reverse. She appears simply as a goddess, like Aphrodite or Isis. I have commented elsewhere on the remarkable

absence of honorary titles in all the early papyri. The many
grades of the official hierarchy which appear in the following
centuries seem as yet unknown. Not only the king and queen,
but the court officials appear without any cumbrous distinctions
attached to their names.

§ 8. The Burdens borne by Agriculture.

What were the actual burdens of the husbandman, and
what reward he got for his labour, will only be gradually
determined, according as we gain more and more knowledge.
Some of the prices given in this papyrus will help us in
this inquiry. Hitherto our evidence comes either from other
papyri on the same subject, or from ancient historians who
tell us of the condition of other Hellenistic lands. The case
of Syria and Palestine, as we find it in the books of Maccabees,
and in Josephus' *Antiquities of the Jews*[1], affords us the closest
analogies. It may not be considered irrelevant, in a general
introduction like the present, to call attention to these parallel
cases, which will help the reader to appreciate the details in
the present document.

But first as regards parallel papyri. In the Petrie collection
there are several which have only become intelligible since
we have examined them by the light of the present text.
Thus the long list of names, and of sums which are multiples
of seven[2], which I had problematically set down as a taxing
list (P. P. II. xxviii.), I found to be a list of retailers of oil, and
of the amounts which they undertake to sell, in accordance with
the express direction of our papyrus (col. 47. 10-15). Another
(xxxix. (a)) is concerned with the amount of croton to be sown

[1] xii. 4 sq.
[2] Cf. Mr. Grenfell's explanation of these figures in Appendix III.

on each farm, and perhaps with the seed to be advanced. As regards the ΕΚΤΗ or ΑΠΟΜΟΙΡΑ on wine henceforth to be paid to Arsinoe Philadelphus, we have not only II. xxx. (e) and xlvi., but the papyrus Q of the Leiden collection, formerly referred to a later date. There is also P. P. II. xxvii. (1), which states the wine produce of a farm, and adds the one-sixth *on fruits and garlands of flowers*, so that this produce is classed with that of the vineyard. This may be the meaning of adding ΠΑΡΑΔΕΙCΟΙ throughout section B of our papyrus to the ΑΜΠΕΛΩΝΕC.

There is also an interesting letter, complete (P. P. II. xi. (6)), calling upon the oeconomus, or perhaps the tax-farmer, to attend on the next day but one, when the vine-grower was going to have his vintage, according to the ordinance in col. 25. Other coincidences are mentioned in Mr. Grenfell's commentary, and in the Appendix to Part II of the Petrie papyri he has made some important corrections, or additions, to my readings of the fragments just cited. Thus the indirect light shed upon the early papyri we have found makes it certain that we shall be able to interpret future discoveries of the same kind with greater certainty, and ultimately reconstruct a definite and connected account of the whole financial system of the Ptolemaic Exchequer.

As regards their external system, we have the curious narrative of Josephus, already cited, from which it appears that as regards Palestine and Coele-Syria, the leading notables went down to Egypt to a yearly auction of the taxes, no doubt arranging on the way to what sum they would bid. But their calculations are upset by the young adventurer who offers the king a far larger sum, gets off giving security by cracking jokes with the king, and, taking an armed force to help him, demands higher taxes, confiscates the property (and even the lives) of recusants, and by remitting to the king a larger sum than he had promised, gains his favour and confidence, and remains controller of the taxes of Palestine for twenty years. Here the King of Egypt does no more than insist upon the punctual payment of a sum fixed at the auction ; he gives, however, military support to his tax-farmer in carrying out any punishment which the latter deems necessary, and even threatens to take up the land and apportion it among new settlers, if his claims are not satisfied. But into the details he seems to make no inquiry.

A very different picture of the taxation of the same province by the Seleucids appears in the documents quoted by Josephus from the books of the Maccabees, and dating a century later. If these documents indeed describe a normal state of things, we need not wonder that the rule of the Ptolemies was more popular in Palestine than that of their rivals at Antioch. The facts come out incidentally in the offers made by rival claimants to the Syrian throne, who are bidding for the support of the Jews. Even if the letters cited are not genuine copies of State documents, there is no reason to doubt that the author of them, especially in the first Maccabees, described an actual state of things. King Demetrius (Soter II, in 152 B.C.) writes (x. 29) : ' And now I let you off, and remit all the Jews from the taxes, and from the price of salt, and from the crowns (the Roman *aurum coronarium*[1]), and what I was entitled to take in lieu of the third part of the sown crops and in lieu of the half of the tree crop.' Many more imposts, such as the tolls on visitors to Jerusalem, are mentioned in the sequel. We have not only these, but

[1] Cf. also Josephus, *A. J.* xii. 3, § 3, for a similar letter from Antiochus the Great to an officer called Ptolemy concerning the Jews. We have here too τοῦ στεφανίτου φόρου, καὶ τοῦ περὶ τῶν ἁλῶν (not ἄλλων, as in most texts).

many other small taxes mentioned in the P. P. II. xxxix. (e) (f)
and in the rest of the collection which Mr. Grenfell is preparing
for publication.

A comparison of the respective burdens which the second
Ptolemy demanded in 260 B.C. and the eighth Seleucid in
150 B.C. is perhaps hardly possible from our evidence. It is
likely, however, that the apparently much greater tax of
50 per cent. on the crop of trees in Palestine may include
the olive-oil crop, whereas this part of the Egyptian revenue
was a seed crop, and, so far as we can see, the cultivator got
a very small share of it. But these details must be left to the
commentator.

§ 9. THE REVISION OF THE DOCUMENT.

The whole document has undergone corrections, as is expressly stated more than once upon the face of it, and as appears
from various erasures and changes, and in Part C from large
additions. We can also show that this revision was carelessly
done. From internal evidence, explained in the commentary,
and from the curious repetition of a chapter (cols. 59 and 60)
without any apparent reason, Mr. Grenfell was led to an acute
conjecture concerning the whole appendix on the nomes which
ensues. He believes that at this point (col. 58) the corrector
desired to fasten on a supplementary roll, containing the revised
list of nomes, but that he made the mistake of allowing the same
chapter to appear twice, immediately before and after his new
junction. The height of the papyrus, which here changes, is
strongly in favour of this hypothesis. It appears from the
fragments Mr. Grenfell has since acquired that another roll of
the same character contained what we desiderated in Part A,
a general account—besides regulations for special taxes—of the

working of the royal and local banks in regulating the accounts of the tax-farming.

Unfortunately these fragments are in such a condition as to make all inferences from them hazardous. But there is one interpretation of cols. 73–8 which is worth setting down here, as it may suggest a new idea in reading other fragments, and will probably be established in course of time, if it indeed has hit the truth. If we were to read the heading ΔΙΑΓΡΑΜΜΑ ΤΡΑΠΕΖΩΝ ΩΝΗΣ, and consider the whole section as one regulating the farming out of local banks by the State, under the control of a central or ΒΑΣΙΛΙΚΗ ΤΡΑΠΕΖΑ in the capital of the nome, we should have found a new sort of tax-farming hitherto unsuspected. The existence of local banks in towns, and even villages, is made certain by 75. 1. The mention of buying the bank seems also beyond doubt (75. 4). It would seem quite reasonable that if so many local banks were required; if it were even necessary to make up accounts in each village daily, as is not impossible (cf. the difficult passage 57. 15–6), some such sub-letting would be almost necessary to avoid an endless staff of Government officials, and if it did take place, it will probably be found that the Jews in Egypt undertook this business.

It is a sad loss that we have not the details preserved which seem to regulate the rate of exchange between silver and copper (col. 76). But of course if the local banks were farmed out, such regulations were highly necessary. I had inferred from the receipts printed in the Petrie papyri (II. xxvi.) that the bank in (the Arsinoite) Ptolemais did business by means of agents all through the province. It now seems very doubtful that this interpretation can be maintained.

The subsequent columns are, if possible, still more disappointing, for here there were regulations affecting the produce from flax, both clothes and sails, for which Egypt was so famous, and which are specially mentioned as an industry of the temples taxed by the Crown in the Rosetta inscription (l. 18). This text, and the earlier inscription known as the Canopus inscription, can now be conveniently consulted in my *Empire of the Ptolemies*.

§ 10. THE LISTS OF THE NOMES.

The problems suggested by the two lists of nomes—the brief enumeration in col. 31, and the longer exposition with their respective burdens in cols. 60 sqq.—are many and interesting. For they do not agree with the earlier and later Greek enumerations—those of Herodotus[1] and of Strabo, still less with the older Egyptian, or the later Roman, as given by the coins of the nomes under the Antonines[2], and by Ptolemy the geographer. It is certain that there were frequent changes in the limitation and arrangement of these counties, as we might call them; the two lists before us are written down in the twenty-seventh year of the same reign, and yet they show some notable discrepancies. It is not therefore surprising that Herodotus, visiting Egypt some 180 years earlier, and Strabo some 240 later, should not agree with either. It was not, moreover, within the scope of Herodotus' account to give an accurate list. We therefore are not surprised that Herodotus, specifying the nomes in which the military caste dwelt (ii. 165), gives only nomes situated in the Delta and

---

[1] All that is to be known concerning Herodotus' list has been gathered by Wiedemann in his excellent commentary on the historian's Egyptian book (II.), pp. 574 sq. and the references there.

[2] Cf. *Coins of Alexandria and the Nomes*, published by the British Museum.

the Theban district. But from Strabo we should have expected the full list; wherefore the commentators on his account have either supposed a lacuna in our texts, or negligence in the geographer, because he names only twenty - four nomes, gathering all those of the southern country (like Herodotus) under the Thebaid, though we know that the old Egyptians counted at least forty. In the most recent atlas of ancient Egypt (published by the Egypt Exploration Fund) there are even fifty enumerated. The two lists before us vindicate Strabo remarkably as regards this supposed omission. They not only agree with him in specifying twenty-four nomes; they also give the Thebaid as the last in the series[1]. Strabo therefore must have copied his list from some financial document such as this, which recognized the whole southern province as no complex of nomes, but as one district under the control of a single governor. It is even easy for us now to lay down the southern boundary of the financial nomes from Strabo's text (xvii. 1, § 41): 'Then comes the Hermopolitic military station (φυλακή)—a sort of custom-house for the produce from the Thebaid—from hence they begin to measure the schoeni of 60 stadia, up to Syene and Elephantine; then the Thebaic station, and a canal leading to Tanis[2].' The two military posts, one

---

[1] There is an interesting parallel in the second-century inscription in honour of Aristides (the rhetor), where ΟΙ ΤΟΝ ΘΗΒΑΙΚΟΝ ΝΟΜΟΝ ΟΙΚΟΥΝΤΕC (unless it only means ΠΕΡΙ ΘΗΒΑC) ΕΛΛΗΝΕC are enumerated after those of Alexandria, Hermoupolis, the ΒΟΥΛΗ of Antinoopolis, and the Greeks of the Delta. *CIG* 4679.

[2] This latter was of course the best mode of irrigating the lower country above the reach of the Nile, the water being drawn from the river at this remote point and brought on the higher level thus secured along the Arabian margin of the Nile valley.

The account of Agatharchides is quite similar (Photius, § 22, in *Geog. Graec.*

to watch imports down the river, the other to watch them coming up the river, are like the custom-houses of jealous' neighbours, such as those of the Servians and the Turks in the present day.

Having recorded this negative agreement between Strabo and the lists in the papyrus, we come to compare them in detail, both as to the number, order, and titles of the nomes. All three agree in giving us twenty-four nomes and the Thebaid. But in the names and the order of the twenty-four they differ considerably, and the whole number is only made up in the second list by counting Memphis as distinct from the Memphite nome. Several of Strabo's names, which we should have thought of old standing, do not appear, viz. Menelaites, Momemphites, Phragroriopolites; but the second and last of these most probably represent the Libyan and Arabian nomes of the papyrus. Moreover, Strabo gives names (Hermoupolis, Aphroditopolis, Kynopolis) to nomes of the Delta which appear in the papyrus as nomes of Upper Egypt. The general order, beginning with the western Delta from Alexandria, and giving the nomes along each of the three great outlets of the Nile, then ascending to Memphis and southward to the Theban custom-house, is the same. So that here the nominal divergence, which amounts to seven new names, may not be a real one. But to identify the seven new names respectively with our lists is not easy.

When we proceed to a closer examination of the two lists (cols. 31 and 60, sqq.) in our papyrus (I will call them *a* and *b*)

Min. i. p. 122, ed. C. Müller, Didot). From Memphis to the Thebaid there are five nomes, one of which is called Φυλακή, or Σχεδία, where the tolls are levied. These are νομοὶ ἐθνῶν. But then follow a list of πόλεις in the Thebaid, in which only one *nome*, the Tentyrite, is mentioned, and Thebes omitted.

we find that there are serious discrepancies not only in the order, but in the names. Were these lists handed down to us in texts of diverse age, we should at once infer that there had been in the interval a formal redistribution of the nomes. Such an explanation is impossible in the case of two contemporaneous lists, unless there were special reasons for the variation in a list required for the oil monopoly only.

The first difficulty is the absence of the *Nitriote* nome from *a*, or rather of this name, for it probably corresponds to either *a* 3 or *a* 6, both unfortunately mutilated. For the second of these I conjectured ΜΕΝΕΛΑΙϹ, i.e. the region about the town called Menelaos, after Ptolemy Soter's brother. This town was certainly situated in or by the Nitrian country, but the form of the ending is without precedent among the nomes, and we know from Strabo's list that there was afterwards a nome called ΜΕΝΕΛΑΙΤΗϹ along the seacoast east of Alexandria. But for the present I have no better suggestion to offer. There is no town-name with this ending to be found in any of the geographies of Egypt. Supposing then that the enigmatical -ΛΑΙΛΙ corresponds to ΝΙΤΡΙΩΤΗϹ in *b*, where shall we place *a* 3? It would appear that the clerk of *b* had absorbed either *a* 3 or *a* 6 in the Libya of his list, and then, finding himself one short of the official number (24), had thrust in ΜΕΜΦΙΤΕΙ—quite out of its place, and properly belonging to ΜΕΜΦΕΙ—to fill it up. There is good reason to identify the ΔΕΛΤΑ of *a* with the ΗΛΙΟΠΟΛΙΤΗϹ of *b*, for Strabo tells us that the apex of the Delta was especially so called, and Heliopolis is situated close to it, though on the Arabian side of the river.

There seems no law or assignable cause for the variations in the order of *a* and *b*. At all events, it may be inferred with certainty that neither was copied from a fixed official list, though there was a general consent that the number of nomes, excluding the Thebaid, amounted to twenty-four.

Thus 5–9, though varying in order, are a group which fairly corresponds in both. *a* 11 and 15 correspond to *b* 14 and 10. *a* 17 and 18 correspond to *b* 17 and 16, except that *a* 17 adds Memphis to its nome, whereas *b* 17 gives only Memphis, while *b* 24 is the Memphite nome, thus bringing the list of *b* up to twenty-four. We now proceed to the country south of Memphis. *a* 19 and 24 (ΕΡΜΟΠΟΛΙΤΗC and ΟΞΥΡΥΓΧΙΤΗC) correspond to *b* 18 and 19. *a* 21–24 agree with *b* 20–23, if the lost *b* 23 be, as I think it must be, the Kynopolite. Both lists end with the Thebaid. It will be found, therefore, that, with many small transpositions, there is nevertheless a general conformity between the lists. The occurrence of Η ΛΙΜΝΗ and of ΛΙΜΝΙΤΗC in *a* 22 and *b* 21 for the subsequent Arsinoite nome, first revealed to us that the complete re-settlement, and the re-naming, of that district did not take place till after the twenty-seventh year of Ptolemy II. Alexandria belonged to no nome, and had a reserved territory in the Libyan nome from which it received produce. This reminds us in a general way of the case of Washington with its territory, which belongs to no State in the American Republic. The use of the large terms Libya and Arabia as names of nomes is also foreign to Strabo and Herodotus, and was probably intended to signify that the desert limits were in each case unfixed[1]. Possibly the

---

[1] In one of the partitions of the empire of Alexander (at Triparadeisus) Ptolemy was granted Egypt and the adjoining countries, especially whatever he could conquer to the west. Hence to claim Libya in these lists may even have had a political origin. In Theban papyri of the next century, such as the Turin papyrus VIII and the B. M. CCCCI, we find Arabia and Libya used simply for the east and west banks of the Nile.

occurrence of the special titles Libyarchs (in this papyrus) and Arabarchs also points to the fact that there was here a military officer instead of a nomarch, as there were certainly desert marauders to be kept in order by what are called in the Petrie papyri ΕΡΗΜΟΦΥΛΑΚΕϹ. I append the two lists, and Strabo's enumeration, of the nomes, for the convenience of those who desire to verify, without trouble, what I have said. The figures after the names in the third list indicate where these names occur in *a* and *b*.

Col. 31 (*a*).	Col. 60 sq. (*b*).	Strabo, xvii. § 18 sqq.
1. ΛΙΒΥΗ	ϹΑΙΤΗϹ ϹΥΝ ΝΑΥΚΡΑΤΕΙ	ΜΕΝΕΛΑΙΤΗϹ
2. ϹΑΙΤΗϹ	ΛΙΒΥΗ ΠΑϹΗ ΧΩΡΙϹ ΤΗϹ ΑΦΩΡΙϹΜΕΝΗϹ	ϹΕΒΕΝΝΥΤΟϹ (8, 5)
3. [ΓΥΝΑΙΚΟ?]ΠΟΛΙΤΗϹ	ΠΡΟϹΩΠΙΤΗϹ	ΕΡΜΟΥΠΟΛΙΤΗϹ [1]
4. ΠΡΟϹΩΠΙΤΗϹ	ΝΙΤΡΙΩΤΗϹ	ΛΥΚΟΠΟΛΙΤΗϹ [1]
5. ΑΘΡΙΒΙΤΗϹ	ϹΕΒΕΝΝΥΤΟϹ	ΜΕΝΔΗϹΙΟϹ (10, 6)
6. ?]ΛΑΙΔΙ	ΜΕΝΔΗϹΙΟϹ	ΛΕΟΝΤΟΠΟΛΙΤΗϹ (11, 14)
7. ΔΕΛΤΑ	ΒΟΥϹΙΡΙΤΗϹ	ΒΟΥϹΙΡΙΤΗϹ ΚΑΙ ΒΟΥϹΙΡΙϹ (9, 7)
8. ϹΕΒΕΝΝΥΤΟϹ	ΑΘΡΙΒΙΤΗϹ	ΚΥΝΟΠΟΛΙΤΗϹ [1]
9. ΒΟΥϹΙΡΙΤΗϹ	ΗΛΙΟΠΟΛΙΤΗϹ	ΑΘΡΙΒΙΤΗϹ (5, 8)
10. ΜΕΝΔΗϹΙΟϹ	ΒΟΥΒΑϹΤΙΤΗϹ ΚΑΙ ΒΟΥΒΑϹΤΟϹ	ΠΡΟϹΩΠΙΤΗϹ (4, 3)
11. ΛΕΟΝΤΟΠΟΛΙΤΗϹ	ΑΡΑΒΙΑ	ΑΦΡΟΔΙΤΟΠΟΛΙΤΗϹ [1]
12. ϹΕΘΡΩΙΤΗϹ	ϹΕΘΡΩΙΤΗϹ	ΦΑΡΒΑΙΘΙΤΗϹ (13, 15)
13. ΦΑΡΒΑΙΘΙΤΗϹ	ΤΑΝΙΤΗϹ	ΤΑΝΙΤΗϹ (16, 13)
14. ΑΡΑΒΙΑ	ΛΕΟΝΤΟΠΟΛΙΤΗϹ	ΓΥΝΑΙΚΟΠΟΛΙΤΗϹ

[1] In the Delta, and not to be identified with the same name in the other two lists, which belongs to Upper Egypt.

Col. 31 (*a*).	Col. 60 sq. (*b*).	Strabo, xvii. § 18 sqq.
15. ΒΟΥΒΑϹΤΙΤΗϹ ΚΑΙ ΒΟΥΒΑϹΤΟϹ	ΦΑΡΒΑΙΘΙΤΗϹ	ΜΩΜΕΜΦΙΤΗϹ
16. ΤΑΝΙΤΗϹ	ΛΗΤΟΠΟΛΙΤΗϹ	ΝΙΤΡΙΩΤΗϹ (? 4)
17. ΜΕΜΦΙΤΗϹ ΚΑΙ ΜΕΜΦΙϹ	ΜΕΜΦΙϹ	ΦΑΓΡΩΡΙΟΠΟΛΙΤΗϹ
18. ΛΗΤΟΠΟΛΙΤΗϹ	ΕΡΜΟΠΟΛΙΤΗϹ	ΒΟΥΒΑϹΤΙΤΗϹ ΚΑΙ ΒΟΥ-ΒΑϹΤΟϹ (15, 10)
19. ΕΡΜΟΠΟΛΙΤΗϹ	ΟΞΥΡΥΓΧΙΤΗϹ	ΗΛΙΟΠΟΛΙΤΗϹ (? 9)
20. ΟΞΥΡΥΓΧΙΤΗϹ	ΗΡΑΚΛΕΟΠΟΛΙΤΗϹ	ΛΗΤΟΠΟΛΙΤΗϹ (18, 16)
21. ΚΥΝΟΠΟΛΙΤΗϹ	ΛΙΜΝΙΤΗϹ	ΗΡΑΚΛΕΩΤΗϹ (23, 20)
22. Η ΛΙΜΝΗ	ΑΦΡΟΔΙΤΟΠΟΛΙΤΗϹ	ΑΡϹΙΝΟΙΤΗϹ (22, 21)
23. ΗΡΑΚΛΕΟΠΟΛΙΤΗϹ	[ΚΥΝΟΠΟΛΙΤΗϹ ?]	ΚΥΝΟΠΟΛΙΤΗϹ (21, 23?)
24. ΑΦΡΟΔΙΤΟΠΟΛΙΤΗϹ ΘΗΒΑΙϹ	ΜΕΜΦΙΤΗϹ ΘΗΒΑΙϹ	ΟΞΥΡΥΓΧΙΤΗϹ (20, 19) ΘΗΒΑΙϹ

§ 11. Conclusion.

Such are the general considerations which the reader may carry with him to the closer study of the text. We cannot claim for it an universal interest such as that aroused by the discovery of lost classical works, or of copies of known literary masterpieces exceptional in their antiquity. But to those who desire a closer insight into the great and highly civilized empire of the Ptolemies, and the causes of its extraordinary wealth, such documents as this are of inestimable value. For they supplement and correct the vague statements of ancient historians, as well as the theories whereby modern scholars have sought to explain away their inconsistencies and obscurities. Moreover to the student of Hellenistic Greek, of that common dialect which pervaded the civilized world for some centuries, such a document affords great additional materials, both in vocabulary and in syntax. It throws new light upon the contemporary documents known as the LXX translation of the Old Testament, and tends to corroborate the dubious traditions of their origin. From all these points of view, the present papyrus affords a supplement of vast importance to our knowledge.

§ 12. APPENDIX ON AN INSCRIPTION FROM TELMESSOS.

There is but one inscription of this period known to me which bears upon the subjects of our papyrus, but its relation to them is so intimate, that I can hardly avoid quoting it here. It was first printed in the *Bulletin de Corresp. Hellénique*, xiv. 162.

ΒΑ]ϹΙΛΕΥΟΝΤΟϹ ΠΤΟΛΕΜΑΙΟΥ ΤΟΥ ΠΤΟΛΕΜΑΙΟΥ ΚΑΙ
ΑΡϹΙΝΟΗϹ ΘΕΩΝ ΑΔΕΛΦΩΝ ΕΤΕΙ ΕΒΔΟΜΩΙ ΜΗΝΟϹ
ΔΥϹΤΡΟΥ ΕΦ ΙΕΡΕΩϹ ΘΕΟΔΟΤΟΥ ΤΟΥ ΗΡΑΚΛΕΙΔΟΥ
ΔΕΥΤΕΡΑΙ (*sic*) ΕΚΚΛΗϹΙΑϹ ΚΥΡΙΑϹ ΓΕΝΟΜΕΝΗϹ
ΕΔΟΞΕ ΤΕΛΜΗϹϹΙΩΝ ΤΗΙ ΠΟΛΕΙ
ΕΠΕΙΔΗ ΠΤΟΛΕΜΑΙΟϹ Ο ΛΥϹΙΜΑΧΟΥ ΠΑΡΑΛΑΒΩΝ
ΤΗΝ ΠΟΛΙΝ ΠΑΡΑ ΒΑϹΙΛΕΩϹ ΠΤΟΛΕΜΑΙΟΥ ΤΟΥ ΠΤΟΛ-
ΕΜΑΙΟΥ ΚΑΚΩϹ [ΔΙΑΚΕΙ?]ΜΕΝΗΝ ΔΙΑ ΤΟΥϹ ΠΟΛΕ
ΜΟΥϹ ΕΝ ΤΕ ΤΟΙϹ ΑΛΛΟΙϹ ΕΠΙΜΕΛΟΜΕΝΟϹ
ΕΥΝΟΙΚΩϹ ΔΙΑΤΕΛΕΙ κ.τ.λ.

Let me dispose of the preamble very briefly. This decree of the city of Telmessos in Lycia is dated 241–0 B.C., shortly after the great campaign of the reigning king, Euergetes I, against Syria, wherein he had established firmly the hold which his grandfather had taken of the coast cities of Caria and Lycia (cf. Petrie pap. II. xlv). I believe the eponymous priest mentioned to be a local priest, not the priest of Alexander,

&c , at Alexandria. It appears that the city of Telmessos had been *handed over* to Ptolemy son of Lysimachus by the reigning king's father, Ptolemy son of Ptolemy, as Ptolemy II was usually called, to distinguish him from his father, Ptolemy son of Lagos. The expression ΠΑΡΑΛΑΒΩΝ is quite vague, used of a son succeeding his father, or a governor receiving authority from the king, or of any other appointment. Here it seems to me clearly to signify a present from the king. This personage had received Telmessos ΕΝ ΔΩΡΕΑΙ. We know that he was a grandee in Asia Minor, for a decree issued by Antiochus II (printed in *DBCH.* xiii. 525), appointing this Ptolemy's daughter, Berenike, priestess of the deified Syrian queen, Stratonike, speaks of him as related to the king in blood (ΤΟΥ ΠΡΟΣΗΚΟΝΤΟΣ ΗΜΙΝ ΚΑΤΑ ΣΥΓΓΕΝΕΙΑΝ); nor is it impossible, though we cannot trace the relationship, that this is more than a mere title of peerage (ΣΥΓΓΕΝΗΣ), and that the person in question may even have been the eldest son of Arsinoe Philadelphus and King Lysimachus of Thrace, who disappears from history without any evidence of his murder by Ptolemy Keraunos, when the younger children were put to death.

At all events this personage, receiving Telmessos from Philadelphus, found it sorely tried by the great wars on the Lycian coast during the early campaigns of Euergetes I.

The inscription proceeds :

ΚΑΙ ΟΡΩΝ ΕΝ ΠΑΣΙΝ ΕΦΘΑΡΜΕΝΟΥΣ ΑΦΕΙΚΕΝ

ΑΤΕΛΕΙΣ ΤΩΝ ΤΕ ΞΥΛΙΝΩΝ ΚΑΡΠΩΝ ΚΑΙ ΕΝΝΟΜΙΩΝ

These are the taxes on fruit trees, which in Syria at one time amounted to 50 per cent. (1 Macc. x. 29), and on pastures.

ΕΠΟΙΗϹΕ ΔΕ ΚΑΙ ΤΗϹ [ΟΙΝ ?]ΗΡΑϹ ΑΠΟΜΟΙΡΑϹ ΚΑΙ
ΟϹΠΡΙΩΝ ΠΑΝΤΩΝ ΚΑΙ ΚΕ[ΓΧ]ΡΟΥ ΚΑΙ ΕΛΥΜΟΥ ΚΑΙ
ϹΗϹΑΜΟΥ ΚΑΙ ΘΕΡΜΩΝ ΠΡΟΤΕΡΟΝ ΤΕΛΩΝΟΥΜΕΝΟΥϹ
ϹΚΛΗΡΩϹ ΚΑΤΑ ΤΟΝ ΝΟΜΟΝ ΤΕΛΕΙΝ ΔΕΚΑΤΗΝ ΜΕΤΡΟΥΝ-
-ΤΑϹ ΝΑΤΑ (*sic*) [ΤΩ]Ι ΤΕ ΓΕΩΡΓΩΙ ΚΑΙ ΤΩΙ ΔΕΚΑΤΩΝΗΙ
ΤΩΝ ΤΕ ΛΟΙΠΩΝ ΤΩΝ ϹΥΝΚΥΡΟΝΤΩΝ ΤΗΙ ϹΙΤΗΡΑΙ
ΑΠΟΜ[ΟΙΡΑΙ] ΑΦΗΚΕΝ ΠΑΝΤΩΝ ΑΤΕΛΕΙϹ

It is from the close connexion of these taxes in our papyrus, and from the importance of wine-taxes, that I supply OINHPAC, not CITHPAC, as do the editors of the text. Then follow the vegetables grown, I think, not in ΠΑΡΑΔΕΙϹΟΙ, but in ΚΗΠΟΙ, viz. millet (of two kinds), sesame, and lupine. On these crops the population had been oppressively taxed and worried by the ΤΕΛΩΝΑΙ, and this *according to the law.* This Ptolemy enacted that they should only pay a tithe (ΔΕΚΑΤΗ) upon them all, and, what was perhaps a far greater relief, should pay it on the areas planted with these crops, and surveyed jointly for the husbandman and the tithe-farmer. So I render the strange word ΝΑΤΑ, which completely puzzled the former editors. Some mistake has been made, as the letters are clear; the smallest change we can assume is of course the most reasonable as an emendation. I propose ΝΕΑΤΑ[1], in which the graver, perhaps because of the pronunciation of the word, omitted the Ε. It means in this sense fallow or ploughed fields, but surely may also mean fields in this condition after the crop is sown. The tithe, therefore, would be estimated on an average yield of the area under cultivation for each sort of produce. It is added that all the subsidiary charges (beyond

[1] I had thought of ΑΝΤΑ (adv.), ΠΑΝΤΑ, ΑΥΤΑ, &c. ΝΕΑΤΑ is marked oxytone in the Lexica.

the tithe) which had been levied on the wheat crop, were also remitted.

I do not believe that any governor deputed by Ptolemy could possibly have made such concessions. The financial officer of the province, O ΕΠΙ ΤΩΝ ΠΡΟΣΟΔΩΝ, would not have tolerated it, especially as it was according to the law enforced by the Egyptians. But if this Ptolemy held Telmessos either EN ΔΩΡΕΑΙ or EN ΣΥΝΤΑΞΕΙ, which latter I take to mean *for a rent*, such benevolences were possible.

I return now to the question of various taxes. The enumeration of the lesser crops is what strikes me as affording a remarkable contrast to the language of our papyrus. Is it possible that all these crops were grown in ΠΑΡΑΔΕΙΣΟΙ? Even if they were, why are they not specified in our papyrus? Is it possible that they were, but that the enumeration is lost in one of the lacunae of the text? These are the difficulties which I still feel concerning this portion of our Revenue text. On the other hand, if my suggestion OINHPAC be adopted, it may be urged that here we have that very combination of wine-tax with other taxes on fruits and vegetables, so that the latter may have been gathered up under one title. I do not feel strongly enough on either side to advocate a decision.

I will only add that my interpretation of the inscription differs widely from that of its first editors, but in no case without having carefully considered their arguments.

J. P. MAHAFFY.

REVENUE LAWS OF PTOLEMY
PHILADELPHUS

ΒΑCΙΛΕΥ[ΟΝΤΟC ΠΤΟΛΕΜΑΙΟ]Υ ΤΟΥ σωτηρος

⟨Πτολεμ[αιου και του υιου] Πτολεμαιου⟩

⟨[. . .] . . . [. . . . .]εις⟩

[. .]τα[. . . . .]

εαν δε τινας των πεπραμε[νων ωνων . . . . . .]

βουληται[ι] πωλ[ει]ν συνθε[. . . . .]

ειν τη[ν πε]πρα[μενην . . . .]

και εξ[εστω . . . .]

οι δε [. . . . .]ι

τοις [. . . . .]

γεγ[. . . . .]

The rest lost.

[τ]ης δ[ε γ]ιν[ο]μεν[ης πρ]οσοδου ταις ωναις

[κ]υριευσ[ο]υσιν οι [αντιγ]ραφεις οι καταστα

θεντ[ε]ς υπ[ο του οικον]ομου

Some lines lost.

]αν εκ πο[. .]ι[

]α λογευματα[

B

1st hand.
Col. 1.
Plate I.
A.

Col. 2.

5

Col. 3.

5

πιπτηι υπα[

]ον εις τας εισ[

The rest lost.

Col. 4.   [ημε]ρολεγδον λογ[ευ]σαμ[εν . . εντο]ς ημερων λ

[εαν] δε πλειους [τω]ν τ[ριακοντα] ημερων

[επε]χωσιν επιλ[ελ]ογε[υ . . . . . . τω]ν πλειρ

[νω]ν τα ανα[. . . . .]

5 [. . .]μμ[. . . . .]

Some lines lost.

]να[

]να και τα πα[

] κατα τον ν[ομον

] τηι αυτηι οικ[

10   α]γορασας [

The rest lost.

Col. 5.   εαν δε ει[ς το βασ]ιλικον φαινωνται οφειλοντες

προς μερος υπαρχετω και τοις καταδ[ι]κασαμε

νοις η π[ρ]αξις

ΔΙ[. . . . .]CIC

5 [. . . . .]κ[. . . . .] των κα

[. . . . .] οικονομωι

[. . . . .]νης

The rest lost.

Col. 6.   εξεστω τοις πρια[μεν]οις παρα των επιλο

γευσαντων λαβειν μ[η]δε εαν εντος των

τριακοντ[α ημερων] ηι

[εα]ν δ[ε . . . .]μεν[. . . . .]

[. . . . .]α   5
[. . . . .]ν
The rest lost.

και μαρτυρων το δε ετερον ασφραγιστον και   Col. 7.
τα [ονο]ματα των πραγματευομενων εις τους
λογους γραφετωσ[α]ν πατροθ[εν] και πατριδος
και περι τι εκαστο[ς πραγ]μ[ατευ]εται

και ει τινων φορτιων [. . . . .]   5
η επ[ι]ζημιο[υ] και τ[. . . . .]
The rest lost.

εαν δε μη συνειδοτων τουτων πρασσετωσαν   Col. 8.
παρα των πεπραγματευμενων

καλεισθωσα[ν δε οι πρια]μενοι τας ων[ια]ς εα[ν] τι εγ
καλεσωσι τοις επιλογευσασι[ν] η τοι[ς υπηρε]ται[ς]
[α]υτων υπερ των κατα την [ωνην εν τωι]   5
[χρονω]ι εν ωι επριαντο την [ωνην   ]
The rest lost.

αφ ης δ αν ημερας την ωνην παραλαβωσιν   Col. 9.
οι εν τωι εμποριωι λ[ο]γευται [εκ]τιθετωσαν
ε[ν τ]ωι τ[. . . . .] δεκ⟨α⟩τον τ[.]ς
[. . . . .]ασιν ελλι[. . .]
Some lines lost.

] τελωνιωι εν ημερ[αις   5
]σον γραψαντες γραμμα[
]ριοις και εαν τι προγραμμα [
] ταις ωναις γενηται γεγρα[μ]μενον
Some lines lost.
B 2

10

] τηι ωνηι γ[

] τους αποδ[

]ινωνται κ[

] ωνην αποτ[·

] δε το[ι]ς του[

] ωνην το δε [

Col. 10. φυλακην δε των εφ[οδω]ν και των λογευτων

και των συμβολοφυλ[ακ]ων κα[ι] των αλλο τι

πραγματ[ευο]μενων [περι] την [ωνη]ν και εξε

[ταξοντων . . . .] τηι ωνηι

5 [. . . . .]σαν υπο

[. . . . . το]ν αντι

[γραφεα . . . .]

Some lines lost.

[. . . . .] περι τη[ν] ωνη[ν . . . .]

[. . . . .]μενης προσοδου [. . . . .]

10 [. . . . . ο αρχωνη]ς και οι κοινωνες ω[. . . . . . .]

[. . . . .]ν μηθεν ανευ το[υ οικονομου]

[η του αντιγραφεως λαμβανετωσαν . . . . . .]

Some lines lost.

[. . . . . . οι τ]ην ωνην εχοντε[ς . . . .]

[. . . . . . ο αν[τιγραφευς εως αν[. . . . .]

15 [. . . . .]

[. . . . .] και οι εφοδοι και οι λοιπ[οι οι πραγ]

[ματευομενο]ι τας ωνας εαν τι τ[. . . . . .]

[. . . . εαν δε] τι ανευ του αντιγρα[φεως]

λαβωσιν η πραξαντες μη α[νενεγκωσι]
προς τον αντιγραφεα απο[τινετωσαν]
εις το βασιλικο[ν πεν]τηκον[τα . . . .]

[ο δε α]ντιγραφ[ευς . . . .]ν

Some lines lost.

[. . . . . αποτινετωσ]αν   5
[. . . . και το βλαβος πεν]ταπλουν
[οι δε πριαμενοι τας ων]ας μη αναφερομενο[ι]
[. . . . . τωι οικον]ομωι η τωι αντι
[γραφει αποτινετωσαν εις το βασ]ιλικον πεντη
[κοντα . . . .]   10

Some lines lost.

[. . . . . τωι οι]κονομωι και τωι
[αντιγραφει πατροθεν] και πατριδος
[. . . . .] τωι λογευτηριωι
[. . . . . . . του αρχω]νου το ονομα και
[των κοινωνων και τ]ων εγγυητων και   15
[των λογευτων και τω]ν υπηρετων των
[γ]ραφεντ[ων επι τηι ωνηι]

οι δε οικονομος και ο αντιγραφευς εαν τιν[α]
λαβωσι πραγματευομενον και μη παρα
δεδομεν[ο]ν εν τηι γραφη[ι α]ν[αγε]τωσαν επι
τον βα[σ]ιλεα πρ]οτερον η [βλαβηναι τι]να υπ αυτου

εαν δ[ε . . . .]εισφ[. . . . . πεπραγμα]τευμε   5
νον [. . . . .]ω

Some lines lost.

[. . . . .] επι

[. . . . .]ηδε

[. . . . .] την

Some lines lost.

10 [. . . . .]τα[. . . . .]

[. . . . .]αστα[. . . . .]

[. . . . .]μωι λο[γε]υται[ς η υπηρ]εταις και

[. . . . . π]οεισθω απο τ⟨·⟩ν [λογευ]ματων

[. . . . . ο] μισθος [λ]ογευτ[ηι εκα]στωι του

15 [μηνος δρα]χμαι τ[ρι]ακον[τα υπ]ηρεταις

[του μηνος δραχμαι ε]ικοσι [συμβο]λοφυλαξι

[. . . . δραχμ]αι δ[εκ]απ[εντ]ε εφοδωι ενι

[. . . . . . κα]τα μηνα δρ[α]χμαι εκατον

Col. 13. [οσου]ς δ[ε δ]ει κατασταθηναι εις εκαστην ωνην

λογ[ε]υτας και υπηρετας και συμβολοφυλακας

διαγραψατω ο τε ο[ι]κ[ο]νομος και ο αν[τιγραφευς]

μετα του αρχ[ωνου]

5 οσαι δ αν ωναι ε[. . . . .]

Some lines lost.

δ[. . . . .]

Some lines lost.

κα[. . . . .] τον αρχ[ωνην . . .]

τ[. . . . .]ακοτε[ς . . .]ω

σ[. . . . .] μηδε οι[. . . . .]

10 νο[. . . . . κοι]νωνειτ[ωσα]ν

μη[. . . . .]ων ος [δ αν] ποιη

ησηι τι [. . . αποτι]σει [εις το] βα[σι]λικον ✗ ε

και εμ φυλ[ακηι εστω ε]ως αν ο βα[σιλε]υς περι

αυτου δ[ια]γνωι   Col. 14.

ΑΠΟΓΡΑΦΗ ΑΡΧΩ[ΝΩΝ οσοι α]ν ωσι

οι βουλομενοι αρχων[ειν απογ]ραφεσ[θωσαν]

προς τον πωλουν[τα . . . . . .]ε δ[. . . . .]

[. . .]νε[. . . . .]   5

Some lines lost.

]οδοις μηδε [

παρευρεσει] μηδεμιαι μη[

]ολεγεσθωσα[ν

Some lines lost.

[. . . . . ταις των αρχ]

ωνων και [των κοινωνω]ν με[τοχ]αις εξεσ[τω]   10

μετεχ[ε]ιν

ος δ αν παρα τ[αυτα η α]γορ[ασηι] η μετ[. . . . .]

η μετεχηι [πραχθησε]ται μ[ν]α]ς τριακ[οντ]α

και τηι επισ[. . . . . . . ο αν] γι[νη]ται

και ο διεγγυω[μενος εαν . .]η μη παρ[αδε]   15

ξηται κοιν[ωνας . . . .]ος μη διδωσιν

αποτει[σ]ει εις το βασιλικον [μν]ας λ   Col. 15.
                                                 Plate II.

[οι] δε μη ωνε[ι]σθωσαν μηδε κο[ινων]ειτωσαν μηδ[ε δι]

[ε]γγυασθω[σα]ν

[. .]οσοι τι των βασιλικων διοικο[υσι και οι χρη]

[ματισ]ται και ο ε[ι]σαγωγ[ευς . . . .]   5

About 8 lines lost.

τ[. . . . .]

δουλος [δε . . . . ει δε μη κο] λαζεσ[θω . . . .]

αν διαφορ[. . . . . απο]τισει δρ[αχμας .]

10 ΠΡΑΞΙC ΤΕΛΩΝ

οι πριαμενοι τας ω[νας πρασσ]εσθωσα[ν τους]

υποτελεις παν τ[ο . . . . . .]ą εκ τω[ν νο]μων

εαν δε τι παρα τα γ[εγραμμε]ṿα ποι[ησω]σιν

αποτινετωσαν ει[ς το βασιλικον ⚹] γ

                                            η

15 και τα τελη οσα αν [ελλιπηι . . . . .] εαṿ [μη]

γραψωσι εν τοις λογ[οις εν ημεραις τρια]κοντ[α]

2nd
hand.   ΔΙΑΛΟΓΙCΜΟC
Col. 16.

[δια]λογιζεσθω δε ο οικονομος και [ο] α[ν]τιγραφευς

PlateIII. προς τους τας ωνας εχοντα[ς καθ εκα]στ[ον]

[μην]ạ προ της δεκατης ισ[ταμενου πε]

5 [ρι των] γ[εγ]ẹνημεν[ω]ṿ εν τ[ωι επανω χρο]

[νωι . . . .]

                             About 7 lines lost.

[. . .]ẹɩ[

                                   α

τα δ εν τωι ενε[στωτι μηνι γεγενημε]ṿ⟨οι⟩

μη προσκατα[χωριζετωσαν εις τ]ην ε[π]ανω

10 αναφοραν μηδε [μεταφε]ṛ[ετωσαν] εξ ετερων

εις ετερα μηδ ει τις τω[ν λογευτω]ν η των

υπηρετων απο της π[ροσοδου] της ων[ης]

λαβων τι διορθουται μη[. . . . . το]υτο ε[ι]ς [το]

ιδιον καταχωριζεσθω

15 οταν δε τον εχομενον δ[ιαλογισμον] πο[ιω]ṿτα[ι]

και το περιον εκ του επ[ανω διαλογ]ισμου

προς την προσοδον προσλ[αμβανετωσ]αν δια
δηλουντες οσον ην το π[εριον εκ] του επανω χρονου

εαν δε ο επανω χρονος εγδειαν ηι π[ε]ποιηκως   Col. 17.
ο δ επιων επιγενημα και απε[χ]ηι ο [ο]ικονο[μος]
πληρες ‘το αδιεγγυον μερ[ος της] ωνη[ς . . . . .]
απο του επιγενηματος τ[. . . . . .]ε[. . . . .]
[. . . . . .]κασιν εκαστωι [. . . . .]   5

About 7 lines lost.

επεχετω [. . . . .]
τοσουτον σ[. . . . .] εις δε [το]
βασιλικον εκ τ[. . . . .] την εγδ[ειαν]
υπερ αυτου [. . . .]α[. . . . .]ω

[ε]αν δε υστερον και εκ [. . . .]ω της ωνης εξ η[ς]   10
το επιγενημα εστιν ε[γδεια] γενηται εστω
αυτωι η πραξις του μ[ετενε]γχθεν[τ]ος επι
γενηματος εκ των ε[γγυων] των εγγεγραμμ[ε]νων
επι τηι ωνηι εις ην το [περιον μ]ετηνεγχθη
προτερον δε εκ του αυ[. . . . . α]ποκαθιστατω   15
το μετενεγχθεν οθεν μ[ετηνεγχ]θη

των δε διαλογισμων ους α[ν ποιη]σηται ο οικονο[μ]ος

προς τ[ο]υς τας ωνας εχοντας παντων αντιγραφα   Col. 18.
εκαστω[ι] των κοινων[ω]ν παραχρημα δοτω
σφραγισαμενος αυτος κα[ι] μα[. .]ε[.]ρας [εχ]ετω δε
και αυτος αντιγραφα σ[φρα]γι[σαμ]εν[ω]ν πα]ντων
των διαλογισα[μ]ενω[ν . . . .]   5

About 7 lines lost.

[. . . . . α]π[οσ]τελλετω δε

C

                    προς
τα[ντιγραφα των διαλογ]ισμων κατα μηνα τον
επι [της διοικησεως τ]εταγμενον και τον
εγλ[ογισ]τ[ην οταν δ]ε ο πεπραμενος χρονος απας
10 διελθηι παρ[εστωσα]ν οι τας ωνας εχοντες παντες
προς τον οικον[ομον εν] τωι εχομενωι μηνι προ της
δεκατης ιστ[αμενο]υ και διαλογιζεσθω προς αυτους
ο οικονομος γ[ενικον] διαλ[ογ]ισμον και τιθεις την τε
τιμην της [προσοδου και] ο δει αυτους δι[ο]ρθωσασθαι .
15 και εις ταυτο [το . . . ανενηνεγμε]νον και εν οις χρονοις
εκαστα και ει [τι απο] των απ[οπρ]αματων η αλλου τινος
ενοφειλεται ο δ[ει τον οι]κονομον πραξαι και το λοιπον

Col. 19. εαν τι προσοφειλωσιν και ποσον εκαστωι τουτων επιβαλλει
και υπο το μερος του ενοφειλομ[ενου] υπογραψατω οσον
                                 και
ιδιαι εχει παρ αυτων η του εγ[γυ]ου εν οις χρονοις και το
λοιπον εαν τι π[ροσο]φ[ειληι] εα[ν δ επι]γε[ν]ημα ηι επιγραψατω
                   About 7 lines lost.
5 [. . . . .]ς ανενεγ[κατω]
[. . . . . . προς το]ν επι της διοικησεως τε[ταγμενον]
[. . . . .]την ο δ επι της διοικησεως τε[ταγμε]
                         τι
[νος επισκε]ψαμενος εαν ηι περιγινομενον εκ [των]
[α]λλω[ν ωνων] εαμ μεν εις αλλας ωνας ενοφειληι
10 κατα[χωρισα]τω εις το ενοφειλομενον εαν δε μηθεν
αλλο ε[νοφειλ]ηι συν[τ]αξατω τωι οικονομωι πραξαντα
παρ ου [προσο]φειλε[τ]αι αποδουναι αυτωι οταν η επι
λογε[υ]σις ηι ο δε οι[κονομο]ς απο[δο]τω εν ημεραις τρισιν
εαν δ [απαιτηθεις μη αποδ]ωι τριπλουν αποτινετω

εισπρα[ξατω δ ο] επι τ[ης διοικ]ησεως τεταγμενος   15

και απ[. . . . .]

οσ[οι δ αν] των τας ωνας εχοντων μη διαλογισωνται προς [τον] Col. 20.

οικον[ομο]ν β[ο]υ[λο]μεν[ου] του οικονομου και παρακαλουντ⟨ε⟩ς

εις τε το βα[σιλ]ικ[ον]

αποτ[ινετωσ]αν μ[νας τ]ριακοντα και ο οικονομος συναναγκασατ[ω]

About 7 lines lost.

. . . .]ω αυτ[. . . . .]

[. . . . .]ρ[.] τ[ο]υ διαλογισμου δου[. . . . . κα]   5

[τα τ]ον νομον

[δοτ]ω δε και ο οικονομος και των εγγ[υητων εκασ]

[τωι] διαλογισμον καθ ον φη⟨σου⟩σιν αυτ[ον α ω]φει[λε]

[πεπ]ραχθ[α]ι εαν δε μη δωι αιτηθεις αυθημερο[ν η τηι]

[υσ]τεραιαι αδικωι πραξει ενοχος εστω   10

ι[τ]

[δια]λογιζεσθωσαν δε παντες κατα ταυτα οσοι τ[ων βα]

[σιλ]ικων π[ωλ]ησουσιν

ΣΥΓΓΡΑΦΩΝ

οι

[οσα δε σ]υγγραφονται οικονομοι η οι αντιγραφεις η οι π[αρ αυ]

[των] οι τα βασι[λ]ικα πραγματευομενοι περι τω[ν εις τους]   15

[. . .]υς·συγκυροντων μη πρασσεσθωσαν οι πραγμα[τευομενοι]

⟨εκ⟩ των συγγραφων μηδε των συμβολων μ[ηδεν]   Col. 21.

[ΚΑ]ΤΕ[Ρ]ΓΩΝ

[καθως γεγ]ραπται εν τωι νομωι τον [οικ]ονομον [. . . .]

About 4 lines lost.

[. . . . . κα]τασταθ[ε . . . .]

C 2

5 τα συντεταγμενα [. . . . . αποτινε]τωσαν
υπερ αυτων οι καταστ[αθεντες . . τ]α δε προσ
τιμα τα γεγραμμενα ε[ισπρασσεσθωσαν] οι πεπρα
γματευμενοι εαμ μη οι κ[ατ]ασ[ταθ]εντες φαινωνται
συνειδοτες αυτοις

10   ΕΚΚΛΗΤΟΙ ΧΡΟΝΟΙ

οσα δ εγκληματα γινεται εκ τ[ων νομων] των
τελωνικων εστω καλεισθαι περι μ[εν . . . .]
οταν βουλωνται υπερ δε των λο[ιπων εγκλ]ηματ[ων]
[οσ]α γ[ι]νεται εκ των νομων των τε[λωνικω]ν υπερ ων
15 μ[. . .]ς ε[ν] εκαστωι των νομων αλλος χρ[ονος ε]κκ[λ]ητος
                                                        τε
τετακται εστω καλεισθαι εν τωι χ[ρονωι] εις ον [αι] προσοδο[ι]

Col. 22. πεπρανται και εν αλληι τριμ[η]ν[ιαι] εαμ μη τις των τι
κοινωνουντων η υπηρετουντω[ν] τη[ι ω]νηι λη[φθ]η
μετα τον γεγραμμενον χρονον ν[. . . . .]
                                ν
[εαν δε τις] τουτω [ληφθηι . . . .]

                    About 4 lines lost.

5 [. . . . .] των [. . . . . πραξατ]ω
[ο] οικονομος παρ[α των . . . .]ρ[. . .] των και των
εγγυων και των [. . . . .]

3rd
hand.
Col 23.
   B.   [. . . . .]ς τα
         [. . . . . . Απολλ]ωνιου του
         [διοι]κητου

β[ασιλευον]τος Πτολεμαιου του Πτολεμαιου

κ[αι του υιου] Π[τ[ολ]εμαιου ετους κζ

[. . . . .]αρ[. . . . .]

4th
hand.
Col. 24.
Plate I.

About 7 lines lost.

[. . . . . του γινο]μενου οινου[. . . . .]

[. . . . την] εκτην παρα δε των κ[. . . . .]

[κα]ι των στρατευομενων και του[s . . . .]

κληρους πεφυτευκοτων και τη[s εν τηι   ]

Θηβαιδι επαντλητης και οσα δ[. . . . .]

διοικειται η σιμαριστου προτερο[ν δ]ιοικε[ιτο την]

δεκατην

Plate IV.

5

των δε παραδεισων εξυντιμησεως τη[s . . . .]

[. . . .]μενης προς αργυριον την εκτην τ[. . . . . .]

[. . .]σιν

10

[ΥΠ]ΕΡ Τ[Ο]Υ ΤΡΥΓΑΝ ΚΑΙ ϹΥΝΑΓΕΙΝ

[οι] δε γεωργοι τα γενηματα τρυγατωσαν

οταν η ωρα [ηι κ]αι οταν αρχωνται τρυγαν

ε[παγ]γελ[λετ]ωσαν τωι διοικουντι η

15

[τωι εχοντ]ι την ωνην και βουλομενου επι

[δειν τους αμπελ]ωνας επιδεικνυτω[σαν]

Col. 25.

About 7 lines lost.

[. . . . . . . τοις την ωνην πριαμε]νοις μνα[s .]

[ο]ταν δε οι γεωργοι οινοποιειν βουλωντ[αι]

παρακαλειτωσαν τον την ωνην διοικο[υντα]

εναντιον του οικονομου και του αν[τιγραφεως]

5

η του παρα τουτων και παραγενομεν[ο]υ οινο

ποιειτω ο γεωργος και μετρειτω τοις με

τροις τοις εν εκαστωι των τοπων υπαρ

10 [χουσ].[ν] εξητασμενοις και εσφραγισμενοι[s]

[υπο του ο]ικονομου και του αντιγραφεω[s]

[και εκ] το[υ] γενομενου μετρου την απομ[οιρ]α[ν]

[α]ποδιδοτω

[οσο]ν [δ] αν των γεγραμ[μ]ενων μη ποιησωσι οι

15 [γε]ωργοι κατα τον ν[ο]μον [δι]πλην την απομ[οι]ραν

τοις εχουσι τη[ν ων]ην απ[ο]τινετωσαν

Col. 26.   [παρ οις δε προυπαρ]χε[ι] οργανα οι[s] οινοποιουσι απογραψασθω[σαν]

[προς τον] διο[ικουν]τα την ωνην οταν παν[. . . . .]

About 7 lines lost.

[. . . . .]α δε [. . . . .]

[. . . . .]ν μελλωσιν [αποδει]

5 [ξατωσαν] το επιβ[λ]ηθεν σημειον ασινε[s ο δε μη]

[απ]ογραψαμενος η μη επιδειξας τα οργ[ανα κατα]

τον νομον η μη παρασχων εις παρασφ[ραγισμον βου]

λομενου σφραγισασθαι η μη απ[ο]δει[ξας την επι]

βληθεισαν σφραγιδα αποτινετω τοις εχουσι [την]

10 [ω]νην οσου αν παραχρημα το βλαβος διατιμησω[σ]ι

[οσ]α δ αν οι γεωργοι προτρυγησαντες οινοποιησω[σι]ν

[. . . . .]ωσαν τον οινον επι των ληνων η επι [των]

[. . . . .] και οταν το πρωτον εκθεμα παραγ[. . . .]

[. . . . . .]νται εν τη[ι] πολει η κωμηι εν ηι εκα[στ]ο[ι]

15 [κατοικο]υσι απογρα[φ]εσθωσαν οι γεωργοι αυθημ[ε]ρο[ν η]

[τηι] υ[σ]τεραιαι και επιδεικνυτωσαν τον οινον [και]

[το]ν αμπελων[α] εξ [ου] προετρυγησαν

[ϹΥΓΓ]ΡΑΦΕϹΘΑΙ

[ο δ ε]χων την ωνη[ν] οταν το πληθος του [. . . . . .]   Col. 27.

[. . . . .] της αναμετρησε[ω]ς [. . . . .]

About 7 lines lost.

[. . . . .]ν της απ[ομοιρας]

[και σφρα]γισ[αμε]νος [της] συγγραφης τ[ο αντιγρα]

φ[ον δοτ]ω τωι γ[ε]ωργωι χειρογραφησα[τω δε]   5

εν τηι συγγραφηι τον ορκον τον βα[σιλικον]

παν τα γενημα κατακεχωρικε[ναι εν τηι]

συγγραφηι και τα προοινοποιηθ[εντ]α κ[αι]

απ[ο]γραφεντα προς αυτον υπο τ[ο]υ γεωργο[υ]

παντα κατακεχωρικεναι και μηθεν νεν[οσ]   10

φισθαι μηδε καταπροιεσθαι την δ ετερα[ν]

[σ]φρ[α]γισαμενου του γεωργου εχετω ο οικονο[μος]

η ο παρ αυτου συναπεσταλμενος χειρογ[ραφη]

[σ]ατω [δ]ε ο γεωργος τον βασιλικον ορκ[ο]ν [π]αν

το γενημα αποδεδειχεναι και τα προοιν[ο]   15

π[ο]ιηθεντα π[α]ντα απογεγραφθαι και την

απομοιρ[αν] την πεπ . . . μ[ε]νην [δ]ικαιως

αναγε[γρα]φηκεναι τα δε αντ[ιγρα]φα σ̣υ̣ν̣

προσεστω ασφραγιστα   Col. 28.

[. . . . .] ομ[. . . . .]

About 7 lines lost.

[. . . . . τοις] εχουσι την ω[νην]

[. . . . . .]ω

[εαν δ αντ]ιλεγωσιν ως πλεον η ελα[σσον]   5

[γι]νεται επικρινετω ο οικονομος και ο [αντι]
γραφευς και καθοτι αν επικριθηι σφρ[αγιζε]
σθωσαν

ο δε τελωνης εαν προς τινα των [γεω]ρ
10 γων μη συγγραψηται βουλομενου [μη] εστω
[α]υτωι τουτων η πραξις
[οι] δε ο οικονομος η ο αντιγραφευς συγγ[ρ]αψα
[σθ]ωσαν προς τον γεωργον και κομισαμενο[ι]
[τη]ν γε[ν]ομενην απομοιραν εις το βασιλ[ικον]
15 [κατ]αχωρι[σ]ατωσαν τοις δε εχουσιν τη[ν]
[ων]ην την τιμην μη υπολογειτω[σαν]

[Μ]Η ΕΠΙΜΙϹΓΕΙΝ

[ε]αν δε τοις ατελεσι τα υποτελη γενη[μα]τα

Col. 29. [. . . . . . .]λ[. .] ως οντα των ατ[ελων επιμισγωσι]

About 7 lines lost.

[. . . . . . οι παραδεισους κεκ]τημενοι απ[ογραψα]
[σθωσαν π]ρος τ[ον] την [ω]νην πριαμεν[ον και]
[τον υπο] του οικο[ν]ομου και του αντ[ιγραφεως]
5 [κα]θεστηκοτα εν τωι τοπωι φραζον[τες το τε]
                                        ικο
αυτων ονομα και εν ηι κωμηι ουσιν και π[οσου τιμων]
ται την προσοδον την εν τωι παρα[δεισωι και εαν]
μεν ευδοκηι ο τελωνης συγγραφην π[. . .]εσθω[σαν]
αυτω[ι] διπλην εσφραγισμενην καθαπ[ερ εν] τω[ι]
10 νομωι γεγραπται και εκ τουτου την [εκ]την
πρασσετω ο οικονομος
[εα]ν δε α[ν]τιλεγηι προς την τιμησιν εξεστω

[τωι τη]ν ωνην εχοντι εγλ[α]βειν τον καρπον ο [δ αν]

[επιβα]λληι αποδιδοτω απο του εμπολωμ[ε]

[νου] καθ ημεραν οταν δε κομισηται ο γ[ε]ωργ[ο]ς   15

[ο]υ ετιματο το πλειον εστω του την

[ω]νη[ν] εχοντος την δε εκτην αποδοτω ο γε

[ω]ργος [τ]ωι [οικονο]μωι εαν δ εκ του καρπου του

πραθεντ[ος η τι]μησις μη εκπ[ε]σηι πραξατ[ω]

ο οικονομ[ος απ]ο του την [ω]νην εχο[ντο]ς και [. .]   20

[. . . . .]ι διορθω[σ]ασ[θω . . . . . .|

[. . . . . .ν[. . . . .]   Col. 30.

About 7 lines lost.

[. . . . . .τ[. . . . .]

[. .]τα[. . . . .]ας εν αλλαις [. . . . . εαν δε]

μητε αυτοι παρ[α]γενωνται εις την ω[νην μη]

τε αλλοι παρ αυτων οι πραγματευ[σομενοι]   5

                κ
κ[υ]ριως εκαστα ⟨τ⟩α⟨κ⟩τα τον νομον η [αλλως]

επικωλυσωσι τους γεωργους επαγγ[ελλοντας]

και παρακαλουντας και συντελουν[τας κατα]

τον [ν]ομον εξεστω τοις γεωργοις [ως γ]εγρα

πτ[αι] παροντων τουτων συντε[λεσ]αι ενα[ν]   10

τιο[ν τ]ου παρα του οικονομου και του [α]ντιγ[ρα]

φεως συναπεσταλμενου εκαστα ποιειν και ειν[αι]

κατα τουτο αζημιους παραγενομενου δ[ε]

[του] διοικουντος την ωνην δηλουτωσαν [το γενη]

[μα και] την αποδειξιν ποιεισθωσαν πα[ραχ ρ η]   15

[μ]α ως υπερ εκαστων διωικηκασιν ο δε π[αρ]α

του οικονομου και του αντιγραφεως γραψαν

D

τες δοτωσαν του τε γενηματος και της απο
μοιρα[ς] τον λογον κατα γεωργον

20 ΑΠΟΚΟΜΙΖΕ[ΙΝ] ΤΗΝ ΑΠΟΜΟΙΡΑΝ
   οι δε γεωργοι τ[η]ν γινομενην απομοι[ρ]αν [τ]ου

Col. 31.   About 7 lines lost.

Plate V. [. . . . . απο]μοιραν εις [το αποδοχι]
ον [. . . . . αποτι]νετω το[ις την ωνην]
εχουσι της ενοφειλουμενης αυτοις απ[ομοιρας την]
τιμην εμ μεν τηι Λιβυηι και τωι Cαιτ[ηι και . . . . .]
5 πολιτηι και Προσωπιτηι και Αθριβιτ[ηι και Μενε]
                    η
λαιδι και Δελτα του με του χ [Ͱ .]
εν δε τωι Cεβεννυτηι και Βουσιριτηι [και Μενδη]
σιωι και Λεοντοπολιτηι και Cεθρωιτ[ηι κα]ι Φαρ
βαιτ[ι]τηι και τηι Αραβιαι και Βουβαστ[ιτ]ηι και
10 Βουβ[ασ]τωι και Τανιτηι και Μεμφιτ[ηι κ]αι Μεμ.φει]
και Λητοπολιτηι και Ερμοπολιτηι κα[ι Οξ]υρυγ[χι]
τηι [κ]αι Κυνοπολιτηι και τηι λιμνηι [κα]ι Ηρακ[λεο]
πολιτηι και Αφροδιτοπολιτηι Ͱ ϛ
[ε]ν δε τ[η]ι Θηβαιδι Ͱ ε εισπραξατω [δ]ε ο [οικο]ν[ο]
15 μος τα[ς] τιμας παρα των γεωργων κ[α]ι κ[α]τα
                   υπερ
χωρισατω εις το βασιλικ[ο]ν της ωνης

                 Α
        ΑΠ[ΟΣ]ΦΡΑΓΙCΜΑΤΟC   κομ[ιζε]
                                 σθω [δ ο οι]
ο δε οικονομος κ[α]ταστ[η]σατω εν εκα[σ]τ[ηι] κω   κονο[μος]
μηι αποδοχια [α]υτος δε ων αν κομιζ[ηται απο]   εκ τ[ων λη]
20 σφραγισμα διδοτω τω[ι γεωργωι . . . .]   25 ιω[ν]

Col. 32.   About 7 lines lost.

[. . . . .]ς συναγομ[εν . . . . .]

παρεχετω [κεραμον] τ[ωι α]ποδοχιωι και [. . . .]

ρον εστω δε ο κερ[α]μος κεραμια στεγνα [. . . .]

πουμενα ικανα τωι οινωι τωι συνα[γομενωι εκ της

ωνης   5

——

ο δε οικονομος και ο αντιγραφευς προ[τερον η]

τρυγαν τους γεωργους εμπροσθεν [ημεραις .]

δοτωσαν τοις γεωργοις τιμην του [κερα]μου ο[ν]

δει εκαστον παρασχειν εις την απομ[οιρα]ν τω[ν]

ιδιων γενηματων την συνταχθε[ισαν] υπο   10

του επι της διοικησεως τεταγμ[ενου] και δ[ι]

αγραψατω την τιμην ⟨τοις⟩ δια της τ[ρ]απ[ε]

[ζ]ης της βασιλικης της εν τωι νομωι

[ο] δε γε[ωργ]ος λαβων την τιμην παρε[χ]ετω κ[ε]

[ρα]μον αρ[ι]στον [ε]αν δε μη δοθηι αυτωι [η] τ[ι]μη   15

τομ [μεν] κεραμον παρεχετω κομιζεσθω δε

απο [της] απομ[οιρας] ης δει αυτον [α]ποδουναι

την τιμην λ[. . . . .]

                     ο η

οινου τ[ου] χ [με . . . . τη ν

απομοιρ[αν . . . .]   20

About 7 lines lost.   Col. 33.

——

[. . . . .]αι μενειν [. . . . . . .]

——

οσος δ αν μ[. . . . .] επισκοπειτ[ω ο οικονομος και]

παραλαμβανω[ν] τ[ον] την ωνην διοικ[ουντα και τ]ον

αντιγραφεα και τον παρεστηκοτα [υπ αυτου πω]

λειτω μετα τουτων διδους τοις [. . . . . . . χρο]νον   5

εν ωι διορθωσονται και πρασσων τας [τιμας . . . .]ε

D 2

τω εις τον της ωνης λογον υπερ τω[ν πριαμενων]
την ωνην

οι δε βασιλικοι γραμματεις απογραψ[ατ]ωσαν [τοις] την
10 ωνην πριαμενοις αφ ης αν ημερας το ε[κθε]μα πο[ιησων]
ται εν ημεραις ῑ οσοι αμπελωνες η [π]αραδε[ισοι εν ε]
καστωι νομωι εισιν και των αρουρων τ[ο] πλη[θος και ο]
σοι αμπελωνες η παραδεισοι των εμ φ[ορολ]ογ[ιαι οντων]
υπ[ο]τελεις ησαν εις τα ιερα προ του κ[α]L

15 [ε]αν δε μη απογραψωσιν η μη δικαιως φα[ιν]ω[ν]τα[ι απο]
[γ]εγραφηκοτες δικηι νικηθεντες αποτινετωσ[αν τ]οις
τ[η]ν ωνην πριαμενοις καθ εκαστον ων αν ελεγχθω[σι] ⊢ '𝈗
και τ[ο β]λαβος διπλουν

οσοι δε των κε[κτ]ημεν[ων αμ]πελωνα[ς η] παραδεισους
20 των εν τη[ι φορολ]ογιαι οντ[ων συνετ]ε[λ]ουν εις τα ιε[ρ]α
την εκτ[ην προ] του κ̄α̅[L αποδιδο]τωσα[ν] τ[ην] εκτη[ν]

Col. 34. [τοις την ωνην πριαμενοις . . . .]

About 5 lines lost.

[οι δε πριαμενοι την ωνην εγγυους καταστη]
[σουσι των εφεικ]οστων αφ [ης αν ημερας αγ]ορασωσ[ιν]
εν ημερα[ις] λ τας δε κατ[αγραφας ποιη]σονται
5 των χρηματων απο Διου εως [. . . . . κατ]α̣ μηνα το
επιβαλλον

οσος δ αν ληφθηι παρ αυτων οι̣[ος εις το βασι]λικον υπο
λογεισθησεται η τιμη εις τας [γινομενας ανα]φορας

ΔΙΑΛΟΓ[ΙϹ]ΜΟϹ
10 οταν δε παντες οι εκ της ων[ης κ]αρπο[ι πωλ]ηθωσιν

παραλαβων ο οικονομος τον ηγ[ορακ]οτα τ[ην ω]νην
και τους μετοχους αυτου και τ[ο]ν αν[τιγραφ]εα δ[ια]
λογισασθω προς τον την ωνην [εχο]ντ[α και τους] μετο
χους και εαν μεν επιγενημα π[ερι]ηι [επιδιαγρ]αψα
τω τωι τε αρχωνηι και τοις με[τ]ο[χοι]ς τ[ο του] επι   15
                μ[ετ]ο
γενηματος εκαστωι κατα την ⟨ωνην⟩ χ[ην επ]ι
βαλλον δια της βασιλικης τραπεζης εαν δ [εγ]δεια
γενηται πρασσετω παρα του αρχωνου κ[αι] των
μ[ε]τοχω[ν] και των εγγυων παρ εκαστου τ[ο] επιβαλλον
την δε [π]ραξι[ν] ποιε[ι]σθω εν τ[ωι εχο]μενωι ενιαυτωι   20
εν τηι π[ρ]ωτ[ηι] τριμηνι[αι]

εα[ν δ]ε μ[η δια]γρ[α]ψη[ι . . . .]

About 8 lines lost.   Col. 35.

[. . . . .] ωνηι [. . . . .]
[. . . . . . εαν] μη αποδωι τ[. . . . .,ται του
το δε καλεισθωσαν οι αδικ[ουμενοι ε]αν απαι
τηθεις μη αποδωι εν ημ[ε]ραις τριακον]τα

About 6 lines lost.   5th
hand.

       ο   Col. 36.
[. .]⟨γι⟩νεσ[θω οπως αν γιν]ηται κ[ατα τα γεγ]ραμμενα   Plate VI.
          ερρωσθε Lκγ Δαισιου ε

τ[ους κατα την χ]ωραν βασιλικους γραμματεις
τω[ν νομων απ]ογραφειν εκαστον ου νομου γραμ
μα[τευει το τ]ε πληθος των αρουρων της αμπε   5
λο[υ και] παρ[αδ]εισων και τα εκ τουτων γενηματα
κα[τα] γεωρ[γο]ν απο του κβL διαστελλοντας

τη[ν ι]εραν γ[ην] και ταυτα εκ ταυτης γενηματα

ινα [η] λοιπη [. . . .]η εξ ης δει την εκτην συναγεσθαι

10 τηι [Φι]λα[δελφωι κ]αι τ[ο]υτων διδοναι χειρογραφιαν

τοι[ς π]α[ρα Cατυρο]υ πραγματευομενοις ωσαυτω[ς]

δε και τ[ου]ς κ[ληρο]υχους τους εχοντας ⟨τους⟩ αμπελω[νας]

η παρα[δεισ]ου[ς ε]ν τοις κληροις οις ειληφασι παρα τ[ο]υ βα

σιλεως και τ[ου]ς λοιπους παντας τους κεκτημενους

15 αμπελωνας η παραδεισους η εν δωρεαις εχοντας η γε

ωργουντας καθ οντινουν τροπον εκαστον το καθ αυ

τον απογραφειν το τε πλ[η]θος της γης και τα γε
                                            την
νηματα και διδον[α]ι τ[ω]ν γενη[μ]ατων εκτην

[Αρσ]ινοηι Φ[ι]λαδ[ελ]φωι ει[ς] τ[ην] θυσιαν κα[ι] την σπ[ο]νδ[ην]

Col. 37.   About 7 lines lost.
Plate
VII.   [. .]ειν δε[. . . . .] αντιγρ[αφ . . . .]

[βασιλε]υς Πτολεμαιος [τοις στρ]ατηγοις και τοι[ς ιππαρχοις]

[κα]ι τοις ηγεμοσι και το[ι]ς νομαρχαις και τοις το[παρχαις και το]ις

[οικ]ονομοις και τοις αντιγραφευσι και τοις βασιλ[ικοις γραμμα]τευσι

5 [κ]αι τοις Λιβυαρχαις και τοις αρχιφυλακιτα[ις πασι   χα]ιρειν

[α]πεσταλκαμεν υμιν ταντιγραφα του προγ[ραμματος κα]θ ο δει

[συ]ντελειν την εκτην τηι Φιλαδελφωι επ[ιμελες ουν υμι]ν γινε

[σθ]ω οπως αν γινηται κατα ταυτα

                    ερρωσθε Lκγ Διου κ[.]

10 [οσοι ε]χουσιν αμπελωνας η παραδεισους τροπωι ωιτ[ινιου]ν
                                            τε
[διδο]τωσαν παντες τοις παρα Cατυρου πραγματ[ευομενοις]

[και το]ις παρα Διονυσοδωρου τεταγμενοις εγλογι[σταις κατα]

[νο]μους χε[ι]ρογραφιας η αυτοι η οι διοικουντες η [οι γεωργου] [ν]τες τα κ[τ]ηματα αυτων απο Ⅼιη εως [Ⅼκα   ]

το τε πλη(θο]ς των γενηματων και εις ποιον ιερον [εδ]ιδο   15

[σ]αν την γινομενην εκτην και ποσον του ενιαυτου ωσαυ

[τ]ως δε και οι ιερεις εκ ποιου κτηματος εκαστος ελαμβ[α]νον

κ[α]ι ποσον οινον η αργυρ[ι]ον του ενιαυτου ομοιως δε διδ[ο]τωσα[ν]

και οι βασιλικ[οι γρα]μματεις [κ]αι οι [. . . . .]

[. . . .] τουτ[ων χ]ειρογραφ[ι]α[ς . . . .]   20

Ⅼκ͞ζ μηνος Λωιου ι͞   3rd
hand.
Col. 38.
Plate I.
C.

δι⟨ο⟩ρθωσ⟨ο⟩μεθα τοις ⟨παρα⟩

Απολλωνιου του διοικητου

About 5 lines lost.   6th
hand.
Col. 39.
Plate
VIII.

[. . . . . του]

μεν [σησαμου τ]ην αρ[τ]αβ[ην την τριακο]νταχοι

νικον κα[θαρον] εις ολμον Ⱶ [η του δε κ]ροτωνος

την αρταβην την τριακον[ταχοινικ]ον καθαρον

εις ολμον Ⱶ δ κνηκου καθα[ρον εις ολ]μον την   5

αρταβην Ⱶ α = κολυκινθινου την αρταβην ʃ—

του εκ του λινου σπερματος ʃ

εαν δ[ε] μη βουληται ο γεωργος δ[ιδο]ναι καθαρον

εις ολμον παραμετρειτω απο τη[ς] αλω καθαρας

κοσκινω⟨·⟩ και προσμετρειτω ει[ς τ]ην αποκαθαρσιν   10

εις ολμον του μεν σησαμου ταις [εκα]τον α͞ρ ζ

και του κροτωνος το ισον της [δε κνηκ]ου α͞ρ η

λαμβανετωσαν δε παρα τω[ν γεω]ργων

εις τας δυο δραχμας τας λογ[ενο]μενας

15 απο του σησαμου και την Ⱶ α [του κ]ροτωνος

σησαμον και κροτωνα τιμης τ[ης εν] τωι

διαγραμματι γεγραμμενης αργυριον

δε μη πρασσεσθωσαν

αλλωι δε μηθενι εξουσιαν εχετωσαν οι γεωργ[οι]

20 πωλειν μ[ητε ση]σαμον μητε κροτω[να]

Col. 40.   About 5 lines lost.
Plate IX. [. . . . . του αν]

[τιγρα]φεως παρ[α του κωμα]ρ[χ]ου κ[αι απο]

σφρ[α]γισμα διδοτ[ωσαν τωι κ]ωμαρχηι ω[ν]

παρ εκαστ[ου] γεω[ργου ελαβο]ν εαν δε μη δωσι

5 το αποσφραγισμα μη προιεσθω ο κωμαρχης

εκ της κωμης ει δε μη αποτινετω

εις το βασιλικον Ⱶ 'Α και ο τι αν η ωνη δια ταυ

τα καταβλαβη πεν[τ]απλουν

πωλησουσι δε το ελαι[ον] εν τηι χωραι (του [μ]εν)

το τε   ν   ν και του κικιος και του κολυκυντινου

10 σησαμινου και το⟨υ⟩ κν[η]κινου προς χαλκον και επελλυχνιου

τομ μετρητην τον [δωδε]καχουν Ⱶ μη

                                                  ε
(του δε κικιος και κολοκ[υντινο]υ και πελλυχνιου)

(τομ μετρητην Ⱶ λ   την δε κοτυλην =

ε[ν Α]λεξανδρειαι δε κ[αι] τηι Λιβυηι πασηι

                 και του κικι[ος]   την δε κοτυλην =

15 του σησ[α]μιν[ο]υ τομ με[τρη]την Ⱶ μη (και του)

                                            την
(κ[ι]κιος τομ μ[ετ]ρητην [Ⱶ] μη) και παρεξουσιν

ἱκανο]ν τοις [βου]λομενοις ωνεισθαι π[ω]λο[υ]ντες

δ[ια χω]ρας εν [π]ασαις ταις πολεσιν [και κω]μαις

[. . . . .] σ . μ[. . μ]ετ[ρ]οις τοις εξετα[σθεισιν] υπο

[του οικονομου και του αν]τιγραφεω[ς]   20

About 5 lines lost.   Col. 41.

συντελε[. . . . . . τα] συντετ[αγμενα] τωι ν[ο]

μαρχηι [ο οικονο]μος και ο αντιγρ[αφευς]

———

αποδειξατωσαν δε τον σπορον τωι διοικουντι

   μετ
την ωνην ⟨δι⟩α του οικονομου και του αντιγραφεως

εαν δε γεωμετρησαντες μη ευρωσιν το πληθος   5

των αρουρων κατεσπαρμενον αποτινετωσαν

ο τε νομαρχ[η]ς και ο τοπαρχης και ο οικονομος

και ο αντιγραφευς εκαστος των α[ι]τιων εις μεν

το βασιλικον ⳨ β και τοις την ωνην εχουσιν

  τε
του σησαμ]ου ο ε[δει λαβειν αυτους της αρ ⊢ β   10

     το
του δε κροτω[νος] της αρ ⊢ α και επιγενημα

του ελαιου κα[ι] του κικιος εισπραξατω δε παρ αυ

των ο επι της διο[ι]κησεως τετεγμενος   εξω ορα

———

ο δε οικονομος [πρ]οτερον η την ωραν καθηκ⟨η⟩ιν
                               ε

του σ[π]ειρεσθαι το σησαμον και τον κροτωνα   15

δοτω τωι προεστηκοτι του νομου νομαρχηι

       εαμ βουληται
η τοπαρχηι ει[ς] τον σπ[ο]ρον του μεν σησαμου

[της αρου]ρα[ς] ⊢ δ του δε κροτ[ω]νο[ς] της αρου

E

[ρας ⊢] β κ[ο]μ[ι]ζεσθω δε απο της αλω αντι του

On the *verso* of Col. 41, to be read after line 13.

20 [. . . . . . .]ων νομων [. . . . .]

πα[. . σ]ησαμον η κ[ροτωνα . . . .] . . .

ταξει ο την ωνην αγορα[σας και]

___

οις προστ[ε]τακται εισπραξας παρ αυτων

[ο ε]πι τη[s] διοικησεως τεταγμενος

25 αποδοτ[ω] εις ους εδει νομους χορη

γηθηναι τ[ο] ση[σ]αμον και τον κροτωνα

___

ο δε οικο[νομ]ο[s]

Col. 42.   About 5 lines lost.

[. . . . .]υ παρα[. . . . .]

τ[ο]ν τ[ην ωνη]ν αγορασα[ντα περι τ]ης τιμης

οταν δε [ωρ]α ηι συναγειν τ[ο] σησ[α]μον και τον

κροτ[ω]να και κνηκον επαγγελλετωσαν

5 οι μεν γεωργοι τωι νομαρχηι και τωι τοπαρχηι

ου δε μη εισι νομαρχαι η τοπαρχαι τωι οικο

νομωι ουτοι δε παρακαλειτωσαν τον την

ωνη[ν] εχοντα ο δε την ωνην διοικων επελ

θων μετα τουτων επι τας αρουρας συντι

10 μησ[ατ]ω

___

οι δε [λαοι] και οι λοιποι γεωργοι τιμασθωσαν

τα α[υτω]ν γενηματα εκαστα κατα γενος

προτ[ερο]ν κομιζειν και συγγραφην ποιεισθωσαν

προς τ[ον] την ωνην εχοντα της τιμησεως

15 διπλ[ην ε]σφραγισμενην [γ]ραφετωσαν δε οι

[λ]αοι [το]ν σπορον ⟨π⟩οσον εκ[α]στο⟨ν⟩ κατεσσπα[ρκε]ν

κατ[α] γενος μεθ ορκου κ[αι] πο[σο]⟨ν⟩ εκαστος [τι]

ματα[ι] και σφραγιζ[εσθω]σαν την συνγραφην

συνεπ[ισ]φραγιζεσ[θ]ω δε και ο [π]αρα του νομαρ

[χου συν]αποσταλεις η τοπ[αρχου]   20

About 5 lines lost.   Col. 43.

[.]σαν και εκ [του . . . . .]ντος σ[. . . . . .]

παραμετρειν [εναντιο]ν των γεωργων   εξ[ω ορα]

δοτω δε ο νομαρχης η ο προεστηκως του νο

μου των αρ[ο]υρων τον σπορον κατα γεωργον προ

τερον η συνκομιζεσθαι τον καρπον ημεραις εξη   5

κοντα εαν δε μη δωι η μη παρασχηται τους

γεωργους εσπαρκοτας το πληθος το διαγραφεν

αποτινετω τωι την ωνην πριαμενωι και επι

τιμα τα γεγραμμενα αυτος δε πρασσετω [π]αρα

[τ]ων γεωργων των ηπειθηκοτων   10

[οσ]οι δ ατελεις εισιν κατα την χωραν η εν δ[ωρεα]ι

[η] εν συνταξι εχουσι⟨ν⟩ κωμας και γην παρ[αμε]

[τ]ρειτωσαν παν το γενομενον αυτοις σησα[μο]ν

[κ]αι τον κροτωνα και τα λοιπα φορτια τα συ[γκ]υ

ρ[ο]ντα εις την ελαικην υπολιπομενοι εις σπ[ερ]μα   15

το ικανον τιμην κομιζομενοι προς χαλκ[ο]ν

του μεν σησ[α]μου της αρ ⊢ ϛ του δε κροτωνος

την αρ ⊢ γ = τη[ς] δε κν[η]κου την αρ ⊢ α εαν

E 2

δε μη πα[ρ]αμετρησω[σι] πα[ν το σ]ησα[μ]ον

　　　　On the *verso* of Col. 43, to be read after line 2.

20 του [δ]ε διαγραφεντος σπαρη[ναι σησαμ]ου

και [κροτω]νος [ει]ς αλλους νομους π[οιησου]

[σι]ν την τιμησιν ο οικ[ο]νομος και ο [α]ντιγρα

φευς και τ[ο] σησαμον και τον κροτωνα πα[ρα]

λαμβανετωσαν παρα των γεωργ[ων]

25 δοτω δ[ε ο νο]μ

Col. 44.　　　　　　　　　　About 5 lines lost.

εργα[στηριον] ειναι και χαρ[α]ξαμ[τες] επισημα

νασθωσαν

οσαι δ εν δωρεαι κωμαι εισιν εν ταυταις δε

ελαιουργιον μηθεν καθιστατωσαν

5 παραθεσθωσαν δε εν εκαστωι εργαστηριωι

και σησαμον και κροτωνα και κνηκον την ικα

νην

τους δε ελαιουργους τους εν εκαστωι νομωι

καταταχθεντας μη επιτρεπ[ε]τωσαν εις

10 αλλον νομον μεταπορευεσθα[ι εα]ν δε τινες

μετελθωσιν αγωγιμοι εστ[ωσα]ν τωι τε διοι

κουντι την ωνην και τωι οικο[νο]μωι και τωι

αντιγραφει

μη υποδεχεσθω⟨σα[ν]⟩ δε τους ε[λ]αιουργους

15 μηθεις ε[α]ν δε τις ειδως υποδεξηται η επι

σταλεν[το]ς αυτωι μη αναγαγη αποτινετω

ε[κ]αστου [ελ]αιουργου ⊢ Γ και ο ελαιουργος αγωγι

μος ε[στω]

About 5 lines lost.

[. . . .] το [. . . . .]

[τ]ου ελαιου μεριζετω [. . . .] και απ[ο του] γε

    κατεργαζομενου

νηματος του ⟨πωλουμενου⟩ ελαιου το[ι]ς ελ[α]ιουργοις

              βſ

του μετρητου του δωδεκαχου ⊢ ⟨γ⟩ τουτου δε

                         αſ—

λαμβανετω ο μεν ελαιουργος και οι κοπεις ⊢ ⟨β⟩   5

             ſ=

και οι την ωνην ηγορακοτες ⊢ ⟨α⟩

εαν δε ο οικονομος η ο παρ αυτου καθεστηκως

   δι

μη αποδωι τοις ελαιουργοις το κατεργον η το

   ε

μεμ⟨η⟩ρισμενον αυτοις απο .της πρασεως αποτι

νετω εις μεν το βα[σιλι]κον ⊢ ʹΓ και τοις ελαιουργοις   10

τομ μισθον και ο τι α[ν η ω]νη δια τουτους καταβλα

βηι διπλουν

εαν δε τα ελαιουργ[ι]α μη καταστησωνται καθο

τι γεγραπται η τα φορ[τ]ια τα ικανον μη παρα

[θ]ωνται και δια ταυτα [η] ωνη καταβλαβηι αποτι   15

[ν]ετω ο τε οικονομος κ[αι ο] αντιγραφευς την εγδει

[αν] την γενομενην [και] τοις την ωνην πριαμενοις

[το βλ]αβ[ος δι]πλουν

[χορηγειτωσαν] δε [ο οι]κονομος κ[α]ι [ο α]ντιγ[ρ]αφε[υς]

[εν εκαστωι εργ]ασ[τ]ηρ[ιωι την κατασκευην]   20

About 5 lines lost.

[. . . . .]ω[. . . . .]

εις τ[ο κα]τεργον κατ[ιω]ν μηθεν επικωλυ[σατω] κα
ταβλαπτων την ωνην

                             τι
εαν δε μη χορηγηι η καταβλαψηι την ωνην κρινεσ
                 επι   και
5 θω επι του τεταγμενου της διοικησεως εαν κατα
ληφθηι αποτεινετω αργυριου ✗ β και το βλα
βος διπλουν

οι δε την ωνην εχοντες και ο αντιγραφευς ο κατασ
τα[θε]ις υπο του οικονομου και του αντιγραφε[ω]ς κυ
                 ελαιουργων
10 ρι[ευσου]σιν των ⟨γεωργων⟩ παντων των εν τ[ωι ν]ομωι
κ[αι τω]ν εργαστηριων και της κατασκευης [και π]α
ρα[σφρα]γιζεσθωσαν τα οργανα τον αργον το[υ χρο]νο[υ]

επ[αν]αγκαζετωσαν δε τους ελαιουργους [καθ] η
με[ραν ερ]γαζεσθαι και συμπαρεστωσαν κατ[εργ]α
15 ζε[σθ]ωσαν δε μη ελασσον την ημεραν του [μ]εν
ση[σ]αμου κατ εκαστον ολμον αρταβης (και τρ[ι]του)
το[υ] δε κροτων[ος] αρ δ της δε κνηκου αρ
απ[ο]διδοτωσα[ν δε] τ[.....] του μεν σησαμου
[των] δ [αρ δραχμας . του δε κροτ]ωνος των [.] αρ
20 ⊢ δ [τη]ς δε κνηκ[ου των . αρ δραχμ]ας η

Col. 47.   About 5 lines lost.

[συντ]αξιν δε προ[ς] τους ελ[α]ιουργου[ς περι τη]ς ρυσεως
του ελαιου μη ποεισθω μητε ο οικονομος μητε ο πρα
γματευομενος την ωνην παρευρεσει μηδεμιαι
μηδε τα οργανα τα εν τοις εργαστηριοις τον αργον
5 του χρονου ασφραγιστα απολειπετωσαν εαν δε συν

τα[ξ]ωνται προς τινας των ελαιουργων η ασφραγιστα

τα οργανα απολειπω[σ]ιν αποτ⟨ε⟩ινετω[σ]αν εις μεν

το βασιλικον εκαστος των αιτιων αργυριου ϰ α

και εαν τι η ωνη εγδε[ια]ν ποιη
      να

ο δε παρα του οικονομ[ο]υ κ[α]ι του αντιγραφεως καθεσ   10

τηκως αναγραψασθω τ[α ο]νοματα των καπηλων

των εν εκαστηι πολει ο[ντ]ων και των μεταβολων
         θ
και συνταξαστω προ[ς α]υτους μετα των την ωνην

πραγματευομενων π[οσο]ν δει ελαιον και κικι λαμβανον
      καθ ημεραν
τες πωλειν εν Αλεξανδρειαι δε συντασσεσθωσαν   15

προς τους παλινπρατ[ο]υντας και συγγραψασθωσαν

[προς] εκα[σ]τ[ο]ν συγγρα[φ]ην προς μεν τους εν τηι χω[ραι]

[κατα μηνα προς δε το]υς ε[ν Α]λεξα[νδρειαι . . . .]

About 5 lines lost.   Col. 48.

υ[πο το]υ οικονομου [και του] αντιγραφ[εως κατ]αχωριζεσ

θω εις την ωνην

οσον δ αν συνγραψωνται οι καπηλοι και οι μεταβολοι

οι εν εκαστηι κωμηι διαθησεσθαι ελαιον και κικι παρακομι

ζετωσαν ο τε οικονος και ο αντιγραφευς προτερον η τον μηνα 5

επιστηναι το πληθ[ος] εις εκαστην κωμην εκαστου γενους

και μετρειτωσαν τοι[ς] καπηλοις και τοις μεταβολοις κατα

π[ε]νθημερον και κομιζεσθωσαν τας τιμας εαμ μεν

δ[υν]ατον ηι αυθημερον ει δη μη εξελθου[σ]ων των πεντε

η[μερω]ν και καταβαλλετωσαν επι την [βα]σιλικην   10

τ[ρα]πεζαν το δε ανηλωμα το εις την [πα]ρακομιδην
δ[ι]δοτωσαν απο της ωνης

την δε συνταξιν ην αν ποιησωνται προς [ε]καστον επι
κ[η]ρυσσετωσαν προτερον η τον μ[η]να επιστηναι εμ
15 προσθεν ημεραις δεκα και γραψαντες εκτιθετωσαν
το ευρισκον εφ ημερας δεκα εν τε τηι μητροπολει και
εν τηι κ[ωμ]ηι κ[α]ι. του κυρωθεντες συγγραφην ποιεισθω
σ[αν]

7th
hand.
Col. 49.

[. . . . .]αι οι ελαιο⟨ο⟩ιργ[οι . . . .]
[. . . . . π]αραλαμβα[ν . . . .]
[τιμης] της γεγ[ραμμενης εν τωι διαγραμματι   ]
[. . . . . π]λειονο[ς . . . .]

About 4 lines lost.

5 το β[. . . . .] εργαζ[. . . . μητε ο]λμους εκ[. . . . .]
μητε ιπωτ[η]ρια μητε αλλο μηθεν των τηι ερ[γασιαι]
ταυτηι συγκυροντων παρευρεσει μηδεμιαι
ει δε μη αποτινετωσαν εις μεν το βασιλικον ✗ ε
και τοις την ωνην πριαμενοις το βλαβος πενταπλουν
10 παρ οις δε προυπαρχει τουτων τι απογραφεσθωσαν προς
                                   παρα
τον την ωνην διοικουντα και προς τον του οικονομου
και του αντιγραφεως εν ημεραις τριακοντα και επι
δεικνυτωσαν τους τε ολμ[ο]υς και τα ιπωτηρια

οι δε την ωνην εχοντες κα[ι ο] παρα του οικονομου
15 και του αντιγραφεως μετε[νεγ]κατωσαν εις τα
βασιλικα ελαιουργια εαν δ[ε τι]ς ευρεθηι σησαμον
η κροτωνα η κνηκον κατε[ργα]ζομενος τροπωι

το σησαμιν[ον] η το κνηκινον τη το

ωιτινιουν το ελαιον ⟨και⟩ κικ[ι] η αλλοθεμ ποθεν ωνου

μενος και μη παρα των την ωνην εχοντων περι μεν

αυτου ο βασιλευς διαγνωσεται αποτινετω δε τοις   20

την ων εχουσι ⊢ ᾽Γ και του ελαιου και των φορτιων

στερεσθω εισπρασσεσθω δε υπο του οικονομου και του

[αν]τιγραφεως εαν δε απρακτος ηι παραδ[οτ]ῳ αυτον

εις [. . . . . βο]υλομενον [. . . . . .]   Col. 50.

τ[. . . . . πραγ]ματευομε[ν . . . . .]

τη[. . . . . . . του οικονομο]υ και του α[ντιγρα]

[φεως . . . . σ[τειλαντ[. . . . . .]

[. . . . .] εαν δε α[. . . . . .]   5

About 3 lines lost.

[. . . . .]μου ελα[. . . . . παρευρεσει]

μηδεμιαι μηδ εις Αλε[ξανδρ]ειαν εισαγεσθαι

εξω τ[ο]υ βασιλικου εαν δε τινες εισαγωσι πλεον

ου μελλουσιν ανηλωσιν εκαστος ⟨την⟩ κατα σωμα

ημερων τριων των τε φορτιων σ⟨ε⟩τερεσθωσαν   10

και των πορειων και προσαποτινετωσαν καθ εκα

στον μετρητην ⊢ ρ και του πλειονος και του ελαισ

σονος κατα λογον

οι δε μαγειροι το στεαρ καταχρασθωσαν καθ η

μεραν [ε]ναντιον του την ελαικην εχοντος   15

αυτο [δε] καθ αυτο μηδενι πωλειτωσαν παρ[ευ]

ρεσει μη[δε]μιαι μηδε συντηκετωσαν μηδε απ[ο]

        ο τε αποδομενος κ[αι ο πρι]αμενος

τιθεσθ[ω]σαν ει δε μη αποτινετω εκαστος

F

καθ εκαστον ων αν πριητα[ι]
τωι τ[η]ν ελαικην πριαμενωι ⟨εκαστην ημεραν⟩ Ⱶ ν
20 οι δ ελα[ι]ουργουντες εν τοις ιεροις τοις κατα τη[ν]
χωραν απογραφεσθωσαν προς τομ πραγματευομ[ε]νον
την ωνην και προς τον παρα του οικωνομου κα[ι] του
αντιγραφεως ποσα τε ελαιουργια υπαρχει εν εκαστωι
ιε[ρω]ι κα[ι] ποσο[ι] ολμοι εν εκασ[τ]ωι εργαστηριωι

Col. 51.   [και ιπωτ]ηρια και επιδε[ι]ξατωσαν τα εργαστ]η[ρ]ια
[και τους ολ]μους και τα ιπ[ωτηρια παρασχε]τω
[σαν εις πα]ρασφραγισμον [   ]
[. . . . .]ωσαν δε ο τε[. . . . .] και
5 [. . . . .] του ελαιου κ[. . . . .]κο
                                       ι
[. . . . .]ην

About 3 lines lost.

εα[ι]ν δε μη] απογρα[φωνται μηδ επ]ιδειξω[σι μηδε
παρα[σχων]ται εις παρασφραγ[ι]ζμον αποτι[νετ]ω
σαν οι επι των ιερων τεταγμενοι εις μεν το βασι
10 λικον εκαστος των αιτιων ✗ γ και τοις την
οσον αν διατιμησωνται
ωνην πριαμενοις το βλαβος πενταπλουν οταν
δε βουλωνται κατεργαζεσθαι εν τοις ιεροις το ελαι
                                  ο
ον το σησαμινον παραλαμβανετωσαν τ⟨η⟩ν την ωνην
πραγματευομενον και τον παρα του οικονομου και
15 του αντιγραφεως και εναντιον τουτων ελαιουρ
γειτωσαν κατεργαζεσθω[σα]ν δε εν διμηνωι οσον
απεγραψαντο ´εις τον ενια[υτο]ν ανηλωθησε[σ]θαι

το δ[ε κ]ικιι το ανηλισκομενο[ν λ]αμβανετωσ[α]ν παρα

των [τ]ην ωνην εχοντων τη[ς κ]αθισταμενη[ς τ]ιμης

ο δ οικονομος και ο αντιγραφευς το ανηλωμ[α] το γινο   20

                             τ

μενον εις εκαστον ιερον τ[ο]υ ⟨δ⟩ε κικιος και του ελαιου

αποστελ[λ]ετωσαν την γρα[φ]ην προς τομ βασιλεα

διδοτωσαν δε και τωι επι της διοικησεως τετα

γμενωι μη εξεστω δε του ελαιου του κατερ

γαζομε[νο]υ εις τα ιερα μηθενι πωλειν ει δε μη στερε   25

σ[θωσαν του ελαιου κ]αι προσαποτινετ[ωσαν του]   Col. 52.

μ[ετρητου ⊦ ρ και το]υ πλειονος και ελ[ασσονος]   Plate X.

κ[ατα λογον]

ο[ι δ[εχοντες την ωνη]ν παραληψοντ[αι . . . . . .]

[. . . . .]ν επι της πρασ[εως . . . . . .]   5

[. . . . .] τον με ⊦ [. . . . .]

Two lines lost.

[. . . . . μη εξεστω]

αναγειν εις την χωρ[ιαν ε]πι πρασει μητε εξ Αλεξαν

δρειας μητε εκ Πηλουσιου μητε αλλοθεν μηδαμοθεν

εαν δε τινες αναγωσιν του τε ελαιου στερεσθωσαν και προσ 10

εισπρασσεσθωσαν του με ⊦ ρ και του πλειονος και

ελασσονος κατα λογον

εαν δε τινες εις την ιδιαν χρειαν ξενικον ελαιον κομι

ζωσιν οι μεν εξ Αλεξανδρειας αγοντες απογραφεσθω

σαν εν Αλεξανδρειαι και καταβαλλετωσαν ⟨εκασ⟩του μετ ⊦ ιβ 15

και το[υ] ελασσονος κατ[α] λογον και συμβολον λ[α]βοντες

αναγ[ε]τωσαν

F 2   .

το τελος
οι δε εκ [Πη]λουσιου αγοντες καταβαλλετω[σαν] εμ
Πηλου[σιωι] και συμβολ[ον λ]αμβανετωσαν

20 οι δε λογ[ευο]ντες εν Αλε[ξ]ανδρειαι και Πηλουσιω[ι]
καταχ[ωρι]ζετωσαν το [τε]λος εις ον αν νομον αγω[σι τ]ο
ελαιον

εαν δε τινες εις την ιδ[ια]ν] χρειαν αγοντες τα τελη μη κα
                              ζ
ταβαλλωσιν η το συμβολον μη κομι⟨ζ⟩ωσιν του τε ελαιου
25 στερεσθωσαν και προσαποτινετωσαν του με Ⱶ ρ οσοι δε των εμπορων

εκ Πηλουσιου ξενικον ελαιον η Cυρον παρακομιζ[ω]σιν εις [Αλ]εξανδ[ρ]ειαν ατελεις
   εστωσαν συμβ[ο]
[λον δ]ε κομιζε[τω]σ[αν] παρα [τ]ου εμ Π[η]λουσιωι καθεσ[τηκο]τος λ[ογ]ευτ[ου]
   και του οικ[ο]νομ[ου κα]θαπερ
[εν] τωι νομωι γεγ[ρα]πται ωσαυτ[ω]ς δε και του απ[...............]ε[...]
   εις Α[λε]ξανδρειαν
[...] και το[υ]του [συμβο]λον κομιζ[ε]τωσαν [π]αρα τ[ου..............]υ
   απ[.....] ε[α]ν δ[ε μη]

Col. 53.   ⟨[....με]νου συμβ⟩
Plate XI. [....μ]ενου συμβολου τω[............. του ελαιου]
[στερε]σθωσαν
[παρα]ληψονται δε οι [εχοντες την ωνην τ]ο προκη
5 [ρυχθε]ν εφ εκαστωι νομ[ωι αποτιθεσθαι σησ]αμον
[και κρο]τωνα αφ ης αν ημ[ερας την ωνην παραλαβ]ωσιν
[εν ημ]εραις γ του σησαμου την αρ Ⱶ . του σ]ησα
[μινο]υ τον με Ⱶ [.. και κροτωνος . και κ]ικιος Ⱶ ιζ

Two lines lost.

[......]μωι[............] τιμης ης[.....] ται αυτοις [....]ρ[....]

[. . . . . .] εις το κζ L και του σησαμου και κροτωνος και κινηκ[ου] τι[μ]ην την 10
γεγραμμε

νη[ν εν τωι] διαγραμματι τωι εκτε[θε]ντι εις το κζL

εαν δε πλειον εγκαταλ[ε]ιπωσιν εξιοντες εκ της
ωνης κομιζεσθωσαν παρα του οικονομου τιμην
⊢ κθ/
του μεν σησαμινου του με (⊢ λα/—ν) του δε κι
⊢ ιζ—
κιος του με ⊢ κ(α =) του δε κνηκινου του με ⊢ (ιη/—)   15
του δε σησαμου της ᾱρ ⊢ η του δε κροτωνος
α=
της ᾱρ ⊢ δ της δε κνηκου ⊢ (α/) οσον δ αν ελαιον
εξ
υποκηρυξωμεν ληψεσθαι εκαστου ν[ο]μου εις
τα[ς] εν Αλεξανδρειαι διαθεσεις ληψομε[θ]α παρ αυ
[κικ]ιος τομ με ⊢ιθ=   ο
των εν τωι νομωι του [με]ν ελαιου τον με τον ιβχ   ⎞
⎛χω[ρι]ς κεραμου ⊢ λα/—[ν] του δε κικι[ος] ⊢ κα =   ⎟ 20
⎝   ν   ⎠
τ[ου] δε κνηκινου ⊢ ιη/— [του] δε κολοκυ[ν]τι⟨κο⟩ου ⊢ ιβ⎠
κ[αι υ]πολογισθησεται η τ[ιμη] τοις εχουσ[ι] τας ωνας
ει[ς τ]ας αναφορας τας γινομ[ενα]ς την δε τ[ιμ]ην των φορ
τ[ιω]ν και το κατεργον και τ[ο] ανηλωμα π[ροα]νηλισκε   25
τ[ω ο] οικονομος

(οσ[ου] δ αν χρειαν εχωμεν ελαιου σησαμινου η κικιος εν Αλε)
(ξ[ανδρειαι προκηρυξ]ομεν επι της π[ρασεως . . . .]   Col. 54.
κα[. . . . .]τον με ⊢ μη) ο[. . . . .]
σθ[. . . . . η]μιολιν τας ελαιο[. . . . .]
δ[. . . . .]ματος λογον τ[. . . . .]
[. . . . .]ενων ε[ν] τω[ι . . . .]   5

Two lines lost.

[. . . . . *εξουσιαν μηδεμιαν*]

εχετωσ[αν] εισαγειν π[αρευρεσε]ι μηδεμιαι εα[ν] δε λη[φθωσ]ιν εισαγοντες

στερεσθωσαν του ελαιου

εαν δε μη δωσιν τον λογον [η μ]η αποδειξωσιν εισαγη

γοχοτες εις Αλεξανδρειαν παν το ελαιον (η εις τους γο)

                                        ου αν μη ενδειξωνται εισα

10 *(μους ληφθωσιν εισαγοντες) του τε ελαιου ⟨στερεσθω⟩*

    γηγοχοτες την τιμην εισπρασσεσθωσαν και

    ⟨σαν⟩ και προσαποτινετωσαν ⟨εις το βασιλικον⟩ εκαστος

                          η

    των μεμισθωμενων τ⟨ω⟩ν κωμην ⳨ *γ*

    υπαρχετω δε η στερεσις εις το βασιλικον και κατα

    χωριζεσθω⟨σαν⟩ εις τη[ν] ελαικην την εν τηι χωραι

15 *παρα[κ]αταστησουσι δε οι πριαμενοι τη[ν ω]νην*

    και αν[τι]γραφεις εν Αλεξανδρειαι και Πηλουσιωι [του] ελαι

    ου του [εκ Σ]υριας αποσ[τ]ελλομενου εις Πηλο[υσιον] και

    Αλεξα[νδρει]αν και πα[ρα]σφραγιζεσθωσαν τα α[ποδ]ο

    χια κα[ι τω]ι ανηλισκομ[ε]νωι παρακολουθειτω[σαν]

20 *ο δε κα[τα]σταθεις αντι[γρα]φευς της ωνης υπο του ο[ι]κονο*

    μου διαλογιζεσθω π[ρος] τον την ωνην εχοντα κ[α]τα

    μηνα εναντιον του αντι[γρ]αφεως γραφετω δε εν τοις λογοις

    τα τε φορτια οσα εκαστο[υ γ]ενους παρειληφεν και οσα

                         [τιμης της εν τωι διαγ]ραμματι γεγραμμενης

Col. 55. *[κατει]ργασται και πε[πωληκε . . . . . . χωρις] του αφαι*

    [ρετου] την τε τιμην τω[ν παρειλημμενων] την εν

    [τωι] διαγραμματι γεγρ[αμμενην . . . . σ]υν τωι

    [κερα]μιωι και τοις λοιποι[ς ανηλωμασι του μεν σ]ησαμου

5 *[της]* a͞ρ *⊢ α του δε κρο[τωνος . της δε κν]ηκου =*

    [του δε κολοκυντινου . του δε εκ του λινου σπερματος .]

[του δε σησαμινου ελαιου των . $\overline{αρ}$ Ⱶ . του δε κικιος των]

ε [$\overline{αρ}$ Ⱶ]α— του δε κνηκ[ινου] των η $\overline{αρ}$ [Ⱶ .] του δε

επ[ελλ]υχνιου των ζ $\overline{αρ}$ Ⱶ α κολοκυντινου των ιβ $\overline{αρ}$ α—

                                    απο

και το συντεταγμενον μεριζεσθαι του επιγενηματος   10

τωι ελαιουργωι και τωι την ωνην διοικουντι και ο τι αν εις

την παρακομιδην των φορτιων γενηται

οι δε μισθοι τοις πραγματευομενοις την ωνην διδοσθω

                      εκ

σαν απο του μεμερισμενου ⟨απο⟩ του επιγενηματος

εν Αλ[εξ]ανδρειαι δε το τε κατεργον του σησαμινου ελαιου και το προπωλητικον   15

και οι μ[ισ]θοι διδοσθωσαν καθοτι αμ προκηρυχθηι επι τη[ς] πρασεως

ZHTHCIC

                        η   ων

εαν δε οι ηγορακοτες την ω[νην] οι ⟨επι⟩ τουτ⟨οι̣ς⟩) υπηρεται

βο[υλ]ωνται ζητειν φαμε[νοι ελ]αιον παρα τ[ισι]ν υπαρχειν

κα[ρπ]ιμον η ελαιουργι⟨ον⟩α ζ[η]τειτωσαν π[αρ]οντος του   20

                η   [παρα τ]ου

π[αρα] του οικονομου ⟨και⟩ του [αντι]γραφεως ε[αν δ]ε παρακλη

θ[εις ο] παρα του οικονου η του [αν]τιγραφεως μ[η α]κολουθησηι

η [μη] παραμεινηι εως αν η ζητησις γενητα[ι α]ποτινετωσαν

τ[οις] την ωνην πριαμενοις την διατιμησιν [οσο]υ αν διατιμη

                και

σωνται διπλην ⟨μη⟩ εξεστω δε τοις την [ων]ην εχουσι   25

ζη[τειν εντος . ημ]ερων   **Col. 56.**

πρ[. . . . .]αι τιμασθω και [. . . . . . .]

ου α[. . . . .]

ος δ[. . . . .] την ζητησιν κ[. . . . .]

                         οτι αν

[. . . . .]ξηι η μη δεξηται

5 [. . . . .] ⟨ϗο⟩[. . . . . . .]

One line lost.

[. . . . .] τῳ [. . .]

τον δε μη ευροντα [α] εφη ζητειν εξεστω [τ]ωι

ζητουμενωι ορκισαι εν ιερωι η μην μηθενος αλλου

ενεκεν την ζητησιν ποιεισθαι αλλα των προσ

10 αγγελεντων και συγκυροντων εις την ωνην

εαν δε μη ομοσηι αυθημερον η τηι υστεραιαι απο

τινετω τωι εξορκιζοντι το τιμημα οσου ετιμη

πριν

σατο ⟨επι⟩ την ζητησιν ποιεισθαι διπλουν

οι δε πριαμενοι την [ω]νην εγγυους καταστη

15 σουσι τω[ν] εφεικοστων και διορθωσονται τα [μ]εν λο

γευμα[τ]α καθ ημεραν [ε]πι την τραπεζ[αν τη]ν

δ αναφορ[αν τ]ην επιβαλ[λ]ουσαν τωι μηνι εν τ[ωι εχ]ο

μενωι [προ] της διχο[μ]ηνιας

20

$$\left(\begin{array}{l} τοις\ ελαιουργ[οις\ τ]ο\ γινομενον \\ διδοναι\ απο\ το[υ\ κα]τεργαζομενου \\ και\ μη\ απο\ του\ α[πο]τιθεμενου \end{array} \right)$$

8th hand. Col. 57. Pl. XII.

[Δ]ΙΟΡΘΩΜΑ ΤΟ[Υ ΝΟΜΟΥ ΕΠΙ ΤΗ]Ι [ΕΛ]ΑΙΚΗΙ

πωλουμεν τ[ην ελαικην την κατα] την χωραν

απο μηνος Γορπι[αιου του . . . . Αιγ]υπτιων

5 Μεσορη εις ετ[η β κατα το εκθεμα] το εκκειμενον

Three lines lost.

πλειον [. .] υ[πα]ρ[ξει] τ[ο] τ[ελος το]υ [τε ση]σ[αμου κα]ι του κρ[οτωνος]

τοις τον εισιοντα χρονον πριαμενοις οσας δ αν αρουρας

απο
ελασσους ⟨παρα⟩δειξωμεν κατεσπαρμενας τωμ προ
κηρυχθεισων εν εκαστωι νομωι παρεξομεν εξ αλλων
νομων το τε σησαμον και τον κροτωνα τον ελλειποντα   10
και απο του δοθησομενου σησαμου και κροτωνος υπαρξει
αυτοις το τελος α/ β ├ του σησαμου και ├ α του
κροτωνος εξ ου δ αν νομου το πλεοναζον του προκη

ρυχθεντος εξαγωμεν σησαμον η κροτωνα ου πραξον
ται το τελος το απο του [σ]ησαμου και του κ[ρο]τωνος οσον 15

δ αν μη δωμεν εις το ε[λλε]ιπον σησαμον και ελαιον αφ ου
το επιγενημα το ισον λ[ηψον]ται οσον απ[ο τ]ου σησαμινου
ελαιου και απο του σησα[μου] εις δε το κικ[ι κ]ολοκυντινον
ελαιον και το απο του λινο[υ σ]π[ε]ρματος κ[ατ]εργασαμενοι
δια των οικονομων μετ[ρη]σομεν αφ ου [το επ]ιγενημα το   20
ισον ληψονται οσον απο [τε] το[υ] κικιος κα[ι απο] του κροτωνος
                                             ουσιν
ελαμβανον τωι δε κατεργασαμενωι επ[ακο]λουθησ⟨ονται⟩
οι την ωνην · εχοντες [και π]αρασ[φρα]γιουντ[αι]

[οσον δ αν εξ εκαστου νο]μου σησαμον η [κροτωνα . . . .]ν Col. 58.
[η ελαιον σησαμινον η κι]κι η το κολοκυντι[νον . . . .]
[ου πραξονται οι πριαμε]νοι την ελαικην εξ [. . . σησαμου . .]
[. . . . . τελος ο]υθεν το δε σπε[ιρομενον σησαμον και κρο]
[τωνα εν τηι αφωρισμενηι] παραληψεται ο [οικονομος και χορηγη] 5
[σει εις το ελαιουργιον το εν Αλεξανδρειαι πωλουμεν δε την]
[ωνην προς χαλκον και ληψομεθα εις τον στατηρα οβολους]
[εικοσι τεσσαρας εαν δε πλειω η ρυσις εγβηι υπαρξει το]
πλ[ειον ε]ις το βασιλικ[ον]

9th
hand.   ΔΙΟΡΘ[ΩΜΑ ΤΟΥ ΝΟΜΟΥ Ε]ΠΙ ΤΗΙ ΕΛΑ[ΙΚΗΙ]

Col. 59. π[ωλουμεν την] ελαικην τ[ην κατα την]

χ῾ωραν απο μηνος Γ]ορπιαιου του [. . . . Αι]

[γυπτιων Μεσορη ε]ις ∟β κατ[α το εκθεμα]

5 [το εκκειμενον   ] παρε[. . . . .]

Two lines lost.

[. . . . . .] αρουρας [. . . . . πλειον . . υπαρ]

ξει το τελος του σ[ησαμο]ν και του κροτ[ωνος τοις τον]

εισιοντα χρονον πρ[ι]αμενοις οσας δ αν αρουρας ελασσο[υς]

αποδειξωμεν κατεσπαρμενας των προκηρυ

10 χθεισων εν εκαστωι νομωι παρεξομεν εξ αλλων

νομων το τε σησαμον και τον κροτωνα τον εν

λειποντα και απο του δοθησομενου σησαμου

και κροτωνος υπαρξει αυτοις το τελος α/ β ⊢

της αρταβης και ⊢ α του κροτωνος

15 εξ ου δ αν νομου το πλεοναζον του προκηρυ

χθεντος εισαγωμεν η σησαμον η κροτωνα ου

πραξονται το τελος το απο του σησαμου και του

κρο[τ]ωνος οσον [δ] αν μη δωμεν εις το ελλειπον

σησ[α]μον και ελαιο[ν] αφ ου και το επιγε[ν]ημα το ισον

20 λη[μ]ψονται οσο[ν] απο του σησαμ[ιν]ου ελαιου

και [του] σησαμου [ε]ις δε το κικι το κολ[οκυ]νθινον ελαι

ον κ[αι τ]ο απο του [λ]ινου σπερματος κ[. . κ]ατεργα

σα[μενοι δια] τω[ν ο]ικονομων μετρη[σομε]ν ου το ε[πι]

γε[νημα το ισον λη]μψονται οσον απο τ[ε του κικιος και απο]

25 τ[ου κροτωνος ελαμ]βανον τωι δε κα[τεργασαμενωι]

επακολουθ[ησουσιν οι την ων]ην

εχοντες και [παρασφραγιουν]ται

οσον δ αν εξ εκ[αστου νομου σησ]αμον

η κροτω[να . . . . η ελαι]ον

[σ]ησαμιν[ον η κικι η το κολοκυ]ν   5

[τινον . . . . ου πραξον]

[ται οι πριαμενοι την ελαικην εξ . . . ση]

[σ]αμου [. . . . .]

τελος ουθεν το δε σπειρομεν[ον· σησ]α

μον και κροτων εν τηι αφωρισμε   10

νηι παραλημψεται ο οικονομος και

χορηγησει εις το ελαιουργιον το εν Α

λεξανδρειαι πωλουμεν δε την

ωνην προς χαλκον και λημψομεθα

εις τον στατηρα οβολους κδ̄ εαν δε   15

πλειω η ρυσις εγβηι υπαρξει το ελαιον

και κικι εις το βασιλικον

EN ΤΩΙ CAITHI CYN NAYKPATEI

   σησαμου ȣ M̄ͣ

   · κροτωνος ȣ M̄ͣ'Αυλγβ'   20

   και ωστ [ει]ς την εν Αλεξανδρειαι

   διαθεσιν [ου] τελος ουθεν πραξεται

   ο τον Ca[ιτη]ν αγορασ[α]ς ȣ M̄ͣχξϛγ'

   και σησα[μου] εις την ε[ν] Αλεξανδρει

   αι διαθεσ[ιν   ] αρ 'Γ   25

Col. 61.

ΕΝ [ΤΗΙ ΛΙΒΥΗΙ ΠΑ]CΗΙ ΧѠΡΙC ΤΗC [ΑΦѠΡΙC]

[ΜΕΝΗC *σησαμου*] ȣ 'Εψ

[*και εν τηι αφω*]*ρισμενηι ο δει* [*χορηγειν*]

[*εις την εν Αλε*]*ξανδρειαι δια*

5   [*θεσιν ου*] *τελος ουθε*[*ν πραξεται ο την*]

[*Λιβυην αγορασας*] ȣ [. .]

[*τον δε κροτωνα ον δει κατεργασθη*]

[*ναι εν τηι ωνηι χορηγησομεν εξ*]

[*αλλων νομω*]*ν αρ*[. .]

10   *ου τελος το γινομενον απο*

του κροτωνος υπαρξει τωι την

Λιβυην αγορασαντι

ΕΝ ΤѠΙ ΠΡΟCѠΠΙΤΗΙ

σησαμου ȣ 'Αω

15   *κροτωνος* ȣ 'Β

και ωστε εις την εν Αλεξανδρειαι

διαθεσιν ου τελος ουθεν πραξεται

ο τον Προσωπιτην αγορασας

αρταβας $\overset{a}{\text{M}}\text{Γχ}$

20   ΕΝ ΤѠΙ ΝΙΤΡ[Ι]ѠΤΗΙ

σησαμου   ȣ *τ*

[*τ*]*ον δε κροτωνα ον δει κατεργ*[*α*]*σθηναι*

[*εν*] *τηι ωνη*[*ι*] *χορηγησομεν εξ* [*αλ*]

[*λων*] *νομ*[*ω*]*ν αρ* 'Δ

25   [*ου τελος τ*]*ο γινομενον απ*[*ο του*]

Col. 62.

[*κροτ*]*ωνος υπαρξ*[*ει τωι την*]

[*Νιτ*]*ριωτην αγ*[*ορασαντι*]

[ΕΝ ΤΩ]Ι ϹΕΒΕΝΝΥΤ[ΗΙ]

[σησ]αμου ℞ [. .]

[και ω]στε εις τη[ν εν Αλεξανδρειαι]   5

[διαθε]σιν ου τε[λος ουθεν πραξε]

[ται ο] τον Ϲ[εβεννυτην]

[αγορασας   αρ . .]

[τον δε κροτωνα ον δει κατερ]

γα[σθηναι] εν τηι ω[νηι. χορηγη]   10

σο[με]ν εξ αλλων [νομων]

αρταβας   Μ̇φ

ου το τελος το γινομενον α

πο του κροτωνος υπαρξει τωι

τον Ϲεβεννυτην αγορασαντι   15

ΕΝ ΤΩΙ ΜΕΝΔΗϹΙΩΙ

σ[ησ]αμου   ℞ Ϛ

κα[ι] ωστε εις την διαθεσιν τη[ν]

εν τοις αλλοις νομοις ου τελος

ου[θε]ν πρᾳξεται ο τον Μενδη   20

σι[ον] αγορασας   ℞ Β

τ[ο]ν δε κροτωνα ο[ν] δει κα

τ[ερ]γ[ασ]θηναι εν τ[ηι ω]νηι

χορηγησ[ομεν εξ αλλ]ων   Col. 63.

νομων [αρ .]φ

ου το τελ[ος το γινομεν]ον

απο του κροτωνος υπαρξε]ι τωι

τον Μεν[δησιον αγορασα]ντι   5

ΕΝ ΤΩΙ Β[ΟΥϹΙΡΙΤΗΙ]

σησ[αμου   ϗ   .]χν
[και ωστε εις την διαθεσιν]
[την εν τοις αλλοις νομοις

10   ου τ[ο] τε[λο]ς ουθε[ν πραξ]εται
ο τον Βου[σι]ριτην αγ[ορ]ασας
κροτωνος [ϗ   . .]
σησαμου   ϗ ’Ατν

ΕΝ ΤΩΙ ΑΘΡΙΒΙΤΗΙ

15   σησαμου   ϗ ’Αφ
και εκ των αλλων νομων
χορηγησομεν αρ ’ϛω
ου το τελος το γινομενον
απο τ.ου σησαμου υπαρξει
20   τωι τον Αθριβιτην αγορασαν
τι κροτωνο[ς] ϗ ’Γψξ
και ωστε ει[ς τ]ους αλλους νομους
αρταβας   ’Γ

Col. 64.   ο[υ τελος ουθεν π]ραξεται
ο τ[ον Αθριβιτη]ν αγορασας

ΕΝ Τ[ΩΙ ΗΛΙΟΠ]ΟΛΙΤΗΙ

σ[ησαμου   ] ϗ φ
5   [και εκ των αλλ]ων νομων
[χορηγησομεν] αρ ’Β
[ου το τελος το γι]νομενον
[απο του σησαμου υπαρξει]

[τωι τον Ηλιοπολιτην]
α[γορασαντι τον δε κρο]   10
τ[ωνα ον δει κ]ατεργασ
θ[ην]αι εν τηι [ω]νηι χορηγη
[σο]μεν εξ αλλων νομων
[αρ]ταβας Ϝφ
[ου το] τελος το γινομενον   15
[το]υ κροτωνος υπαρξει ·
τωι τον Ηλιοπ[ο]λιτην αγο
ρασαντι

ΕΝ ΤΩΙ ΒΟΥΒΑCΤΙΤΗΙ ΚΑΙ
ΒΟΥΒ[Α]CΤΩΙ   20

σησαμου   ʚ 'Α
κ[αι] εκ των αλλων νομων

[χορηγη]σομεν [αρ . .]   Col. 65.
[ου το τε]λος το γινο[μενον απο το]υ
[σησαμ]ου υπαρξει [τωι τον Βου]
[βαστι]την και Βου[βαστον αγο]
[ρασαν]τι τον δ[ε κροτωνα ον δε]ι   5
[κατεργ]ασθηναι εν [τηι ωνηι χορ]η
[γησομε]ν εξ αλ[λων νομων]
[αρταβας   . .   ]
[ου το τελος το γινομενον απο]
τ[ο]υ κ[ροτωνος υπαρξει τωι τον]   10
Βουβ[αστι]την και Β[ουβ]αστ[ο]ν
αγορα[σα]ντι

EN THI APABIAI

σησαμου   ४ 'Αμ

15   και ωστε εις τους αλλους νομους

αρουρας   'B

ου τελος ουθεν πραξ[ε]ται ο την

Αραβιαν αγορασας το[ν δε] κροτω

να ον δει κατεργα[σθ]ηναι εν

20   τηι ωνη[ι] χορηγησομ[ε]ν εξ αλ

λων νομων   αρ 'Γψ

Col. 66.   ου [το τελος το] γινομεν[ον υπαρ]

ξε[ι τωι την Α]ραβιαν αγ[ορασαντι]

EN T[ΩΙ CEΘP]ΩΙΤΗΙ

ση[σαμου] ४ [. .]

5   κ[αι ωστε εις το]υς αλλου[ς νομους]

ου [το τελος ο]υθεν πρα[ξεται]

ο [τον Cεθρωιτ]ην αγορα[σας]

[αρουρας   . .   ]

[τον δε.κροτωνα ον δει κατερ]

10   γ[ασθηναι εν τηι ωνηι χορη]

γησομεν εξ [α]λλων ν[ομ]ων

αρταβας   'Ευξ

ου τελος το γινομενον [α]πο

του κροτωνος υπαρξει τωι

15   τον Cεθρωιτην αγορασ[α]ντι

EN TΩΙ TANITHI

σησαμου   ४ 'Αυλ

κα[ι] ωστε εις τ[ο]υς αλλους νομους

ου τελος ουθεν πραξεται [ο] τον
Τανιτην αγορασας ১ 'Αφο   20
τον δε κροτωνα ον δει κατε[ρ]γασ

θηναι εν [τηι ωνηι] χορη   Col. 67.
γησομεν [εξ αλλων] νομων
αρταβ[ας]   'Εμ
ου το τε[λος το γινο]μενον
απο του [κροτωνος] υπαρ   5
ξει τω[ι τον Τανιτ]ην
αγορασα[ντι]

[ΕΝ ΤΩΙ ΛΕΟΝΤΟΠΟΛΙΤΗΙ]

[σησαμου   ১ . .]
[και ω]σ[τε] εις τους αλ[λους]   10
νομους ου τελος ουθεν
πραξετα ο τον Λεοντο
πολιτην αγορασας ১ Σμ
τον δε κροτωνα ον δει κα
τεργασθηναι εν τηι ωνηι   15
χορηγησομεν εξ αλλων
νομων   αρ 'ϛΣ
ου το τελος το γινομενον
απο του κροτωνος υπαρξει
τωι τον Λεοντοπολιτην   20
[α]γορασαντι

[ΕΝ ΤΩΙ ΦΑ]ΡΒΑΘΙΤΗΙ   Col. 68.

[σησαμο]υ   ১ [. .]
[και ωστε] εις τους α[λλους]

II

5 [νομους ο]υ τελος ο[υθεν]
  [πραξετ]αι ο τον Φ[αρβαι]
  [θιτην αγ]ορασας [�733 . .]
  [τον δε κ]ρο[τ]ων[α ον δει κα]
  [τεργασθηνα]ι εν [τηι ωνηι]
  [χορηγησομεν εξ αλλων]
10 [νομων αρ . .]
  [ο]υ το τ[ελ]ος τ[ο γινομε]
  νον απο του κροτωνος υ
  παρξει [τ]ωι τον Φαρβαιθι
  την αγορασαντι

15 ΕΝ ΤѠΙ ΛΗΤΟΠΟΛΙΤΗΙ
  σησαμου ʘ υπ
  κροτωνος ʘ φν
  και ωστε εις την διαθεσιν
  την εν τοις αλλοι νομοις
20 ου τελος ουθεν πραξεται
  ο τον Λητοπολιτην αγο
  ρασας ʘ 'ΑΣν

Col. 69. ΕἸΣ ΜΕΜΦ[ΙΝ ΔΕΙ Χ]ΟΡΗΓΕΙ[Ν]
  [Ε]Κ ΤΗΣ Λ[ΙΜΝΗΣ]
  σησα[μου αρ] 'ΔΣ
  κροτω[νος αρ . .]
5 ου τελ[ος ουθεν π]ρα[ξεται]
  ο την ελ[αικην τη]ν ε[ν Μεμ]
  φει αγ[ορασας]

[ΕΝ ΤΩΙ ΕΡΜΟΠΟΛΙΤΗΙ]

[σησαμου ৬ ..]

και εκ των αλλω[ν] νομων   10

χορηγη[σ]ομεν αρ M̅'Β̅ͣ

ου το τελος το γινομενον ·

απο του σησαμου υπαρξει

τωι τον Ερμοπολιτην

αγορασαντι και τον κρο   15

τωνα ον δει κατεργαζεσθαι

εν τηι ωνηι χορηγησομεν

εξ αλλων νομων αρ M̅'Β̅Τ̅ͣ

ου το τελος το γινομε[νον α]

πο του κροτωνος υπαρξ[ε]ι   20

τωι τον Ερμοπολιτην αγο

ρασαντι

[ΕΝ] ΤΩΙ Ο[ΞΥΡΥΓΧΙ]ΤΗΙ   Col. 70.

[σησαμου ৬] 'Αω[.]

[τον δε κροτωνα] ον δε[ι]

[κατεργασθηναι εν] τηι [ω]

[νηι χορηγησομε]ν εξ α[λ]   5

[λων νομων αρ] 'ϛχ[.]

[ου το τελος το γινομενον]

[απο του κροτωνος υπαρ]

[ξει τωι τον Οξυρυγχι]

[την αγορασαντι]   10

H 2

ΕΝ ΤΩΙ ΗΡΑΚΛΕΟΠΟ[ΛΙ]ΤΗ[Ι]

σησαμου   ℔ 'B
και εκ των αλλων νομων
χορηγησομεν   αρ 'Βω

15   ου το τελος το γινομενον
απο του σησαμου υπαρξει
τωι τον Ηρακλεοπολιτην
αγορασαντ[ι] και τον κροτω
να ον δει κατεργασ[θ]ηναι εν

20   τηι ωνηι χορηγησομεν
[ε]ξ [αλ]λων νομων αρ 'Θφ

Col. 71.   [ου το] τελος το [γινομεν]ον απο
[του κ]ροτων[ος υπαρξ]ει τωι
[τον] Ηρακλε[οπολιτη]ν αγο
[ρασαν]τι

5   ## [ΕΝ ΤΗΙ] ΛΙΜ[ΝΗΙ]

[σησα]μου [℔ . .]
[κροτωνος ℔ . .]
[και ωστε εις τους αλλους]
[νομους ου τελος ουθεν]

10 ε].]π̣α̣ι   [πραξεται ο τον Λιμνι]
    γ
. . . Μ   την αγορασας ℔ [. .]
    σησαμου   ℔ 'Ητ

ΕΝ ΤΩΙ ΑΦΡΟΔΙΤΟΠΟΛΙΤΗΙ

σησαμου   ℔ χλ

15   τον δε κροτωνα ον δει κα

τεργασθηναι εν τηι ω
νηι χορηγησομεν εξ αλ
λων νομων αρ 'ΒΣ
ου το τελος το γινομε
νον απο του κροτωνος   20
υπαρξει τωι τον Αφρο
διτοπολιτην αγ[ο]ρασαντι

[ΕΝ ΤΩΙ ΚΥΝΟΠΟΛΙΤΗΙ]   Col. 72.

[σησαμου   ☙ . .]
[και εκ των αλλων νομων]
[χορηγησομεν   αρ . .]
[ου το τελος το γινομενον]   5
[απο του σησαμου υπαρξει]
[τωι τον Κυνοπολιτην]
[αγορ]ασαντ[ι και τον κρο]
[τ]ωνα ον δει κ[ατεργασθη
[ναι] ☙ [. .]   10

ΕΝ ΤΩΙ ΜΕΜΦΙΤΗΙ ΧΟΡΗ ΓΗCΟΜΕΝ ΕΚ ΤΗC ΛΙΜΝΗC

σησαμου   αρ 'Βυ
κροτωνος   αρ 'Βρκ
ου τελος ουθεν πραξεται   15
ο την ελαικην την εν
τωι Μεμφιτηι αγορασας

ΕΝ ΤΗΙ ΘΗΒΑΔΙ

σησαμου   ☙ 'Γτν
κροτωνος   ☙ Μ̇'Αωϟ   20

καὶ ὥστε εἰς [τ]ην [διͺ]αθε[σ]ιν τ[ην]
ἐν Ἀλεξανδρ[ε]ιαι
κροτωνος ৬ 'Θξζ

10th hand.
Col. 73.
D.

ΔΙΑ̣[ΓΡΑ]Μ̣ΜΑ ΤΡΑΠΕΖω[Ν]

[πωλουμ]εν τας τραπ[εζας . . . .]
[. . . κα]τα την χωρ[ιαν . . . .]
[. . . . . .]ιβικην τρα[πεζαν . . . .]
5 [. . . . . .] ϵγληψοντ[. . . . .]
[. . . . .] παρα[. . . . .]

The rest lost.

Col. 74. παραληψονται δε και οι οικονομοι και οι πρασσ[οντες τι]
των βασιλικ[ω]ν παρα των καταβαλλοντω[ν τα . . . .]
ματα καθοτι κα̣ι̣ τ[η]ν̣ [τρ]απεζαν γεγρα[πται]
παραλαμβα[νε]ιν [. . . . . .]υσι παντε[ς . . . . . .]
5 ρα[. . . . .] αλλωι [. . . . .]
εξ[. . . . .] δ αγοραζει̣ν̣ [. . . . .]
βιζ[. . . . . παρ]ευρεσει μη[δεμιαι]
οσο[. . . . .]

The rest lost.

Col. 75. [αι εν ταις] πολεσιν η κωμαις τραπεζαι βασιλικαι μη υπ[. . .]
ενην
[. . . . . α]ναφερετωσαν επι την αποδεδειγμ τραπεζαν[. . .]
[. . . . εν ημ]εραις δεκα εαν δε μη ανε[νεγκ]ω[σιν] αποτινετω[σαν]
[τωι τη]ν τραπεζαν ηγορακο[τι καθ εκα]στην ημεραν ⊦ [. .]
5 [. . εξε]στω δε τοις τρ[απεζιταις παρα] των καταβαλ[λοντων]
[. . . . . .]ν αργυ[ρι . . . . λ]αμβανοντω[ν . . .]
[του βασι]λικου ε[. . . . . ε]αν δε τι μ[. . . .]

[. . . . . .]ιν η μολυ[βδ . . . .]ν η[. . . . . .]

[. . . . . .]ηλου[. . . . .]

[. . . . . .]πρου[. . . . .]   10

The rest lost.

[. . . . .]ατα παρασφραγιζεσθω δε ο ηγορακως την Col. 76.

[τραπεζαν και . . .]κιμον παρεχετω οταν δ επιπαραριθμειν

[. . . . . ο] την τραπεζαν αγορασας και τον χαλκον παρα

[ριθμειτω λα]μβανων επι τωι στατη[ρι προς αλλ]αγην οβολους

[. . αλλωι δε μη]θενι εξεσθω εγδε[. . . . .] εαμ μη συντα 5

[ξηται προς το]ν ηγορακο[τα την τραπεζαν εαν δε αλι]σκηται

[. . . . .]στερεσ[θω . . . .]ωι την

[. . . . .] Ⱶ κ [. . . . .]τι

[. . . . . δ]ιδοτω ν[. . . . .]

[. . . . .] προς α[. . . . .] 10

The rest lost.

[. . . . . . ωι αν γραφηι] παντα χαλκον διδοναι χρηματιει   Col. 77.

[. . . . .]   ωι δ αν γραφ[ηι] παν αργυριον υπολο

[γειν . . . .]ου δει τον χαλκον δοθηναι τον

[. . . . .]ο διαγραφετω δε εις το β[ασ]ιλικ[ο]ν

[. . . . . α]γοραιοι και οι γε[. . . . .] 5

[. . . . .]ου και οι λ[. . . . .]

[. . . . .] εμπορων [. . . . .]

[. . . . .]ν Ⱶ δ χα[λκ . . . .]

[. . . . . λα]μβανετω [. . . . .]

The rest lost.

τω[. . . . .]η δεδανεικεναι αυτους επι τ[. . . .] Col. 78.

ενε[. . . . .] χειρογραφησατωσαν οι δεδανει

κοτ[ες . . . . μη] προιστασθαι αλλα δεδανεικε[ναι]

επ[ι . . . .]ος απογραψασθωσαν κα[. . . .]

5 ε[. . . . .]ντες   αποδε[. . . . . .]

ε[. . . . . μ]ηθεις [. . . . .]

The rest lost.

Col. 79.
E.
              About 4 lines lost.
                            ] αυτον
              The rest lost.

Col. 80.
                        αν[   ]

ΝΟΜΟC ΔΕΚΑΤ[   ]

οι πρια[μενοι   ]ετωσαν αυτους [

τ[υπ]αρχετω τη[ι

5 η[   ]φης δ ανα[

και [   ]ων τ[

τη[

και τω[

[.]α[

              The rest lost.

Col. 81.
              ] τωι νομωι εξ α[

              ]ι τωμ πλοιω[ν

              ] τον νομον τ[

              ]θω δε εν ημερ[αις

5   ]μηι και αργ[

       ο οικονο]μος και ο αντιγρα[φευς

              ] παρ αυτοις [

              ] τους υ[

              The rest lost.

] των σωμα[των

εα[ν] δ̣ α̣[   ]μιας συγγ[

γραφει[αντιγ]ραφευ[s

αυτοις κ[   ]φαις πρα[

και ον[   ]μενου και [5

η το[   ]σθωσαν τ[

]μενων μη δω[

]εστω[

The rest lost.

]η τοιαγ[   ] Μεσορει και [

]αρχησ[   ] τους αλ[

] ταις κ[   ] απο

]νομενον [   ]ν οι λοιπ[οι] δε[

]ομων τω[ν   ] συναναγ[5

]ινο[. .] εν[   ] επανα[

ο] δε οικονομος [   ] εισδιδοτω δ[

] ατελη πα̣[   ]ει μηνα κα̣[

]ι του κατα̣[

]ν λαμβαν[10

The rest lost.

]τωι την ω[νην εχον]τι την δε ε[

του την ων]ην εχοντος [. . . . . . συνε]πισφρα[γιζεσθω δε

ο αν]τιγρ[α]φε[υ]s και σ[. . . . .]μω[

]νηται αποδ[. . . . .] χρη[

] αποσφραγισμ[α . . . .] εα[ν δε μη   5

] πραξατ[ω παρα του την ωνην εχον]τος και [

I

]ερος εκαστοι μ[. . . . .]η αποδωι τ[

]αι εν τωι νομω[ι . . . . . . δικηι] νικηθεις απο[τινετω

σ]υν τοις τη[ν ωνην εχουσι

10   ]THCIC [

]σαν τη[

The rest lost.

Col. 85.

] επιτιμ[. . . . . .] πραχθεντ[

] βασιλικον πα[. . . . . .]αν το τε[

]ου διδοσθω τ[. . . . . . . ε]χοντι τ[

]ν εστω του βα[σιλ . . . .] ο δ[

5   γ]ραφα [. . . . .] ετιμη[

]ν ναυτειαν [. . . . .] σωματο[

]εισтερι[. . . . . ε]πιτιμου ε[

]HCIC ΤΕΛω[N . . . . . τας ω]νας εχοντω[ν

τ]ων οφειλοντω[ν

10   ] απογεγραμ[μεν

] κωμηι ου οι[

The rest lost.

Col. 86.

]τι κα[	]ιστι αφ ης αν ημ[ερας
]ηγμα[	]ι εκαστης ημ[ερας
μη]νος Μεχειρ[	] προεντες κατ[
λ	
] αλοι υπερ αυτ[ων	]εις της ωνης ε[
5]ς υποτελεσι πρ[	]κοτας ητ[
]αν επι του διοικ[ητου	]πα[. . .] οδ[
]ο διοικητης[	]ατωσαν
] οι δ εγκαλουντε[ς	]σεν αφ ου[
]αρχας και κ[	] τους εν τοις[

]ν τετα[.]μα[.]τη[   ] ομνυω βασι[λεα   10
δικαιω]s την απογραφ[ην   των χρημ]ατων των υ[παρχοντων
μοι α]πογεγραφηκενα[ι   ] απο του [
   απ]ογραφην εξ αλλ[
   ]εσθαι μηθεν[.
   ] και εκ του διαγ[15

The rest lost.

[. . . . .] την [   ]ν[.]   4th
[. . . . .]χιαι και ο[ι] τοπαρ[χαι   ] ⊢ Σ   hand.
[. . . . .]. . . εις τον λινον κ[   ]τω[. .]εσ[. . .]   Col. 87.
[. . . . . .] τοπαρχια[   ]ο[. .]κω[. . .]
[. .]ηναι λινου εν τωι μ[   ]ηι ενω[   ]   5
   ινο
[. .]υς αρουρας κατ[γ]ραφεντος[   ] του βασιλικου με
τωι οικονομ[ωι   ]τω αυτ[   ] και ευφαντω[. .]
εαν δε ον[   ]μητ εις τε[. .]
αποδειξηι[   ] παραδεχεσ[. . . . .]
νετω εις το [βασιλικον   ]εια π[α]ρα[. . . .]   10
νιηρα κατα[   ]τω ⊢ ʼΑ

επιμελ[   ]σομεναι ωι[. . . .]
   ο
και αντ[ιγραφευς   ]εαν βουλων[ται]
                                    σ
                        ] πωλη⟨λ⟩ουσι τ[. . .]
                        ]να [. . . . . . .]   15

The rest lost.

εκα[   ] της διοι   Col. 88.
[κησεως   ]ητω ποι
                        ]

I 2

5

]νται εκ τε πω
}γμενων γινε[. . .]
]αν δ εχετωσαν
]ις αν βουλωντα[ι
π]ωλειτωσαν [. . .]
]τωσαν τ[. . .]

10

]εως εκαστ[. . . . .]
]ν δε λοιπων τ[. . .]
] και την τιμ[. . . .]
]δοτω ο τετ[. . .]
αντ]ιγραφεω[s . . . .]

The rest lost.

Col. 89.

] και των π ε ω[
] εαν δε αντιλεγη[ι
π]ρος τ[ο] παραδειγ[μα

β͘

]ειςθω σημαινεσθω δε ε[

5

] εαν μη παραδι[
παραδει]γμα ο τε οικονομος κ[
δι
•] παραδοντες κ[
]τωσαν κατα[
τε]ταγμενο[

10

]ντα γινεσ[
] επι της κατ[
] το συμβολον [
Ε]λευσινι κα[
δει]κνυτωσ[αν

The rest lost.

]ης εσφραγισ[
]κων μη παραδι[
]ν μεν παρ[α]δο[
]ν ιστον των αν[
]μα προς το πα[5
]υς πα[
        ]υσις κ[
      τη]ς διοικησε[ως
      ]κριθηι κατα[

The rest lost.

] τον οικονομον τ[Col. 91.
πω]λειτωσαν εις την χω[ραν
    ]ωνται   [
γεγ]ραφθω δ εν τωι συμ[βολωι
τ]ο ονομα του εμπ[ορου   5
    ]ωι κοιτ[
υ]φαντα[.] και ει[
εμ]πορον επανα[
        δι
] αποδο(υ)ναι τ[

The rest lost.

] και παι[11th
    ] εκ της [hand.
] επιστολης αυ[Col. 92.
]ωι ομφαλω[ι

The rest lost.

<table>
<tr><td>12th
hand.
Col. 93.</td><td>

εις Cεβεννυ[τον και] Πηλουσιον [

εαν δε τ[. . . . . .]αγηι εν τ[.]τη[

τεταγ[με . . . . .] τωμ μεν εις Αλε[ξανδρειαν

ας των δ[ε εις Πηλ]ουσιον ολυμπ[Σε]

5 βεννυτ[. . . . . .] επιθαλασσιαν τ[

περι μεν [αυτου ο β]ασιλευς διαγνω[σεται εισπρασσεσ]

θω δε τ[. . . . . .]ν και προσεισπ[ρασσεσθω

κ[. . . . .] τọ [ο]νομα [

[. . . . .]ετạ[

10 [. . . . . εκ]αστην ημ[εραν

[. . . . .] του εμποριου [

[. . . . .]νοντων [

</td></tr>
</table>

The rest lost.

Col. 94.

            ] υπογεγραμ[μ]ενης

            ]ν̄ τον ιστον ⊢ κε

            σ]υν τωι τριηραρχηματι

            ]ν και χειρωμα κατ[. . .] τα

5   τον ι]στον ⊢ κε ταλ[. . . . .]υσι

            τρι]ηραρχηματι [   ]

            ] περιζωματ[

            πρ]ασσων τιμ[

            ]θησουσι [

10   ] τυλειω[

            } και [

            ]ν τιμη[

            ]ησουσιν [

The rest lost.

σωτ[
συ[
τε[
. . [
Ͱ ιη [
σω[
ρωσε[
ωμ[
τε[

```
        ]                    Col. 95.
        ]
        ]
        ]οι
Ͱ      ]β—                        5
        ] Ͱ β—c
        ]υσι Ͱ ρκ
        ]ρει Ͱ ρπ
        ] λινου το
        ] τελος                   10
        ]ο ταλαν
        ]ησουσι Ͱ [. .]
```

The rest lost.

ετελει οσο[υ] δ αγ χρειαν εχω[
σεται τω[ι οι]κονομωι παρα[
         τιμης
τρηραν ηγ[ορα]κοτων το[. . .]λα[Col. 96.

ο⟨ι⟩ ·δε οικονο[μος] και ο αντιγραφ[ευς
εκ δε [. . . . . .]νεψαν κατα[5
       ]Ͱ ν[
       ]μα[

The rest lost.

    οικ]ονομου και αντιγ[ρα]φεως και τ[. .] Col. 97.
   ο βασι]λευς διαγνωσεται της [. . . . .]
     ]ετω στερησις κ[. . . . .]οπρασσε
     ]εντες του ⚹ Ͱ Ἀ
     ]θεις επι των [. . . . . Α]λεξαν 5

[δρει   ] λαβων την λινο[

            ]ν αμναιον καθ[

            ]ην ταις τοις συ[

                ]ενοις εις το βα[σιλικον

10   σ]ταλεντος υ[

             ]οραιον λ[

             ] εις δε [

             ]ν ανε[

           The rest lost.

Col. 98.

]ê γ $α^ν$ ⊢ [   ]κο

]ις ιη̂ $α^ν$ κς αλλω[ν   ]

]$α^ν$ ⊢ μ αλλων $α^ν$ ⊢ [   ]ων ιη̂

]ν $α^ν$ ⊢ ζ χιτωνων [   ]$α^ν$ ⊢ ζ

5   ] οσου αν καθ[   ]

       ] το τελος π[   ]

       ]ων των κατ[   ]

       ] εικοστην [   ]ν

       ] και των α[   ] τ[ω]ν οθονιω[ν]

10   ] το βασιλικ[ον

           The rest lost.

10th hand.
Col. 99.

          ]. . .[. .]ς [μ]ηθεν [. .]

          ]μενος το συμβολ[ο]ν

          ]⟨οι εν ταις⟩

          ]ων προσορμισθω συν[. .]

5   ]ων οθ[ο]νιων οι δε πλειονα[. .]

          Αλε]ξανδρειαν [. . .]

          ]τω μηδε κωλ[. . . . .]

] της παρ[. . . . .]

] την συντ[. . . . . .]

12th
hand.

The rest lost.

ε[

εις τα[

των α[

των δε α[

σχοινι[

10th
hand ?
Col. 100.

5

The rest lost.

About 6 lines lost.

Col. 101.

ε]ξαιρε = c

] επι

]μος

]

]λεντων

5

The rest lost.

[. . .] αλλ[.]ιν τ[

[. . .]μνημα ου αν[

πορωι ων τον ισο[

παραδειγμα του [

τυλειων δε του [.]υ[

τιμη λινου [

προσκεφαλαι[

μον[

κ[

ΔΙΟCΠ[

Col. 102.

εμ]

5

10

The rest lost.

K

Col. 103.   On the *verso* of Cols. 99–100.

]ιεμενοι την [τιμη]ν των [β]υσσι[ν]ων και τ[ων

]στυππεινων και ερικων τα μεν αλλα χ[

δι]αγραμματι τ[ωι] εκκειμενωι επι τη[ι ο]θο[ν

γ]εγραπται εν τω[ι . . . .]αματι τουτωι χρησονται του [

5   π]ραξονται δε [. . . . .]ουμενων τωμ μεν [

.τ. . .ν. . . . .] το λινον εκ τιμησεως π[

]ενου παρακα[

]ων αλλων γεν[

α]ποδομενου δε [

10   ] των δε ανδ[

]ης λοιπης [

]ασαντες [

]νται προς [

The rest lost.

Col. 104.   On the *verso* of Cols. 98–99.

] και ο αντ[ιγραφευς . . .]τωσαν τωι
τα συν

]σφραγισμ[. . . . .] γεγραφθω δε
και

] και μεισκα[. . . . .] τουνομα

πατροθεν κ]αι πατριδος [και ε]κ ποιας πολεως

5   ] ποσου ε[. . . . .]σι τα τελη

]αν[. . . . .] σφραγιδα

The rest lost.

Col. 105.   On the *verso* of Cols. 97–98.

[τα]λαντα πεν

[τ   ] το δε πεμπτ[ον]

[. . .] ροσ[.   ] εκ της χωρα[ς]

οι δε[   ]ọ πραξαν[. . . .]

τον[5

τωι εμπ[

τωσαν [

λοιπον εφ[

τραπεζ[

οι δε εισ[10

The rest lost.

On the *verso* of Col. 97.   **Col. 106.**

παντων [

συντελουγ [

[ι]ερεων και τω[ν

ταυτα τ[

[. . . .]αν δε τηι[5

[. . . .]σεσθωσαν [

[. . . . .]ται οι [

[. . . . . .]σαν προς τ[

[. . . . . .]ιs υπαρχει[

[. . . . . .] των υφαν[τ   10

[. . . . . .]εσεται[

[. . . . .]ντ[

The rest lost.

On the *verso* of Cols. 95–96.   **Col. 107.**

τα εν εμποριωι τελη ε[των την]

ωνην ε[χο]ντων εξ ου αν νομο[υ
_____
μεριζε[σθ]ωσαν δε απο της τ[

την [. . . . . . ι]ερεων των κατ Αλεξα[νδρειαν

K 2

5 [. . . . .]ηθεντων

[. . . . .]ου γινομενου τ[

[. . . . .]ν μερος δια[

[. . . . .] τους δε αγο[

[. . . . .]εντες επ[

10 [. . . . .] της φυλ[

[. . . . .]οσ[

The rest lost.

Frag. 1.   Tops of columns.

(a)]κον πραξ[
 ]λη εκαστ[
 ]εντ[
 ] το επι[
5

(b)] . γρυ . . . [
 ]πωλα[
 ]δεν τ[

(c)] εκ του νομου [
 ]ων εν τωι ν[
 ]ανται μ[
 ] τους εχ[
 ] παρ αυτ[
συ]μβολον [
 ]γωσιν [
 ] εισαγ[

(d)]αν λειας δια[
 ] εν τη[ι υ]στε[ραιαι
 ] εαν δε τι[
 ]σηται απ[
5 ω]νην εχ[
 ]των [
 ] επι[
 ]ροι ωσ[
 ]τ[

(e) [Υ]ΠΕΡ ΑΝΑΦΟ[ΡΩΝ
διορθωσον[ται
τιμην [
απογ[
το[
ωσ[
λογε[
σου [
σε [

(*f*)]ες εν τοις [(*g*)]φον και θεα . εσ[
]ηι συγγραφηι   π]εποι[η]σθαι [
]ελης του ε[γρ]αφηι μηθεν [
]υσιν απ[γρ]αμμ[. .]ε[
]αρ[γρ]αμμα[5
]οισ[   ]   [
]σεσ[   ]   [
]εκα[   ]ν συ[
]ων ε[   ]ων κ[
                     ]αι κα[10

Frag. 2.

Tops of columns.

(*a*) blank   (*b*)]ωτης   (*c*)]αραζουσι
                 ]εως   ]ν απ[
                 ]του   ]νεντ[
                           ]οι οτι ουκ ει[
                           ]ειαν αποτιν[5
                           ]ξ[. . .] εκ τη[
                           ]ιν   [
                              ]τα[

(*d*)]ν απεγραψαντ[ο   (*e*) διδοτω[(*f*) την] ωνην εχοντα [
]σειν απεγραψα[ντο   τιμην τ[   ]ρουμενων των [
] τον νομον α[νιζομεν[   ]με[. .]ν και ει [
] και συμβολο[εαν δε αγ[   ]εμ μηνι Χ[οιαχ
]ν μετα[επικριν[   ] μηνι Χοιαχ[5
  εαν
] και εισετ[εις την κ[   ]υς κα[
ε]παγγειλ[[ ] εξεστ[ω   ]εως κα[
]υτες [[   ]νων[
                 [. . .]ησ

(g)]μου [. .]
   ]ς κληρο[. .]
   ]εξω
   ]ερ και
5   γε]γραπται
   ] νεμοντες
   ] και οι
     απο
   ]α τελου[. . .]

(h)]οις νε[
   ] ιδιοις [
   ]ιδ[

(i) blank

Frag. 3.   Tops of columns.

(a)]ηι κα[
   ]τη[
   ]ς λεια[
   ]ιοτι δου[
   ]ην εν[

(b)]ενων[
  οι]κονομ[
   ]κ αυτο[
   ]μη ε[

Frag. 4.   Middles of columns.

(a)]στου[
   ]φεσθαι τ[
   ]σαν κατ[
   ]μενους [
5 ν]ομαρχηι [
   ]ν εκαστος [
   ] πλει[
   ]εστρα[
   ]τομ[
10   ] κατ[

(b)]του[
   ]νωι χρονωι[
   ]τον πρα[
   ]ω ε[.]τ[
   ]μη λαμβα[ν
  επ]ιτιμον πρ[
   ] δεκα[
   ]ον η[
   ]εις το βα[σιλικον
   ]ς τοις [

(c)]τωσαν
  οι]κονομου
   ] μηνος
   ] Τυβι
   ]νται μη
   ]
   ]ν εξ [. .]
  ε]πιτιμ[. .]
   ] τηι[. .]

(d)]δεκα αν[
]   [
α]ποδε[
]τισα[
]ηι απο[
]ημε[
]   [
]ς [
]τυ[
]ναι[

(e)]οι επι[
]ρημεν[
]αι υποζ[
]ρατεια[
]οι μελ]
]εν τρε[
]ασω[
]η ε[
] δε τα[

(f)]ε[
]ντο ε[
]κν[
] αποτ[
]τες κα[5
]του αγ[
]ν με[
] τη[
   10

(g) οι[
οι[

(h)]υ[
]υντ[
] αν δε οι [
] του [
]α[
]σιν [
]ς συν[
] μητροπ[ολ
]στο[
]υ[
]μα[
]οτι[

(i) αν]τιγραφ[
] παρα των
]ς ενιαυ[
]ραις τ[
]ν του[5
]του ε[
]ον[
ω]νην αγο[ρα
]υσιν οι α[
]ος το[10
]οικιαι[
] δε παρα[

(k) blank

(l)]δε
]ου εν
κ]ςL
Μ]εσορη
] κεL
]

(m)]τ[.]
] καθοτ[ι]
]την
] και τα
]ς εαν   5
]η

(n) blank

]   ]ατι

]ων   ενν]ομιον

]ς   ]τε

10   ]ωι

Frag. 5.   Middles of Columns.

(a)]ν αντιγ[ραφ   (b) τ]ρεφομε

     ] εννομοι κ[   ]ωι τρεφο

     ]ρος τους ε[   ]αι τηι

     ]ην αυτ[   ]ατα

5   ]ης απογρ[   ]σαι τη[.]

     ] γενηται[   ] προεσ

       ]ι εν[   ] προβατ[. .]

       ]σ[

(c)]ρα τα[(d)]οι την ω[νην

     ] νεμε[   ] τοις λογ[

     ]ασθω το[   ] γινεσθαι [

     ]   εαν[α]λλοις [

5   α]ντιγ[ραφ   ]ιν εν ημ[

     ] της λε[   ]αρ[.] εκα[

     ] επαγγ[

Frag. 6.   Bottoms of columns.

(a)]νη[. . .]   (b) blank   (c)

     ]ν κομ[. .]

     ] χαλκου[. .]   ] τ[ο] ενν[ομιον

     ] παρακ[. .]   ] πραξον[

5   ]ατ[.]ν   ]μενα α[

     ]την εκτ[. .]   υ]περ Βερε[νικης

     ]αν εις Αλε[ξαν]   ]υσιν απ[

     ] εγγυους   ]αλεις και π[

] του οικονομου   ] μηνος δυσ[

] κατα τριμη $\overline{\kappa\rho}$[μη]νος Μεχιρ κα[10

εγ]γυον παρα μον . .   οι[   ]ωι κϛL εις μηνα [

]ο καθεστηκως   το[ως δε] Αιγυπτιοι αγουσι [

]αν δε οι ζυ $\overline{\kappa\alpha\iota}$ [   ] της αυτης λειας [

] του κατερ[γ]ου   μην[   ]ξαι το εννομιον

(d)   ]κιαι κα[(e)   (f)

] τον νο[

]ημε[

]ν[.]ετ[

απ]οτινετ[ω   γ]ραφον α[

                     ]βαλοντ[5

] και τοις [   ]η παρα [   ] τοι[

]φου το ενν[ομιον   ε]στω του β[   ]το[

] τωι τετ[   ] μη δωι α   ]εια γε[

]ϛ του[   ] μη δωι   ]ος δ αν[

]υς απογραφεν[   ] αλλοι τινες   ]ν γεγραμ[μεν 10

(g)   (h)   ]λα[

                     ] ελαμβαν[

                     ]ν ζυτοπ[

                     ]ησωντα[

                     κ]ωμηι εφ ημ[5

                     τ]ριμηνον συ[

                     ]ηι το τε ετος και [

                     ]εν και την κωμην ε[

εχ[ο]νομα και [. . .] παρα[

σφραγι   ]σιν ημ[. .]ε[. .]ϛ την [10

LIST OF ABBREVIATIONS USED IN
THE COMMENTARY.

A : cols. 1–22.

B : cols. 23–37.

C : cols. 38–72.

D : cols. 73–78.

E : cols. 79–107 and Fragments.

Lumb. or L. Professor G. Lumbroso.

L. Rec. Prof. Lumbroso's 'Recherches sur l'économie politique de l'Égypte sous les Lagides.' Turin, 1870.

L. P. 'Les papyrus grecs du Musée du Louvre et de la Bibliothèque Impériale,' Notices et Extraits, vol. xviii. part ii. Paris, 1866.

M. Professor J. P. Mahaffy.

P. P. 'The Flinders Petrie Papyri,' edited by Prof. Mahaffy. Dublin. Part I. 1891, Part II. 1893. Part II is meant unless the contrary is stated.

P. P. App. 'Appendix to the Flinders Petrie Papyri.' Dublin, 1894.

Rev. M. E. Revillout.

R. E. Revue égyptologique.

Wilck. or W. Professor U. Wilcken.

W. Akt. Prof. Wilcken's 'Aktenstücke aus der Königlichen Bank zu Theben,' in Abh. der Kön. Akad. der Wiss. zu Berlin. 1886.

W. G. G. A. Prof. Wilcken's review of 'The Flinders Petrie Papyri' in Göttingische Gelehrte Anzeigen 1895, No. 2.

W. Ostr. Prof. Wilcken's forthcoming 'Griechische Ostraka.'

A. E. F. 'An Alexandrian erotic fragment and other Greek papyri, chiefly Ptolemaic,' by B. P. Grenfell. (In the press.)

Numbers enclosed in brackets [ ] refer to columns.

COMMENTARY.

———•———

[1.] 1. On the formula and the correction see Introd. p. xix sqq. It is possible that σωτηρος was written by the first hand. But if so, it is absolutely certain that he wrote it as a correction, for σωτηρος not only projects at the end of the line, but is written in smaller and more cursive letters, especially the τ, which lacks the right-hand portion of the cross-bar. There is no other instance of τ written thus in [1]–[15], though this is very far from proving that σωτηρος must have been written by another scribe, since [1]–[15] are written in a hand even more formal than most hands in the papyrus, and we cannot say what this writer's natural hand would be. But though on palaeographical grounds alone even a moderate degree of certainty is unattainable, on other grounds there is a strong probability that the writer of σωτηρος was a different person from the writer of [1]–[15]. B and C were corrected in the office of Apollonius the dioecetes of the Fayoum, see notes on [23] 1 and [38] 1, and it is therefore likely that A was corrected there also. It is even possible that a note stating this before [1] has been lost, but the fact that the papyrus begins with the opening formula is not likely to be a mere coincidence, though see note on [73] 1. Still if A was corrected in Apollonius' office, the presumption is all in favour of the corrector here being different from both the writer of [1]–[15] and the writer of [16]–[22]; and the few corrections in A, when not clearly made by the two scribes themselves, may all have been written by the corrector of C, who in addition probably inserted [31] 21–25, the only correction in B not made by the writers of B themselves.

L 2

The first three words, which are, like the headings, e.g. [5] 4, [15] 10, written in larger characters than usual, have been printed in capitals.

2. Πτολεμαιου at the end is quite discernible; the vestiges at the beginning are consistent with Πτολεμαιου, but that is all.

3. We should expect the year to be mentioned, cf. [24] 2, but the papyrus is hopelessly effaced. The eponymous priesthoods were probably not mentioned in [24], so that it is not likely that they were mentioned here.

[2.] 1-4. This section perhaps refers to a second auction after the ωνη had been already bought; cf. L. P. 62 [3] 14-16, and Josephus, A. J. 12. 4. 4.

3. εω cannot be the end of πωλειν : see note on [13] 11.

The subjects discussed in A, so far as they can be traced, are arranged on the whole in chronological order. [2] is concerned with the auction : [4]-[8] apparently have to do with the relations between the outgoing and incoming tax-farmers : [9]-[15] 9 with the conditions under which the new farmers and their subordinates entered office : [15] 10-16 with the collection of taxes : [16]-[20] are concerned with the monthly and the final balancing of accounts. The last three headings, συγγραφων, κατεργων, and εκκλητοι χρονοι, stand somewhat apart. A chronological order is also observed in B, and in [44]-[48] of C, where the subject is the manufacture of oil ; but in [39]-[43], regulations concerning the oil-producing plants, little order of any kind is traceable, and [49]-[56] are arranged on a different system.

[3.] 1-3. 'The antigrapheis appointed by the oeconomus shall take charge of the revenue payable to the different companies of tax-farmers.'

2. Cf. [12] 2 and [21] 4, both passages referring to payments of salaries in which οι κατασταθεντες αντιγραφεις perhaps reappear. Subordinate antigrapheis appointed by the oeconomus and antigrapheus, with other duties, occur in [46] and the succeeding columns, cf. [55] 21, and an antigrapheus της ωνης appointed by the oeconomus is mentioned in [54] 20. Not only are the subordinate agents or representatives of the oeconomus and the antigrapheus (himself the alter ego of the oeconomus) called antigrapheis, but even the tax-farmers appoint

antigrapheis, see [54] 16. It is remarkable that the βασιλικη τραπεζα is never mentioned in A, although the money payments were made to it, see [31] 16 note, and [56] 16. Of course mentions of the bank may have been lost, though the columns dealing with the διαλογισμος are fairly complete. But the explanation is, as W suggests, that A deals with the tax-farmers in their relations to the government officials; the relations of the officials to the banks are discussed in D, the διαγραμμα τραπεζων. See also note on [7] 5.

4-7. The position of this fragment, as well as the corresponding one [4] 6-10, is uncertain, except in so far that both belong to the first four columns.

[4.] 1. Possibly a reference to arrears of taxation, which were to be collected in thirty days: cf. [6] 2.

[5.] 1-3. 'If they are discovered to be in debt to the Treasury, those who secured their condemnation shall have a share in exacting the payment.'

2. If καταδικασαμενοις be correct, the δ is written much smaller than the usual δ in this hand, and is more like σ. Possibly this section has something to do with the informers, who were rife in the next century, see L. P. 61. 15-16 μαλιστα δε των συκοφαντειν επιχειρουντων τελωνων (so the facsimile) αυτοι τε παραφυλαξασθε και πασι τοις κατα μερος διαστειλασθε περι των αυτων μη παρεργως. υπαρχετω is more than a mere equivalent for εστω, cf. [17] 11 and [28] 10, and the meaning perhaps is that the persons in question were not only to join in exacting the payment, but to keep a share of it.

4. ΔΙ[ΕΓΓΥΗ]ΣΙΣ would just fit the lacuna: cf. L. P. 62 [3] 6. The appointment of sureties is not decreed by any provision in A which has been preserved, unless [9] bears on that subject; but the sureties are mentioned several times. The heading is here a substantive in the nominative, as usual: cf. [14] 2, [15] 10, &c. The genitive is found in [20] 13, [21] 2, and [31] 17: the infinitive with υπερ in [24] 14; with μη in [28] 17; the infinitive alone in [26] 18, [30] 20; υπερ with the genitive in Fr. 1 e.

[6.] 1-3. 'It shall (not?) be lawful for the tax-farmers to receive payments from those who collected the arrears, even if it be within the thirty days.'

1. οι επιλογευσαντες. The term is new; from [8] 4–6 it appears that they like the λογευται had υπηρεται, and that their services were required when the ωνη was changing hands. Cf. [19] 13, where επιλογευσις probably means 'supplementary collection of taxes,' i. e. 'collection of arrears.' Assuming μη to have been lost before εξεστω at the end of [5], the sense may be that the tax-farmers were allowed thirty days in which to collect arrears (cf. [4] 1), but the arrears had to be paid not to the tax-farmers but to the oeconomus direct, cf. [18] 17 and [19] 11. On this theory, however, we should expect πεπραγματευμενοις, not πρια-μενοις, cf. [8] 2. M. suggests that 1–3 are complete in themselves, the sense being that the new tax-farmers might receive the arrears left by their predecessors, but not until the thirty days had elapsed in which the outgoing tax-farmers might settle their accounts. This gives a more satisfactory meaning; cf. L. P. 62 [4] 10–12. But instances in the papyrus of a section beginning without a connecting particle are rare, and there is no instance of such an ellipse of a verb after μηδε.

The πρακτωρ is never mentioned in the Rev. Pap., though the office existed at this time; see P. P. 42. 2, and Leyden pap. Q. 2. As Revillout has pointed out (R. E. ii. 140), his services were only required when some extraordinary payment, e. g. of a fine or arrears, was made. The P. P. quite confirm this view. Then what was the relation of the πρακτωρ to οι επιλογευσαντες? The use of the aorist participle is in favour of the term not being an official title; cf. [52] 20 οι λογευοντες i. e. λογευται, and [18] 8 ο επι της διοικησεως τεταγμενος i. e. the διοικητης, though ο αγορασας is found as often as ο ηγορακως την ωνην.

[**7.**] 1–4. '(The one copy shall be sealed and contain the names of the . . . . .) and of the witnesses, the other shall be unsealed; and they shall enter in their books the names of the persons employed, with their fathers' names and their original homes, and the nature of each person's employment.'

1. Cf. [27] 5 and 18 τα δε αντιγραφα συνπροσεστω ασφραγιστα.

2. οι πραγματευομενοι is a general term including all persons connected with farming the taxes, [12] 2, but with especial reference to the λογευται, υπηρεται, &c., [10] 3, 17. Cf. οι τα βασιλικα πραγματευομενοι, i. e. the government officials, [20] 15. In C οι πραγματευομενοι την ωνην are identical with οι πριαμενοι.

3. γραφετωσαν: the subject is the tax-farmers; see [15] 16. Cf. [54] 22 and L. P. 62 [4] 18. The official document of the oeconomus is a γραφη, [12] 3.

πατριδος: Egyptians, as well as the foreign settlers, could be tax-farmers in the second century B.C.; Lumb. Rec. p. 322. But πατριδος points to the fact, already traceable in the Petrie papyri, that most, if not all, tax-farmers in the third century B.C. were foreigners.

5. φορτιων: [1]-[22] no doubt apply equally to taxes in kind and taxes in money; hence the brevity and indefiniteness of [15] 10–16, the section dealing with πραξις τελων. The fact that taxes in kind as well as in money are meant helps to explain the absence of any mention of the royal banks (cf. [3] 2 note), which only received taxes in money, [31] 16 note.

[8.] 1–2. 'But if these persons did not connive at it, they shall exact the payment from the outgoing tax-farmers.'

1. Cf. [21] 4–9. If there is a real parallel between the two passages, τουτων may be οι κατασταθεντες (sc. αντιγραφεις; see [3] 2), and μη goes with συνειδοτων, not with εαν.

3–6. 'Let the tax-farmers bring an action, if they have any complaints to make against the collectors of arrears or their subordinates in matters connected with the farming of the taxes during the time in which they were engaged in buying the tax.'

3. καλεισθωσαν: cf. [21] 12 and [35] 3. In all these cases the word may be passive.

4. υπηρεται in A are always mentioned together with the λογευται; see [12] 12, [13] 2, and probably [11] 16 and [16] 12. They are a distinct class, subordinate to the λογευται and receiving two-thirds of their pay ([12] 15). Cf. the ταγματικοι υπηρεται in Wilck. Akt. viii. 2. In [22] 2 οι υπηρετουντες are all those connected with the farming of the taxes, other than οι πριαμενοι.

[9.] 1. παραλαβωσιν: the subject is probably the tax-farmers.

2. το εμποριον: cf. [107] 1 τα εν εμποριωι τελη, which seems to show that there were some taxes specially connected with the εμποριον. Otherwise one might conjecture that the notice was put up in the *bazar* as being the most frequented place.

3. Possibly ε[ν τ]ωι τ[ελωνιωι ... το επι]δεκατον, referring to the εγγυοι.

Cf. L. P. 62 [1] 13–15 εγγυους καταστησουσιν . . . . . των επιδεκατων. But in [34] 3 and [56] 15 the amount of the caution-money has to be only one-twentieth greater than the sum promised by the tax-farmers.

It is difficult to see any reason for the correction of the a in δεκατου, unless, because from the way in which it was joined to the κ by the first hand, it might be read as a ζ. Cf. [31] 17 and [52] 24, where there are equally unnecessary corrections, and not improbably [15] 15.

5–8. The middle fragment in this and the succeeding columns is much nearer to the lower piece than to the upper.

[10.] 1–4. 'They shall appoint a guard for the inspectors, the tax-collectors and the guardians of the vouchers, and all others engaged in the tax-farming . . . .'

1. φυλακην, sc. καταστησουσι. In the provinces the tax-farmers were sometimes assisted by troops in collecting the taxes, Jos. A. J. 12. 4. 5, and Lumb. Rec. p. 325. φυλακη is used in Leyden pap. O for the office of the συγγραφοφυλακες; cf. συμβολοφυλακες here. But as the εφοδοι are found in connexion with φυλακιται in App. II (4) 10, I prefer to take φυλακη in its ordinary sense. The εφοδοι were important officials, judging by the amount of their pay, [12] 18. Their title is still frequently found in the Berlin Urkunden of the Roman period.

[10.] 8–[11.] 10. The structure seems to be as follows: (a) [10] 8–12, a regulation applying to the tax-farmers, 'The chief farmer and his associates shall not receive any payments except in the presence of the oeconomus and antigrapheus.' The penalty for disobedience is probably that fixed in [11] 5–6. (b) A regulation that the tax-farmers should report what they received either to the oeconomus or to the antigrapheus. [10] 14–15 may be the conclusion of this rule, the penalty for disobedience being fixed in [11] 7–10. (c) and (d), parallel regulations for the εφοδοι and others, [10] 16–18: the penalty is fixed in [10] 18–[11] 3.

[10.] 10. κοινωνες: in the other places where the word is used the papyrus is mutilated or consistent with the commoner form κοινωνος.

11. ανευ: cf. [25] 6 and [30] 10. Payments in money did not pass through the hands of the tax-farmers; see [31] 14 note. The presence

of a government official, but not the presence of the tax-farmer, was essential in all payments of taxes.

16. Perhaps [ωσαυτως δε], and then εαν τι τ[ων τελων] πραξωσιν.

[11.] 1. α[ι̇ενεγκωσι]: cf. [11] 7. Perhaps 'pay as an αναφορα,' see [19] 5 note.

3. There are great difficulties in the way of supposing the name of a coin to have been lost after πεντηκοντα here and in line 10. 50 talents are too much, 50 drachmae too little, so that the only alternative is 50 minae, which M. would adopt. But (1) 50 minae seem an inadequate fine, and when this amount is expressed, it is called 5000 drachmae, not 50 minae. (2) As the amount appropriated by the tax-farmers might vary, we should expect a sliding scale, not a fixed sum, for the penalty. (3) The custom of the papyrus, to which in A there is no exception, is that where there is no article the number comes *after* the noun. Therefore on the whole, since this offence would be one of the most serious which the tax-farmers or their subordinates could commit, I prefer πεντηκονταπλουν here and in line 10, though there is no instance in the papyrus of a fine larger than five-fold, when calculated in this way.

[11.] 11–17.

11. Perhaps ονοματα παραδωσουσι, as Mr. Kenyon suggested to me: cf. [12] 2.

17. The exact position of the fragment containing ραφειτ in relation to the preceding line is doubtful. επι τηι ωνηι, cf. [17] 13, Wilck.

[12.] 1–6. 'If the oeconomus and antigrapheus discover any person employed in farming the taxes whose name has not been entered in the list, they shall bring him to the king before he has been able to injure any one.'

1. οἱ δε οικονομος: cf. [28] 12, where οι δε ο, whatever we may think of the Greek, is necessary, and [96] 4, where οι δε οικονομος και ο αντιγραφευς is corrected.

4. [βλαβηναι τι] Wilck. For an instance of an unlicensed taxcollector, see the complaint of the cobbler, P. P. xxxii (1).

[12.] 11–18.

11. Possibly οι κατ]αστα[θεντες, see [3] 2 note; and then τοις εν εκαστωι νο]μωι.

M

13. Probably π]οεισθω and εστω δε] in line 14. The λογευται, υπηρεται, &c. were to be paid out of the sums collected. But nowhere in A or B is there any mention of a μισθος for the tax-farmers, nor did they receive a μισθος in the second century B.C.; cf. note on L. P. 62 [5] 3. And as the account of the διαλογισμος, where it would certainly have been mentioned, is fairly complete both in [16]-[20] and [34]-[35], we may conclude that the tax-farmers received nothing but the surplus above the sum which they had contracted to pay to the government: see [19] 4 and [34] 13. The position of the contractors for the oil monopoly was different; there was hardly any room for an επιγενημα in the sense in which it is employed in A and B, and even if there was such an επιγενημα, it is doubtful whether they received it; moreover they had definite administrative duties to perform. Hence they received a μισθος, [39] 14 note.

15. Cf. App. ii. (4) 5, 8 ως του μηνος. In 17 a number has perhaps been lost: cf. εφοδωι ενι.

[13.] 1–4. 'A list of all the collectors required for each farm, and their subordinates and the guardians of the receipts, shall be drawn up by the oeconomus and antigrapheus acting in conjunction with the chief farmer.'

1. εκαστην: this shows that A is quite general and applies to all ωναι throughout the country.

2. συμβολα: cf. [21] 1, [52] 16, 24.

[13.] 7–[14] 1. A regulation forbidding certain persons to farm the taxes: cf. [15] 2 sqq. The penalty is fixed in line 11 sqq.: 'Whoever disobeys any of these rules shall pay 5 talents to the Treasury and shall be kept under arrest until the king decides his case.' This is the only passage in the papyrus where the absence of a law of *habeas corpus* is conspicuous; but cf. P. P. iv. (7) 5. Imprisonment was but rarely employed as a punishment, though it is no doubt implied in [12] 2 and [49] 20.

11. ιη. It is possible that the corrector, whether he be the scribe himself, or, as I think, another person, intended to alter ποησηι to ποιη; cf. for the omission of the ι adscript [22] 2 note. But it is more likely that he wished to correct the spelling, and divide the word differently, ποιη|σηι instead of πο|ησηι, though instances of the division of a word

between two vowels are not uncommon in B and C, e.g. [29] 17 γε|ωργος, [54] 16 ελαι|ου. In the division of words the practice of the scribes was to divide a word at the end of a syllable, except in some cases where the last letter of a syllable was a consonant. Thus we find [52] 10 προσ|εισπρασσεσθωσαν, [56] 9 προσ|αγγελευτος, [36] 5 γραμ|ματευει, and probably even αρχ|ωνων [14] 9, [46] 4 κρινεσ|θω (cf. 46. 8, where σ is attracted to the preceding vowel, κατασ|ταθεις). On the other hand, the tendency to end with a vowel and begin the next line with a consonant is shown by [21] 7 πεπρα|γματευμενοι, [30] 9 γεγρα|πται, [37] 7 γινε|σθω, &c.

The fragment containing]ων ος[and]βα[in line 12 has disappeared.

12. There seems to be insufficient room for τουτων.

[14.] 2–5. 'Registration of chief tax-farmers. Intending chief tax-farmers shall register themselves before the official who holds the auction . . .'

3. αρχων[ειν]: Wilck. The verb is not found elsewhere in the papyrus, but αρχων[αι] would be very awkward here.

4. τον πωλουντα: there was no special πωλητης in Egypt, the auction being held by various officials, though generally by the oeconomus, [20] 12. Cf. L. P. 62 [7] 19–[8] 4, where οι πωλουντες are the oeconomus and probably the βασιλικος γραμματευς, for in [8] 13 of that papyrus the officials who hold the auction are subordinate to the επιμελητης as well as to the διοικητης. In pap. Zois it is Dorion, ο γενομενος επιμελητης προς την εγληψιν της νιτρικης, who holds the auction. Cf. the papyrus published by Rev. R. E. vii. 40, where the oeconomus was probably the auctioneer. In [57] 3 πωλουμεν, it is the king who speaks; cf. [53] 18 note.

[14.] 9–[15] 1.

9. [αρχ]|ωνων suits the context, though there is no other instance of a word divided in such a way that there is a consonant at the end of a line and a vowel at the beginning of the next, except in the case of a word compounded with a preposition : see [13] 11 note.

12. μετ[αγορασηι] is too long for the lacuna. Possibly μετ[αλαβηι].

16. διδωσιν appears to be a mistake for διδωι, unless the subject is not ο διεγγυωμενος, but οι κοινωνες.

[15.] 2–9. 'They shall be ineligible for becoming either chief tax-

M 2

farmers, or associates, or sureties.   (Likewise) crown officials, the chrematistae, the eisagogeus . . . .'

3. M. suggests taking οσοι τι κ.τ.λ. closely with the preceding lines, but there is no parallel instance in the papyrus of an unfinished line in the middle of a sentence.   Probably a division-line between lines 3 and 4 has been lost, and οι δε refers to the persons mentioned in [14].   But in any case the meaning of lines 4 sqq. is that οσοι κ.τ.λ. are not to take part in the tax-farming.

5. The εισαγωγευς is always mentioned in connexion with the chrematistae in Ptolemaic papyri: see L. Rec. p. 184.

7–9. Apparently a regulation forbidding a slave to take part in farming the taxes.   Though the slaves of the government officials are included, cf. M. Introd. p. xxxi, this regulation was probably quite general.

[15.] 10–16. 'Exaction of taxes.   The tax-farmers shall exact from those who are subject to taxation all the (taxes) in accordance with the laws.   If they disobey this rule in any particular, they shall pay a fine of 3 talents to the Treasury, and (twice?) the amount of the deficiency, unless they enter in their books within 30 days the taxes that are wanting.'

12. παν: the meaning is that the tax-farmers were to grant no remissions of taxation: cf. L. P. 62 [1] 9–13, where διπλας would suit the lacuna in line 12, as διπλα is possible in line 15 here; and pap. in P. P. App. p. 3, the complaint of Apollonius, a tax-farmer, against Philo, his associate, οτι ανευ ημων . . . . . . [προ]ξενει τους υποτελεις του φυλακι[τι]κου εις το ιδιον και εξ ελαττονος (not εξ εαυτου) συνχωρησεις ποιειται.   (In line 5 of that document read υπομνηματα for υπομνημα.)

Though α before εκ is doubtful, παντ[ας τα τελ]η is impossible.

15. The letter written above the line may be α.   But if it is η, it is still possible that the first hand had written μη: see [9] 3 note.

[16.] 'Balancing of accounts.   The oeconomus shall hold a balancing of accounts with the tax-farmers every month before the 10th with reference to the sums received during the previous month . . . . . They shall not add the sums received in (the current month?) to the instalment belonging to the previous month, nor take sums which belong to one instalment and credit them to another, and even if one of the tax-collectors or of their subordinates pays back (?) a sum which he has received from the revenue of the farm, this shall not be credited to his separate account. But when the next balancing of accounts takes place, they shall add to the revenue of the month the amount which was left over from the previous balancing, making clear the amount of the sum left over from the previous period.'

1. διαλογισμος : cf. [34] 9, [54] 20, and L. P. 62 [4] 13.

8. The meaning of the paragraph depends on what these sums were which were not to be put down to the account of the previous month, but were to be carried on to the next reckoning. I conjecture that they were sums received between the end of the month and the day on which the διαλογισμος was held, i. e. εν τωι ενε[στωτι μηνι.

9. The subject of the imperatives here, as in lines 10 and 17, is probably the oeconomus and antigrapheus : cf. line 15 with [17] 17.

10. For the meaning of αναφορα cf. [34] 7, [53] 24, [56] 17, pap. Zois i. 31 τεταχθαι την πρωτην αναφοραν, αι δ αναφοραι εταχθησαν in an unpublished Petrie papyrus, and L. P. 62 [4] 4. That αναφορα refers to the monthly instalment of revenue payable by the tax-farmers is quite clear, but it is difficult to decide whether it means the actual sum paid, or the account of it. In spite of the two instances where τασσεσθαι is used and where actual payment must be meant, and [56] 17, q.v., I think that αναφορα here means the account of the instalment. For the taxes collected were sent εις το βασιλικον, [28] 14 note, and the actual payments might be made on any day. The αναφορα seems to be the account of the payments during a month added together.

11. These four lines are very difficult. διορθουσθαι, cf. [56] 15, is the term used for paying off the balance of the αναφορα, if it did not reach the required amount. It is possible that λαβων refers to the μισθος of the λογευται, see [12] 13–16. π[ροσοδον]: Lumbroso.

13. εις το ιδιον : cf. [19] 3, which shows that the tax-farmers had a separate, as well as a general, account with the oeconomus, and [54] 12 note.

16. It is not clear whether το περιον εκ του επανω διαλογισμου is identical with το περιον εκ του επανω χρονου in line 18, and whether one or both are equivalent to επιγενημα in the next column, i. e. the surplus of the taxes actually received over the amount, or, as the αναφοραι were monthly, over the twelfth part of the amount which the tax-farmers had

contracted to pay to the government. If το περιον refers to the same sum in lines 16 and 18, it means the surplus carried over from the previous month as distinct from the προσοδος or receipts for the current month. If however, as seems probable, there is a distinction between το περιον in the two cases, το περιον εκ του επανω διαλογισμου may refer to the sums mentioned in line 8, while το περιον εκ του επανω χρονου would mean the surplus left over when the accounts of the last month were settled. In either case therefore το περιον εκ του επανω χρονου probably means the επιγενημα; cf. [17] 14, where it is probably used as a synonym for it.

[17.] 1–16. 'But if the previous period has produced a deficit, while the next month produces a surplus, and the oeconomus receives in full that portion of the deficit in the farm which was not covered by surety . . . from the surplus . . . But if subsequently a deficit occurs in the farm which produced the surplus, the oeconomus shall exact payment of the surplus which had been transferred to another farm, from the sureties inscribed on the register of the farm to which the surplus was transferred ; but first . . . let him restore the surplus (?), which was transferred to another farm, back to the farm from which it was transferred.'

1. Three cases are contemplated : (1) 1–5, when a period of deficit was followed by a period in which there was a surplus : of the course to be pursued by the oeconomus we are ignorant, but a balance of some kind must have been struck, so that the sureties were not made liable for the whole deficit; (2) 6–9, when a period of surplus in one farm coincided with a period of deficit in another : in this case the surplus and deficit were allowed to balance each other, i.e. the surplus was lent to the farm which required it, instead of the deficit being at once made good by the sureties ; (3) when the period of deficit occurred in the farm which had produced a surplus, but had lent it to meet the deficit of another farm. In this case the oeconomus had first to recall the surplus (15–16), in order to meet the deficiency in the farm which had lent its surplus. By doing so he of course caused the deficit in the other farm to reappear, and it was therefore necessary to call upon the sureties of that farm to meet the deficit (13–14). Cf. for this balancing of surpluses against deficits L. P. 62 [6] 4–7.

3. το αδιεγγυον : apparently a deficit might be so great that the

sureties failed to cover it. Yet in [34] 3 and [56] 15 the sureties have
to be one-twentieth greater, presumably, than the sum due from the
tax-farmers; cf. L. P. 62 [1] 13, where they have to be one-tenth
greater. The question of the sureties and their relations to the tax-
farmers presents many difficulties, see note on [34] 4. αδιεγγυον is
apparently equivalent to ανεγγυον, as there seems to be no difference
between εγγυασθαι and διεγγυασθαι, εγγυησις and διεγγυησις, wherever they
occur in the Revenue papyrus, L. P. 62, and pap. Zois.

8. Possibly εκ τ[ου περιοντος], if το περιον is right in 14.

9. The piece of a letter after]α[will not suit φ; therefore μεταφερετω
will not do. There is not room for καταστησατω or καταβαλλετω.

10. εκ [της α]υτης is inadmissible, nor is αδιεγγυον the word lost in 15.

[**17**.] 17-[**18**] 9. 'Copies of all the balancings of accounts held by
the oeconomus with the tax-farmers shall be sealed by him and given at
once to each of the associates, ... and the oeconomus also shall have
copies which have been sealed by all those who took part in the
balancing, ... and he shall send the copies of the balancings every
month to the dioecetes and eclogistes.'

3. The letter after αυτος may be η, and it is not certain that any letter
is lost after κα, though if so, it can only be ι. The word, whatever it
is, has nothing to do with μαρτυρας. εχετω: cf. [27] 12. Each party
had a copy sealed by the other, after the manner of modern agreements,
as Mr. Kenyon suggests.

6. αποστελλετω: cf. [51] 22, where it is opposed to διδοναι. While
αποστελλειν implies distance, and therefore we may conclude that the
dioecetes and eclogistes were not always accessible to the oeconomus,
διδοναι is not always to be taken literally, e.g. [36] 8. On the dioecetes,
see note on [38] 3.

9. εγλογιστην: cf. [37] 12 τοις υπο Διονυσοδωρου τεταγμενοις εγλογισταις,
and Tobit i. 22 Αχιάχαρος δὲ ἦν ὁ οἰνοχόος καὶ ἐπὶ τοῦ δακτυλίου καὶ διοικητὴς
καὶ ἐκλογιστής. The eclogistae were accountants or paymasters, who
probably had a central office at Alexandria controlled by Dionysodorus,
and branch offices in the country. One of these was probably the
λογιστηριον in the Fayoum mentioned in P. P. 25, line 23, and 26, line 4.
The simple word λογιστης however is not found in the Revenue pap. or
in the Petrie papyri, and in a papyrus of the thirtieth year of Phila-

delphus published by Rev. R. E. 1882, p. 268, where he reads πεπτωκεν Θεωνι λογειστηι δια Διονυσοδωρου των Στρατωνος υπηρετων, Wilck. tells me that λογευτηι is the correct reading; cf. [8] 4 note. The eclogistae are not mentioned in the papyri of the next century, but cf. B. M. pap. xxiii. 41 for the verb εγλογιζεσθαι meaning 'pay.' Later, εγλογιστης is used for a 'tax-collector,' i.e. λογευτης; cf. the edict of Tiberius Alexander, C. I. G. 4957, line 36.

[**18.**] 9-[**19**] 4. 'When the period for which the tax was sold expires, the tax-farmers shall all come to the oeconomus before the tenth day of the following month, and he shall hold a general balancing of accounts with them, in which he shall state both the value of the revenue received, and the balance which they have still to pay, together with the sums which have already been reported as paid and the dates of the payments, and whether from the sub-letting of the farm or other quarters any debts are owing of which it is the duty of the oeconomus to exact payment, and the remainder still due, and how much is each tax-farmer's share of the debt ; and underneath the share of the debt he shall write the amount which he has received separately from them or the surety, with the dates of the payments, and the remainder still due ; but if there is a surplus, the oeconomus shall set it down to the credit of the tax-farmers.'

10. παρεστωσαν προς : cf. Xen. Cyr. 2. 4. 21. παρ[αγενεσθωσα]ν is too long.

13. γενικος λογος is found in papyri of the Roman period.

14.-[**19**] 1. οφειλωσιν, deal with the collective account of the tax-farmers, [19] 1 και ποσον-[19] 4 with the separate accounts of each tax-farmer with the oeconomus. Both sections may be sub-divided into (1) the liabilities of the tax-farmers [18] 4, corresponding to [19] 1 και ποσον εκαστωι τουτων επιβαλλει; (2) the sums either already paid to the oeconomus or for the collection of which he was responsible, [18] 15-17 πραξαι, corresponding to [19] 2-3 ; (3) the balance due to the oeconomus, [18] 17 και το λοιπον εαν τι προσοφειλωσιν, corresponding to [19] 4 εαν τι προσοφειληι.

τιμην της προσοδου : even where taxes were paid in kind, the accounts of the tax-farmers were kept in money, see [**33**] 2-8, [**34**] 7-10, and cf. [**53**] 23. διορθωσασθαι : cf. [**16**] 13 and [**56**] 15.

15. ταυτο apparently for τουτο. M. suggests ηδη for the lacuna. ανενηνεγμενον: cf. [11] 1, [19] 5 notes.

16. αποπραματων: cf. L. P. 62 [3] 17. L.'s suggestión (Rec. p. 324) that it refers to the sub-letting of the farms is a perfectly satisfactory explanation of that passage, but if αποπραμα is right here and has the same meaning, it is curious that there should be no other reference to this subject in A, mutilated though these columns are.

[19] 3. εγγυου: the singular, because each tax-farmer had only one surety; see P. P. xlvi, where Theotimus is surety for Philip, and pap. Zois, where Thanoubis is surety for Dorion. The ωναι which were sold separately for each nome, see L. P. [1] 1, [57] 12, 14, [60] 23, &c., were subdivided among the different members of the company, each of them being especially responsible for a district, cf. [54] 12 note, though the whole company was liable for the failure of one of its members, L. P. 62 [6] 14–15.

4. προσοφειληι: if this is right, the letters must have been very cramped. The subject is not the εγγυος, but the tax-farmer.

επιγραψατω: here the oeconomus only credits the surplus to the tax-farmers; cf. [34] 14, where the payment is made through the royal bank. But from line 9 it appears that the payment is authorized by the dioecetes.

[19.] 5–16. 'The oeconomus shall report . . . to the dioecetes; and the dioecetes shall examine his books to see whether there is a surplus in the receipts from the other farms; and if there is a surplus due from him to other farms, he shall balance the arrears against this surplus, but, if there is nothing due from him to other farms, he shall order the oeconomus to exact the arrears and pay them over to him when the collection of arrears takes place. The oeconomus shall pay the arrears to the dioecetes within three days, or, if he fails to pay them over on demand, he shall be fined three times the amount, and the dioecetes shall exact the payment from the oeconomus, . . .'

5. ανενεγκατω: cf. P. P. 47. 9, and 122. 5 ανενεγκωμεν επι τον διοικητην, in both cases meaning 'report,' not 'pay,' and [11] 7.

12. προσοφειλεται: i.e. the tax-farmer; cf. lines 1 and 4.

επιλογευσις: cf. οι επιλογευσαντες [6] 2 note. While the oeconomus was responsible for the payment of arrears not only from the tax-

N

farmers but in some cases from the tax-payers ([18] 16–17), this is not inconsistent with supposing that the actual collection of the arrears from the tax-payers was in the hands of οι επιλογευσαντες: see note on [30] 5.

15. εισπραξατω: i.e. from the oeconomus, not from the debtor; cf. [41] 12.

[20.] 1–12. 'Any tax-farmers who fail to balance their accounts with the oeconomus, when he desires them to do so and summons them for the purpose, shall pay 30 minae to the Treasury and the oeconomus shall at the same time compel them to balance the account . . . The oeconomus shall also give to each of the sureties an account of his balance, stating that the surety has paid what he owed. If the oeconomus when asked fails to give the account on the same day or the one following, he shall render himself liable to proceedings for malversation. Balancings of accounts shall be held in the same manner by all officials who shall put up to auction any of the Crown revenues.'

3. Though τε is written above εις το, it ought strictly to come after αποτινετωσαν, unless a second fine has been lost.

11. παντες: see note on [14] 4.

[20.] 13–[21] 1. 'Concerning contracts. With respect to all contracts made by the oeconomi or antigrapheis or their agents, being officials of the Crown, in matters connected with . . ., the officials shall not exact any payment from the tax-farmers for the contracts or receipts.'

13. Cf. [30] 5 μητε αλλοι παρ αυτων οι πραγματευσομενοι, κ.τ.λ.

15. Possibly εις τους λογους; there is scarcely room for εις τους διαλογισμους. Though]υς is doubtful,]ις or ων]ας is impossible. The meaning of this section, as was suggested by L., is that the government officials were not to charge the tax-farmers anything for drawing up or sealing the contracts and receipts.

[21.] 2–9. 'Concerning wages . . . the appointed antigrapheis shall pay instead of them . . . but the additional penalties which have been decreed shall be exacted from the outgoing tax-farmers, unless the antigrapheis are discovered to have connived at the fraud with them.'

2. The spaced and enlarged letters indicate that the word is a

heading, and therefore cannot be taken with the preceding genitives. Though the τ is rather doubtful, no other compound of εργον except κατεργον occurs in the papyrus. Cf. [45] 8 and [55] 15, where it means wages for piece-work. Lines 4–9 are not inconsistent with such a heading; cf. τα συντεταγμενα with [55] 10 το συντεταγμενον μεριζεσθαι, and οι καταστα-θεντες with [3] 2 and [12] 12.

7. Cf. [8] 1–2, from which I have conjectured εισπρασσεσθωσαν, though it is rather long for the lacuna.

[21.] 10–[22] 7. ‘Times for appeal. When disputes arise out of the laws concerning tax-farming, the Crown officials may bring an action … when they choose, but when disputes arise out of the laws concerning tax-farming, and a different time for appeal has been appointed in each law, the Crown officials may bring an action, both in the period for which the revenues have been sold and in the next three months, unless one of the associates or subordinates connected with the tax-farming is discovered after the three months have elapsed to have peculated . . .’

10. εκκλητοι χρονοι : cf. Dio Cass. 51. 19 εκκλητον δικαζειν, and 52, 22 τας δικας, τας τε εκκλητους και τας αναπομπιμους . . . κρινετω.

11. νομων τελωνικων : cf. line 14 and Dem. 732. 1. M. however objects to νομων here, and suggests μεν τουτων in line 12, referring to the word lost here. But the phrase is certain in line 14.

As L. acutely observed, νομοι τελωνικοι is really the title of A. Moreover that throughout the Revenue papyrus we have the laws of Philadelphus, i. e. the πολιτικοι νομοι of Pap. Taur. i. [7] 9, is shown, as he remarked, by the various cross-references from one section to another as νομος. See (1) [25] 15 κατα τον νομον, i. e. the preceding section : (2) [26] 7 κατα τον νομον, i. e. [26] 1–5 : (3) [29] 10 καθαπερ εν τωι νομωι γεγραπται, i. e. in [27] : (4) [30] 6 and 9 κατα τον νομον, i. e. [24]–[30] : (5) [52] 28 καθαπερ εν τωι νομωι γεγραπται, i. e. [52] 17–18. In [4] 8, [20] 6, and [21] 3, there are also cross-references which, owing to the lacunae, cannot be verified. Cf. also [57] 1 and the crowning instance [80] 2 where there is the heading νομος δεκατ[ων?]. It was therefore a series of documents like the Revenue papyrus, to which L. P. 62 [1] 6 referred, κατα τους νομους και τα προσταγματα και τα διαγραμματα και τα διορθωμεθα (i. e. διορθωματα). For besides νομοι, there are examples of the other three in the Revenue papyrus; see [39] 1–7 διαγραμμα, [37] 2–8 προσταγμα, and [57] 1 sqq., διορθωμα.

15. The first word is not κυριος, for no letter which reaches far below the line is admissible. It is just possible that νομων in this line means 'nomes,' but it is very unlikely, both on account of the context and because we should in that case expect εν εκαστωι νομωι: cf. [53] 5, 18, &c.

[22.] 2. ληφθη: if this conjecture is correct, the ι adscript is omitted, a rare occurrence in this century. But see [44] 16 αναγαγη, [47] 9 ποιη, [40] 8 καταβλαβη. It is noticeable that all the cases are the 3rd person singular of the subjunctive.

3. M. suggests νοσφισαμενος: cf. [27] 10.

4. This line is perhaps the protasis to which 5–7 are the apodosis. The rest of the column is blank.

[23.] 1. There is a foot of blank papyrus between this column and the one preceding, so that this note refers to B, not to A. Cf. [38], a similar entry prefixed by the same writer to C, and notes ad loc. There is little doubt that [23] refers to the revision of B in the office of Apollonius, the dioecetes of the Fayoum, though the few mistakes which occur are not corrected, and the only change is the insertion of [31] 21–25; cf. note on [48] 9.

[24.] 1–2. 'In the reign of Ptolemy the son of Ptolemy, and the son of Ptolemy, the twenty-seventh year.'

2. For the formula cf. [1] 1, P. P. xxiv, and M.'s and my corrections in P. P. App. pp. 5–6. In line 4 of that papyrus θε[ω]ν α[δελφων is right. For the various meanings attached to the υιος Πτολεμαιου see Rev. R. E. i. 1; Krall, Sitzungsb. Wien. Akad. 105, 1884, p. 347 sqq.; Wiedemann, Rhein. Mus. 1883, pp. 384–393; and Philol. 1888, pp. 81–91; Wilck. on Arsinoe Philadelphus in Pauly-Wissowa's Encyc.; and Introd. p. xix. sqq., where M. propounds a new explanation for the disappearance of Euergetes' name from the formula after the twenty-seventh year, a fact already known from demotic ostraca, see Rev. Proc. Soc. Bibl. Arch. 1885, p. 138.

[24.] 4–13. 'They shall receive for the tax on vineyards from ... the sixth part of the wine produced, and from the ... and the soldiers who have planted vineyards . . ., and owners of land in the Thebaid, which requires special irrigation, or of land . . . the tenth part of the wine. For the tax on orchards in accordance with the method of valuation (hereinafter described) they shall receive the sixth part of the produce in silver.'

4–10 deal with the απομοιρα (see [25] 12, [27] 17, &c.) from vineyards, which was generally a sixth, but in the case of the favoured classes in 5–9 a tenth part of the produce, and was paid under ordinary circumstances in kind, but sometimes in money, see [31]; while the απομοιρα from παραδεισοι, 11–13, was in all cases a sixth, and was always paid in money.

5. Possibly κ[ατοικων, but this term has not yet been found in papyri of the third century B.C. κ[ληρουχων (cf. [36] 12) is not likely, as they are probably the persons meant in the next line.

6. The absence of των before του[shows that πεφυτευκοτων and στρατευομενων refer to one and the same class of owners, and the tense of πεφυτευκοτων points to the land not having been cultivated before. Therefore, accepting Prof. Petrie's theory that the κληρουχοι in the Fayoum received land reclaimed from the lake, I think that the cleruchs of P. P. are included in this class, if not directly referred to by it. Perhaps του[s βασιλικους], cf. [36] 13, or even του[s εν τηι λιμνηι], cf. [69] 5 note. But I think that M. is hardly justified (see Introd. p. xxxix) in using the fact that the Revenue papyrus comes from the Fayoum as an argument for supposing that only the cleruchs of P. P. are meant here. The Revenue papyrus gives the law for the whole of Egypt, and is not more concerned with the Fayoum than with any other nome. In any case this passage strongly confirms Wilcken's theory (G. G. A. 1895, no. 2, p. 132) that the cleruchs in P. P. were, at any rate nominally, active soldiers, and not mere pensioners : cf. P. P. xxxi. 5–6.

8. επαυτλητης : i. e. land on the edge of the desert, out of reach of the inundation, and irrigated probably by the *sakiyeh*, or wheel with buckets attached. Cf. Diodorus' (1. 34) description of the κοχλιας.

9. διοικειται is clearly opposed to προτερον διωικειτο, but the sense depends on the word lost in the lacuna. Cf. [37] 13, where οι διοικουντες κτηματα are 'land agents,' opposed to 'landlords' and 'tenants.'

Σιμαριστου : cf. App. II (1) 1, where Σιμαριστου is followed by the fraction for one-fourth, and then δια γραμματε[ων. Underneath are two columns, one of dates, the other of figures, which, to judge by the fractions, refer to artabae, as Wilck. pointed out to me. The quarter in question is probably a tax, cf. κ' for εικοστον in P. P. 151. 15, and the amounts are large, showing that the tax was an important one. The occurrence of the form Παχωνς in that papyrus is, according to Wilck., in favour of assigning it to the earlier rather than to the later part of the third century B.C., so that it is probably nearly contemporary with the Revenue papyrus. But the meaning of Σιμαριστου is equally obscure in both cases, though it is probably a proper name, for a Simaristus who wrote a treatise ' on Synonyms ' is frequently mentioned by Athenaeus, e. g. 99 c. M. suggests that here it is the name of a god.

10. δεκατην: cf. P. P. xliii (*b*) where the heading of a tax list on produce of vineyards, palm groves and fruit trees, i.e. απομοιρα, is εκτης και δεκατης, and see note on line 13. Elsewhere when the amount of the tax on the produce of vineyards is stated, it is always a sixth, cf. [37] 19 note. It appears that while the tax of a sixth was a legacy from the time when the απομοιρα was paid to the temples, the payment of a tenth by certain favoured classes was a change instituted by the government; [33] 21 note, and [36] 18.

11. Perhaps υπογεγραμ]μενης or υποκει]μενης. In any case the reference is probably to [29], q. v. There is no other instance in the papyrus of such a spelling as εξυντιμησεως for εκ συντιμησεως.

12. προς αργυριον is opposed not only to payment in kind, which is allowed in the previous section concerning vineyards, but to payment in copper, cf. [40] 10 προς χαλκον and App. III, and notes on line 13 and [37] 19.

13. Perhaps ταξυυσιν or τιμησουσιν. The subject may be either the tax-farmers or the government officials.

As the reader will have noticed in Introd. p. xxxiii, Mr. Mahaffy and I differ as to the meaning of παραδεισοι. He thinks that their produce was only grapes, while I think that palm trees and fruit trees of all kinds are meant. The distinction everywhere drawn between αμπελωνες and παραδεισοι, especially in the mode of valuation and taxation, cf. [29], seems to me hardly accountable, if wine was obtainable from παραδεισοι. Why should the government insist on money-payment of the tax on wine produced in παραδεισοι, but not on wine produced from αμπελωνες? On the other hand if the produce of παραδεισοι was miscellaneous, the reason for the difference is obvious. The wine would keep, but fruit would not, and therefore the government required the tax to be paid in money. With regard to the αναδενδρας (cf. Introd. *l. c.*), a single instance of this mode of culture in the Fayoum does not seem to me to justify the supposition that it was universal in the rest of the country. The Fayoum, then as now, contained an unusual number of trees; and since the απομοιρα was a tax on produce, not on land ([33] 13 note), there is no difficulty in supposing that wine obtained from αναδενδραδες, the amount of which I believe to have been very small, was included in the wine obtained from αμπελωνες. Secondly, Mr. Mahaffy adduces the contrast drawn between παραδεισος and κηπος in P. P. xxii, the contrast between παραδεισος and φοινικων in P. P. xxxix (*i*), and the mention of σικηυηρατον in P. P. xliv. As in P. P. xxii. I have made a number of corrections, I give the important part, line 4 sqq. εαν δε τις παρα ταυτα κριηηι η κριθηι ακυρα εστω εαν εμβηι βους η υποζυγιον η προβατον η αλλο τι [. . . . . . .]νον εις αλλοτριον κληρον η παραδεισον η κηπον η αμπελωνα η κατανεμηι η καταβλαψηι αποτεισατω ο κυριος τωι βλαφθεντι το βλαβος ο αν καταβλαψηι εκ κρισεως προ κρισεως δε μηθεις ενεχυραζετω μηδε αποβιαζεσθω μηδεν παρευρεσει μηδεμιαι εαν δε τις τουτων τι π[οι]ησηι (?) αποτεισατω παρα χρημα ⊢ 'A. The distinction drawn between παραδεισος and κηπος does not militate against my theory, for if as I think the παραδεισοι contained palms and fruit trees, the κηποι may have contained vegetables and flowers. P. P. xxxix (*i*) however seems at first sight to contradict it, for whether this taxing list refers to απομοιρα or, as I think is more probable, to φορος (see note on [33] 13), φοινικωνες are distinguished from παραδεισοι. But cf. P. P. xliii (*b*), where Wilck. has made an important rectification, showing that xliii (*a*) 24–44 really belong to the bottom of xliii (*b*). There seems to me to be no doubt that the tax in xliii (*b*) is the απομοιρα, see notes on line 10 above, [31] 16, and on [33] 13, yet in addition to αμπελωνες we have ακροδνα and φοινικωνες mentioned, but no παραδεισοι. Now if the tax on αμπελωνες is here the απομοιρα, it is necessary to suppose on Mr. Mahaffy's theory that the παραδεισοι have for some reason been omitted, and that φοινικωνες and ακροδνα, which have no right to be there, have been inserted instead. But if παραδεισος is a general term including both φοινικωνες and ακροδνα, the omission of παραδεισος in xliii (*b*) is explained, and even the difficulty in xxxix (*i*) disappears. If a person had only palm trees he paid the tax on palms,.

if he had only fruit trees he paid on fruit trees, cf. εκτη ακροδυων in a Ptolemaic ostracon, Wilck. Ostr. 1278. παραδεισος being a wider term includes both. Cf. P. P. xxvii (1), in which a man pays the sixth in kind on wine and in money on ακροδυα, στεφανοι, which must mean flowers, and another word which is lost. There can be little doubt that this tax too is the απομοιρα, and that the sixth paid in money means the tax on παραδεισοι. This leads to the remaining difficulty, the absence of any enumeration of the different kinds of produce, which are on my theory classed together under the general term παραδεισοι. But the government did not fix the amounts to be grown or even the assessment of the crop, see [29]. The oeconomus looked on while the tax-farmer and tax-payer fought the question out, and was certain to get the full amount of the tax in any case, [31] 14 note. Nor can I see any difficulty in the use of καρπος in [29] 13 as a general term for the different varieties of produce. There seems to be no special reason for enumerating the different kinds, since the word παραδεισος, however obscure to us, must have been perfectly intelligible to the people for whom the law was written. But we are at liberty to suppose that a complete list was given at the top of [29] which is lost, though I do not think that this supposition is necessary, cf. [36] 6 note. That παραδεισοι contained φοινικωνες, ακροδυα, and στεφανοι seems to me certain from the instances in the Petrie papyri quoted above, and it is possible that λαχανα, 'vegetables,' were also included; cf. B. M. pap. cxix of the second century A.D., a taxing list on αμπελοι (so Wilck. for ακανθα), ακροδυα, λαχανα, and φοινικωνες, a classification very like the Ptolemaic, and note on [37] 19 for an instance of απομοιρα in the Roman period.

[24.] 14–[25] 3. 'Concerning the gathering and collection of the vintage. Let the cultivators gather the produce when the season comes, and when they begin to gather it, let them give notice to the manager of the farm or tax-farmer; and if he wishes to inspect the vineyards, let them exhibit them to him.'

From this point to [29] 1 the subject is the tax on vineyards, as is shown by the numerous references to wine, and by the tax being paid in kind. The tax on orchards is discussed in [29]; [30]–[33] 8 revert to the tax on vineyards; [33] 9–[35] are general.

15. γεωργοι are 'cultivators' in the widest sense, whatever their

position in the scale of society may be; cf. [29] 2, 15, where one of οι παραδεισους κεκτημενοι is a γεωργος. The word for the 'fellaheen' is λαοι, [42] 16.

17. Though ο διοικων is here distinguished from ο εχων την ωνην, if that be the right conjecture, the distinction is one of names, not of persons: cf. [42] 8, where ο διοικων is identical with ο εχων. The fact seems to be that οι ηγορακοτες or αγορασαντες, οι πριαμενοι, οι εχοντες, οι διοικουντες, οι πραγματευομενοι are mere synonyms for τελωναι, a term which only occurs in [28] 9 and [29] 8, perhaps, as M. suggests, because it was unpopular. Where the singular of any of these expressions is used, the 'tax-farmer,' whether αρχωνης or μετοχος, is generally meant. Sometimes however one of them is equivalent to αρχωνης, e.g. [34] 10-14, where ο ηγορακως, ο εχων, and αρχωνης are interchanged.

[25.] 1. βουλομενου: if the tax-farmer did not come, the γεωργοι might take matters into their own hands, [30] 4-13.

επι[δειν: cf. P. P. xxiii (2) 3 εφιδειν του σπορου. An example of notice being given in accordance with this regulation is P. P. xl (*b*), a letter from Dorotheus to Theodorus, no doubt a tax-farmer, γινωσκε με τρυγησοντα, κ.τ.λ.

3. Probably the end of a regulation fixing the penalty in case the γεωργοι failed to give notice to the tax-farmer.

[25.] 4-16. 'When the cultivators wish to make wine, they shall summon the tax-farmer in the presence of the oeconomus and anti-grapheus or their agent, and when the tax-farmer comes, let the culti-vator make wine, and measure it by the measures in use at each place, after they have been tested and sealed by the oeconomus and anti-grapheus; and in accordance with the result of the measuring let him pay the tax. If the cultivators disobey the law in any of these particulars, they shall pay the tax-farmers twice the amount of the tax.'

7. παραγενομενου; sc. του διοικουντος; see [30] 13.

8. μετροις: the utmost variety in respect of measures of capacity is found in Ptolemaic Egypt. Hence the necessity, when metretae or artabae were mentioned, to specify which metretes or artaba was meant; see [31] 6, [39] 2, [40] 11. The variations were not only between the measures commonly used in different places, which are referred to here, but also between different measures used in the same place, as is shown

by the ever-recurring formula in Ptolemaic and even later contracts for loans of wheat, αποδιδοτω . . . . μετρωι ωι και παρειληφεν.

10. εξητασμενοις : cf. [40] 19 and Leyden pap. Q, a receipt, as Wilcken has pointed out, for the κεραμιον (i. e. απομοιρα) τηι, not τωι, Φιλαδελφωι. No special δοκιμαστης is mentioned in the Revenue Papyrus, as there.

[26.] 1–10. 'Those persons who already possess instruments for making wine, shall register themselves before the tax-farmer, when . . . and when they intend to make wine, they shall exhibit the seal which has been stamped upon the instruments, unbroken. Any person who fails to register himself, or to produce his instruments for inspection as the law requires, or to bring them to be sealed up when the tax-farmer wishes to seal them, or to exhibit the seal stamped upon them, shall pay to the tax-farmers the amount of the loss which the tax-farmers consider at the moment that they have incurred.'

1. Cf. [49] 10–13 and [50] 21–[51] 11, parallel regulations concerning the οργανα for making oil.

4. Perhaps οταν οινοποιειν μελλωσι]ν, cf. [25] 4.

7. παρασφραγισμον: cf. [51] 3, 8, and [46] 11 παρασφραγιζεσθωσαν τα οργανα τον αργον του χρονου, which explains this passage. παρασφραγισμος and παρασφραγιζεσθαι are used for sealing up something, i. e. putting it aside for the time : cf. [54] 18 and [57] 23.

10. Cf. [51] 11 and [55] 24, where the tax-farmers are allowed to demand as much compensation as they like ; but see also [56] 13, where the tables are turned upon them.

[26.] 11–17. 'If the cultivators gather the vintage and make wine before the tax-farmer comes, let them (keep ?) the wine at the vats or . . ., and when they hear (?) the first notice of the auction announced in the town or village in which they live, they shall register themselves on the same day or the one following, and shall exhibit the wine which they have made, and the vineyard from which they have gathered the crop prematurely.'

12. Faint traces of what are about the fourth and fifth letters of the first word are visible, and they will not suit σφραγιζεσθωσαν, αποτιθεσθωσαν, or κομιζετωσαν. δει]κν[υτωσαν would be consistent with them, but does not suit the context.

13. I have taken το πρωτον εκθεμα as referring to the proclamation of

he highest bid on the first day of the auction by which the απομοιρα was sold, and suggest παραγ[γελεν πυθω]νται, since ορω]νται is not satisfactory. This is a mere guess, but for εκθεμα and εκτιθημι in the sense of proclamation of a bid see [48] 16 and probably [33] 10; cf. P. P. 44. 20, L. P. 62 [8] 2 and 10. The length of time during which the taxes were put up to auction is not stated in any part of the Revenue Papyrus which is preserved, but in the next century it was ten days, L. P. [8] 11, and in [48] 16, at the auction held by the contractors for the oil monopoly, ten days are the period. If εκθεμα means 'proclamation' or 'edict' generally, without reference to the auction, it is difficult to see what πρωτον refers to.

15. κατοικουσι: cf. L. P. 63. 100 των εν ταις κωμαις κατοικουντων λαων. απογραφεσθωσαν: sc. προς τον εχοντα την ωινην, cf. [27] 9.

[26.] 18-[28] 1. 'Agreements . . . The tax-farmer shall seal the copy of the agreement and give it to the cultivator. In the agreement the tax-farmer shall declare under the royal oath that he has entered in the agreement the full amount of the produce, including all wine made prematurely and reported to him by the cultivator, and has not peculated any of it, nor let it out of his possession. The other agreement, after it has been sealed by the cultivator, shall be kept by the oeconomus or his representative; and in this agreement the cultivator shall declare under the royal oath that he has exhibited all the produce, and reported all the wine made before the proper time, and has honestly entered in the agreement the (due) amount of the tax. And there shall in addition be copies of both agreements, which shall not be sealed.'

5. There were two separate συγγραφαι (cf. [29] 9, [42] 15 διπλην), one written by the tax-farmer, of which the original was no doubt kept by the oeconomus, cf. line 12, and a sealed copy was given to the cultivator, while the other was written by the cultivator, and kept by the oeconomus; and there were besides unsealed copies of the second συγγραφη, of which one was no doubt kept by the tax-farmer, another by the cultivator, perhaps also of the first συγγραφη, of which one might be required for the tax-farmer.

6. For examples of the βασιλικος ορκος see Wilck. Akt. no. xi; P. P. xlvi (a); a demotic papyrus in Rev. Nouv. Chrest. Dém. p. 155 (cf. note on [39] 8); and probably App. ii (2).

7. παν τα : a mistake for παν το, cf. line 15. The few blunders made by the writer of [24]–[35] are not corrected : but see [31] 17.

11. καταπροιεσθαι : cf. [40] 5 προιεσθαι εκ της κωμης.

την ετεραν : P. P. xxvii (*a*) and xxx (*e*) are examples of this συγγραφη, in which payment is made in wine, cf. [31] 16 note, though there is no royal oath.

13. συναπεσταλμενος : i. e with the tax-farmer ; so in [42] 20.

18. συν was deciphered by Wilck. from the very faint traces.

[28.] 5–8. 'But if the tax-farmer and the cultivator have a dispute, the one saying that the produce is more, the other that it is less, the oeconomus shall decide the question, and the agreements shall be sealed in accordance with his decision.'

5. Cf. [29] 12 sqq. the parallel regulation for παραδεισοι.

9–16. 'If the tax-farmer fails to make an agreement with the cultivator, when the cultivator wishes him to do so, he shall not exact payment of the tax. But the oeconomus and antigrapheus shall make an agreement with the cultivator, and having conveyed the requisite amount of wine to the royal repository, shall enter it as having been received, but shall not put down the value of it to the credit of the tax-farmers.'

10. Quite a different meaning is obtained by taking βουλομενου with what follows, and referring it not to the cultivator but to the tax-farmer, but this suits neither the construction nor the context. The other explanation is much more satisfactory, that lines 15–16 are the punishment which the tax-farmers incur, if they fail to come to an agreement with the cultivator.

12. οι δε ο: cf. [12] 1.

14. το βασιλικον : a perfectly general term, comprehending all places where taxes were kept : see Rev. R. E. vii. 90. When the taxes were in money, το βασιλικον is equivalent to the βασιλικη τραπεζα ; cf. Wilck. Akt. p. 49, and [31] 16. But taxes in kind were taken to υποδοχια, [31] 2, 19, and [50] 8 ; or ταμιεια, P. P. 108. 5 ; or θησαυροι, W. Ostraca 709, 725.

16. τιμην. The wine was sold before the διαλογισμος took place, [33] 2–8 and [34] 10. Hence the accounts were kept in money, cf. [18] 14, and App. ii (5).

υπολογειτωσαν: cf. P. P. 14. 3 υπολογησαι εις τα αλικα; P. P. 84. 18 υπολογησα (sic) εις τον της ελαικης λογου το εις φορετρον; and [34] 6, [53] 23 υπολογισθησεται

[28.] 17-[29] 1. 'Against confusion of produce. If the tax-farmers mingle taxable produce with produce exempt from taxation, as if it belonged to this class, . . .'

17. Cf. L. P. 62 [6] 15 for ατελειαι wrongly awarded by the tax-farmers, and [15] 12 note.

[29.] 2-21. 'Owners of orchards shall register themselves before the tax-farmer and the local agent of the oeconomus and antigrapheus, stating their names, the village in which they live, and the sum at which they assess the revenue from the produce in their orchard. If the tax-farmer consent to the assessment, they shall (make) a double agreement with him, sealed, as the law requires, and the oeconomus shall exact the sixth in accordance with the terms of it. But if the tax-farmer object to the assessment, he shall be allowed to seize the crop, and shall pay the cultivator by instalments from what is sold from day to day; and when the cultivator has recovered the amount at which he assessed his crop, the surplus shall belong to the tax-farmer, and the cultivator shall pay the sixth to the oeconomus. On the other hand, if the crop when sold does not reach the amount of the assessment, the oeconomus shall exact the deficit from the tax-farmer . . .'

2. Cf. [33] 19; but, apart from my conjecture in line 7, the fact that here the tax is a sixth and is paid to the oeconomus direct, and therefore in money, cf. [24] 12 and [31] 16, makes it certain that the tax on παραδεισοι, not on vineyards, is meant, and that this column describes the συντιμησις referred to in [24] 11.

6. τιμωνται: middle not passive, cf. [56] 6, for the cultivators made their own assessment, which the tax-farmers might accept or reject. Cf. [42] 17, where τιμαται is probably passive.

7. Cf. [39] 16 τιμης της εν τωι διαγραμματι γεγραμμενης, from which it might be conjectured that παρα[is the beginning of some word meaning 'law' or 'edict.' But (1) there is no room for γεγραμμενης; (2) if παρα be the beginning of παρα[γραμματι or some such word, the reference is to something not contained in the papyrus, which is very unlikely, especially as [24] 11-13 so far from explaining this passage probably refers to it for

explanation; (3) the fact that the tax-farmer could reject the assessment if he chose implies that it had only been provisionally fixed. Hence, in spite of the difficulty of the phrase, I prefer την προσοδον την εν τωι παραδεισωι. This use of προσοδος, meaning the land from which the προσοδος was derived, may be compared with the use of ωνη in [30] 4, [32] 4, and [34] 9 for the land, the tax on which was farmed.

2. διπλην: see note on [27] 5.

12. Cf. [28] 5–8. The exercise of the tax-farmer's right to seize the crop was purely voluntary: cf. P. P. part I. xvi (2), where a γεωργος makes an agreement with the oeconomus and topogrammateus to pay part of the tax on his παραδεισοι, but refers the rest, περι ων αντιλεγω, to a certain Asclepiades; and P. P. xxvii (1), where the γεωργος, after stating his assessment of the produce from his vineyard, fruit trees, &c., says εαν δ επι[γενημα] (Wilck.) γενηται προσανοισω μ[ετα] χειρογραφιας ορκου βασιλικου.

17. την εκτην: presumably on the correct assessment.

19. πραξατω: sc. the difference between the real value of the crop and the tax-farmer's valuation of it, not the tax, which must have been paid by the cultivator as before. εκπεσηι is very doubtful, and there is room for another letter in the lacuna.

[30.] 3–19. 'If the tax-farmers fail either to come in person or to send representatives to carry out duly all the requirements of the law, or in any other way hinder the cultivators when giving notice, or summoning the tax-farmer, or paying the tax in accordance with the law, the cultivators shall be allowed in the presence of the agent of the oeconomus and antigrapheus, as the law prescribes the presence of these two officials when payments are made, full power of action, without incurring any penalty by so doing. But when the tax-farmer comes, they shall show him the produce and bring evidence at once to prove that they have done all that was required, and the agent of the oeconomus and antigrapheus shall give the tax-farmer a written account both of the produce and of the tax, cultivator by cultivator.'

1. From [30] to [33] 8 the subject reverts to the tax on vineyards.

5. πραγματευ[σομενοι]: Wilck. In this class would be included the λογευται and υπηρεται, mentioned so often in A; cf. [56] 18 and [52] 20, 27. Elsewhere in B and C the subordinate officials of the ωνη are not

distinguished from οι πριαμενοι. Similarly the oeconomus could have performed in person only a small part of the duties assigned to him; the rest must have been done by his agents.

9. ως γεγραπται: i. e. in [25] 6.

10. παροντων τουτων: cf. P. P. ix, a petition from two peasants to Theodorus, asking him to write to Theodorus the oeconomus, in order that they may receive permission εις οργυας ρ το γινομενον καταγαγειν εις το υποδοχιον.

12. εκαστα ποιειν: to gather the crop, make wine, and pay the απομοιρα.

13. αζημιους: this refers to the penalty fixed in [25] 15.

15. πα[ραχρημα]: Wilcken.

17. γραψαντες δοτωσαν: the plural is a mistake, as only one person is meant, see line 11 and [46] 8, [47] 10, &c. Cf. [55] 22 for a precisely similar error.

[30.] 20-[31] 16. 'Transport of the tax. The cultivators shall transport the due amount of wine to the royal repository . . . (if any of them fail to do so) he shall pay the tax-farmers the value of the tax which he owes them. This value is in Libya, the Saite, . . . polite, Prosopite, Athribite nomes, the district round Menelaus, and the Delta, . . drachmae for each metretes of eight choes; in the Sebennyte, Busirite, Mendesian, Leontopolite, Sethroite, Pharbaethite nomes, Arabia, the Bubastite nome and Bubastus, the Tanite, the Memphite nome, with Memphis, the Letopolite, Hermopolite, Oxyrrhyncite and Cynopolite nomes, the Lake district, the Heracleopolite and Aphroditopolite nomes, six drachmae for each metretes; and in the Thebaid five drachmae. The oeconomus shall exact the different values from the cultivators and pay them over to the Treasury to the credit of the tax-farmers.'

[30.] 21. The connexion between this line and the *adaeratio* of the next column is probably that the cultivators had to bring the απομοιρα to the υποδοχια (though see [31] 19 note), within a fixed time, under pain of being compelled to pay the money equivalent if they failed to do so. This explains both αποτινετω in [31] 2, which always implies paying as punishment of some sort, and ενοφειλουμενης, which implies that the payment was in arrear.

[31.] 4. τιμην: the figure in line 13 might be δ, but it is more likely that the scale is a descending than an ascending one, and ς is much more probable. Here therefore the figure is probably greater than 6.

On the value of wine in this century, see (1) P. P. Introd. p. 32, where the price of ⅓ χους is 5 obols, and therefore the price of a metretes at the same rate would be 13 drachmae 2 obols; (2) App. ii. (5), where the prices of a metretes vary between 5 and 11 drachmae προς χαλκον, the average being between 7 and 8, i. e. nearly 7 silver drachmae, see App. iii; and (3) L. P. 60 (*bis*) 15–16, of the third century B.C., where the price of 16 cotylae is 6 drachmae, and in the next line 11 cotylae at (ανα) 2¼ obols each are worth 4 drachmae and ¾ obol. The price of a metretes of 8 choes would at the same rate be 36 drachmae, and even if the prices in 60 (*bis*) are προς χαλκον, cf. App. iii, there is here a great divergence from the other prices. But then as now the price of wine of course depended on the age and vintage.

5. . . . . πολιτηι: see Introd. p. xlviii. Γυναικοπολιτηι, cf. Strabo 803 b, is the most likely, if we are to look for a name not included in the other list, [60]–[72]. Ηλιοπολιτηι, cf. [64] 3, appears to correspond to Δελτα in line 6. It is possible that the difference between this list and that in [60]–[72] is due to the different periods at which they were originally made. The list here cannot have been made out much before the twenty-seventh year (see [38] 1 note), while the other list may have been based upon an older classification.

[Μενε]λαιδι: cf. Strabo xvii. 23. Whether M.'s conjecture is right or not, the Nitriote nome, cf. [61] 20, must be meant here, unless it was omitted in this list. Δελτα: cf. Strabo xvii. 4, and see Introd. l. c.

The metretes of 8 choes was used for wine, cf. [32] 19, while the ordinary metretes of 12 choes was used in measuring oil, [40] 11 and [53] 20, and cf. note on [25] 8. The chous approximately six pints.

12. λιμνηι: cf. [71] 5 and 11. The Fayoum received the title of the Arsinoite nome between the twenty-seventh and probably the thirtieth year of Philadelphus, when the new title occurs in a letter among Cleon's correspondence, P. P. 8. 2, in which Apollonius was still dioecetes of the Fayoum, cf. [23] 2 and [38] 3. See also P. P. 36. 9 η αυτου γη εν τηι λιμνηι αβροχος εστι. If the whole district is meant here, as seems probable, the date of the change may be after Mesore of the twenty-

ninth year. But the old name may have continued in occasional use for a time after the Arsinoite nome became the official title; cf. App. ii. (2) 13 ἐν τῶι λιμνίτηι, where the Fayoum appears to be meant, in a papyrus which cannot be earlier than the twenty-seventh year of Philadelphus.

14. When the tax was paid in money, not in kind, it was exacted by the oeconomus, not the tax-farmer; cf. [29] 10 and [48] 1, 8. Even when it was paid in kind, the presence of the tax-farmer was not essential and the tax could under certain circumstances be paid direct to the oeconomus or his agent, [28] 9-16, and [30] 4-13. If the tax-farmers were thus often reduced to the position of being mere spectators of the payments, and were sometimes not even that, it may be asked what purpose did they serve? It was certainly not to save the government trouble in collecting the ἀπόμοιρα, since their presence could be dispensed with at the least provocation, while nothing could be done without the oeconomus or his agents. But the tax-farmers were necessary for two reasons, first because they enabled the government to make an accurate estimate beforehand of its revenue, and secured it against loss from a sudden fall in the value of crops; and secondly because the complicated system described here, of which the central fact was the separation of tax-farmer and tax-collector, rendered it as certain as any system could render it, that the Treasury received what was due, the whole of what was due, and nothing but what was due. For if the oeconomus attempted to defraud the government either by granting exemptions or by peculations, the loss would fall on the tax-farmers, who would then lose their surplus (see [34] 14), and therefore had the strongest motive for seeing that the oeconomus kept the accounts correctly, since every payment that was made to the oeconomus belonged to them. On the other hand it was impossible for the oeconomus to exact more than the legal amount of the tax, because the amount was fixed by a contract between the tax-farmer and the cultivator over which the oeconomus had no control. And if the tax-farmer tried to extort more than what he was entitled to, in one case, by the no less ingenious than equitable arrangement described in [29] 13-20, he would find the tables turned on him; and in the other, [28] 5-8, he would have to submit his demands to the oeconomus, who, having no interest in allowing the tax-farmers to

P

increase their surplus at the expense of the tax-payers, and having been expressly forbidden to take any part in tax-farming himself, [15] 4, would have no motive for giving an unfair decision. So far as mechanical safeguards could go, the interests both of the Exchequer and the tax-payers were protected at every point. How the system worked we have little means of judging, but it is probably more than an accident that the Petrie papyri contain no complaints against unjust taxation, for in P. P. 122 it is probably not the tax-farmers who are to blame, but the ελαιοκαπηλοι, cf. [48] 4, and the writer of the papyrus in P. P. App. p. 3 only complains of wrongly awarded remissions of taxes. Cf. note on [39] 14 for the position of the farmers of the oil monopoly, which was somewhat different.

15. τιμας: the plural because the price varied in the different nomes ; cf. [33] 6.

16. το βασιλικον means here the royal bank, cf. [34] 17. In practice the απομοιρα on vineyards was often paid in money during the third century, and in the next century all the evidence points to exclusive payment in money; see [37] 19 note.

[31.] 17–25. 'Stamping of receipts. The oeconomus shall establish repositories for the wine in each village, and shall himself give a stamped receipt for what is brought, to the cultivator . . . (The oeconomus shall transport the wine from the vats (?)' added by the corrector).

17. For the correction of the third a in αποσφραγισματος cf. note on [9] 3.

19. κομιζηται is passive, for the transport was usually done by the γεωργος, cf. [31] 21 note and P. P. ix quoted in note on [30] 10. αυτος means that the oeconomus was to seal the receipt himself, cf. [18] 2 σφραγισαμενος αυτος. κωμαρχηι is possible in line 20, cf. [43] 3.

24. The meaning of this addition by the corrector is very obscure. It is difficult to take κομιζεσθω in any other sense than transport, but see previous note. The first two letters of 25 are very doubtful: Wilck. thought they were not νω but γεω, in which case γεωργων can hardly be avoided. But this suits neither εκ, nor, so far as I can see, the context, and I have therefore conjectured ληνων, which may refer to the exceptional cases mentioned in [26] 11–17.

[32.] 'The cultivator shall provide pottery for the repository, and

... and the pottery shall consist of water-tight jars, which have been tested and are sufficient for the wine payable to the tax-farmers. The oeconomus and antigrapheus shall, .. days before the cultivators gather the crops, give them the price of the pottery which each cultivator has to provide for the tax in wine upon his own produce; this price shall be fixed by the dioecetes, who shall pay it to the oeconomus and antigrapheus through the royal bank in the nome; the cultivator, on receiving the price, shall provide pottery of the best quality; and if he does not receive the price, he shall nevertheless provide the pottery, but shall recover the price of it from the tax which he has to pay in money.'

2. M. suggests κη]ρον, and διασκο]πουμενα in the next line; cf. [25] 10 note.

3. κεραμος: cf. [55] 4, P. P. xxx (c) and my corrections in P. P. App. p. 7, and App. ii (5).

4. εκ: possibly υπερ, but cf. [34] 10, and [29] 7 note.

5. Cf. [48] 15. The απομοιρα των ιδιων γενηματων appears to be the ordinary tax on vineyards payable in wine while the απομοιρα 'of which he has to pay the value' is the tax on vineyards when payable in money, see [31] 4, and perhaps the tax on orchards besides. How the case of a cultivator who paid the whole of his tax on vineyards in wine and yet had no orchard, was to be met, if he did not receive the price, is not explained; but I suspect that the case is not mentioned, either because it was not important, or because it was not likely to occur. There are several places where, if the letter of the papyrus be observed, there are inconsistencies or omissions, the importance of which it is easy to exaggerate: cf. note on [42] 4.

10. την συνταχθεισαν I have taken with τιμην not with απομοιραν. Besides. the awkwardness of the intervening accusative, it may be objected that the price appears to be fixed in 18–19, and therefore was not fixed by the dioecetes. This however is not an insuperable difficulty, even if 18–19 do not refer to something else; and it is not so great as the difficulty of taking συνταχθεισαν with απομοιραν, seeing that the απομοιρα was fixed in [24] by law, and that this is the only mention of the dioecetes in [24]-[35]. Moreover if the dioecetes is the subject of διαγραψατω, it implies that he fixed the price of the pottery; and the fact that the singular is used not the plural, cf. 8 δοτωσαν,

makes it difficult to suppose that the oeconomus is the subject, the antigrapheus being omitted. Equally abrupt changes in the subject are not rare in the papyrus, e. g. [54] 18, [49] 20, [48] 13, [34] 4. δοτωταν here means that the money was given outright not as a loan, cf. [41] 16, and [43] 2, for otherwise there would be no reason for the cultivators subtracting the price from the amount which they had to pay.

11. διαγραψατω: see note on [34] 14. The expression 'the royal bank in the nome' might seem to imply that there was only one, but there were royal banks even in the villages, [75] 1.

17. I have taken τιμην as the object of αποδουναι not of κομιζεσθω, for which την τιμην has to be supplied: cf. [43] 16 and [48] 8. If τιμην be taken with κομιζεσθαι, and ης as an accusative attracted into the genitive, the απομοιρα in line 17 is the same as the απομοιρα in line 9, and in both cases means the tax on vineyards paid in kind, contrasted with the tax paid in money, which is in some respects more satisfactory.

18. Perhaps λαμβανετω δε. The price in question is probably that which the γεωργος was allowed to subtract from the απομοιρα ης δει αποδουναι την τιμην, if he did not receive the price of the jars.

19. Cf. note on [31] 6.

[33.] 2–8. 'The oeconomus shall examine the (wine) . . . and taking with him the tax-farmer, the antigrapheus and his agent, shall jointly with them sell the wine, giving the (tax-farmers?) time in which to settle their accounts. He shall exact payment of the amounts and shall put them down in the account of the tax-farmers to their credit.'

2. οσος: sc. οινος or καρπος; cf. [34] 10.

6. διορθωσονται, i. e. 'pay off the balance of what they owe' to the Treasury; cf. [56] 15, which shows that the tax-farmers are meant. καπηλοις, cf. [47] 10, is less likely, and κ does not suit the vestiges of the first letter. Perhaps τελωναις, cf. [28] 9.

7. λογον: i. e. at the royal bank; cf. [31] 16. [αποτιν]ετω would suit the lacuna, but it is not the right word, as there is no question of a penalty here. We should expect καταχωριζετω, cf. [31] 16, for which there is not room. Wilck. suggests [προσθ]ετω.

[33.] 9-[34] 1. 'The basilicogrammateis shall, within ten days from the day on which they proclaim the auction, notify to the tax-farmers

how many vineyards or orchards there are in each nome, with the
number of arourae which they contain, and how many vineyards or
orchards belonging to persons on the tribute list paid the tax to the
temples before the twenty-first year. If they fail to make out the
list, or it is discovered to be incorrect, they shall be condemned in
a court of law, and pay the tax-farmers for every mistake of which
they are convicted 6000 drachmae and twice the amount of the loss
incurred by them. All owners of vineyards or gardens on the tribute
list who paid the sixth to the temples before the twenty-first year,
shall henceforward pay it (to the tax-farmers).'

10. εκθεμα : see [26] 13 note, and cf. [48] 16. Here too there is
nothing in the papyrus for εκθεμα to refer to, unless it be the auction.
Though ten days, as was shown, was probably the time during which
the tax was put up for sale, it is not clear whether that has anything
to do with the ten days here. The absence of πρωτον, cf. [26] 13, and
the fact that the tax-farmers had already entered upon their duties,
line 9, are in favour of εκθεμα referring not to the proclamation of
the highest bid on the first day of the auction, or to a proclamation
that there was going to be an auction, but to the proclamation of the
final result.

13. φορολογια : cf. Ros. stone 12, απο των υπαρχουσων εν Αιγυπτωι
προσοδων και φορολογιων τιιας μεν εις τελος αφηκεν αλλους δε κεκουφικεν ;
a second century B.C. fragment, *Notices et Extraits* xviii. (2) p. 413,
αναγραφει εις [τας] φορολογιας ; and B. M. pap. 401. 14, see M. *Hermathena*,
vol. ix, no. xxi, και γης χερσου και αλλης εκτος φο(ρο)λογιας. It is
probable that the φορολογιαι were taxes on land, classified according
to the different kinds of produce, but not, as the απομοιρα, taxes on
the produce itself. In that case the φορολογια here would be the list
of cultivators of vineyards and orchards who paid φορος, not a list
of all landowners, much less a list of all inhabitants. Cf. (1) P. P.
xliii (a) φορος αμπελωνων ; the fact that the cultivators had to pay
φορος on the land as well as απομοιρα on the produce is clearly shown
by the recurrence of some names found in this list in the companion
document xliii (b) (see note on [24] 14), εκτης και δεκατης i. e. απομοιρα.
Cf. Αντιπατρος Δημητριου Βερενικιδος αιγιαλου in (a) 1 and (b) 51 : as there
is probably nothing lost between Δημητριου and Βερενικιδος, it appears
that he paid 20 drachmae as φορος, but only 17 drachmae 4½ obols

for απομοιρα, and therefore in his case φορος was a slightly heavier tax than απομοιρα, but whether he paid the sixth or the tenth as the latter tax we do not know. Cf. also (a) 17 Αντιδωρος και Ηγημ[ων] το παρα Πασιτος [του] Πασιτος with lines 13–14 of the second column belonging to the εκτη και δεκατη, but not printed by M., Αντιδωρος και ..... Πασιτος; and (a) 4 Πετε[σουχος] Ψεναμουνιος και Μαυρης Τεωτος Αλεξανδρου νησου κη, i.e. 28 drachmae, with (b) 56, Πετεσουχος Ψεναμουνιος και Μαυρης Ιμουθου αμ(πελωνος) Αλεξαν(δρου) νη(σου) ο, i.e. 70 drachmae.

(2) P. P. xxix (a), a taxing list on vineyards, from the mentions of the various κληροι suits φορος better than απομοιρα, even apart from the heading χω(ρος?) αμπελωνων.

(3) P. P. xxxix (i) is also, I think, an account of φορος, not απομοιρα; for there is no reference to wine, cf. xliii (a) 30 which belongs to the εκτης και δεκατης, not to the φορος (24. 14 note); and αμ(πελωνος) του προτερον οντος Πτολεμαιου, which is the correct reading in lines 5–6, suits φορος better than απομοιρα. The following corrections have also occurred to me:—1. πρωταρχου . . . Πηλ[ου]σιου. 3. Πηλουσι ſ. 4. Αρμαις . . . 11. Αλεξανδρου ν⁷. 12. Πυ[θ]ων? . . . Θεαδελφειας πδ/–. 14. Ονητωρ . . . 16. Θοτορταιος . . . Πηλουσιου. 17. Τεως. 18. Αγαθων. 19. Π[ε]τοσιρις.

A conclusion which might be drawn from 9–23 is that owners who were not on the tribute list, if there were any such, e.g. those εκτος φο(ρο)λογιας, were not subject to the tax of a sixth. But in [36] 12–16 it is most explicitly laid down that all cultivators of vineyards or orchards whatever were to pay the tax, except the priests, who, if the strict letter of the papyrus is to be observed, seem exempt from both taxes. But l. 31 of the Rosetta stone shows that before the ninth year of Epiphanes a tax of a κεραμιον on each aroura of αμπελιτις γη belonging to the temples was levied, and it is not likely that in Philadelphus' reign they escaped this κεραμιον, which I suspect took the place of φορος in their case.

14. There can be little doubt that the year is the same as that in line 21. Though the a there has been mostly broken away, what is left will not suit β, and [36] 7 shows that from the twenty-second year onwards the tax was paid to the government, not to the temples.

17. 6000 drachmae instead of 1 talent is remarkable, but there is no doubt about the cipher, which recurs in [67] 17 and [70] 6.

21. The δεκατη, cf. [24] 10, is here ignored as in [36] 18 and [37] 16,

probably because the tax was a sixth both when paid to the temples and when first appropriated by the government. The payment of a tenth by certain privileged classes was instituted between the twenty-third year, see [36] 2, and the twenty-seventh. Perhaps [33] 19-[34] 1 represent the law as it was first promulgated, and have been allowed to remain unmodified. But for the emphatic language of [36] and [37] I should be inclined to think that the δεκατη was simply omitted because the vast majority of the tax-payers paid a sixth. Here, however, I think the inconsistency has a real meaning.

The use of the εκτη for the tax on vineyards as well as on παραδεισοι removes any doubt as to the identity of the εκτη in [36]-[37] with the απομοιρα, which is moreover proved by other papyri, see note on [37] 19. Much as the Egyptian fellah has been able to endure, he could hardly have borne a tax of a sixth besides φορος and απομοιρα, to say nothing of οινολογια which is coupled with απομοιρα in Wilck. Ostr. 711, of the third century B.C., and which, since the payment is in kind, must be a tax on produce.

[34.] 1. τηι Φιλαδελφωι is possible, cf. [36] 10.

2-6. 'The tax-farmers shall within thirty days from the day on which they purchase the tax, appoint sureties for a sum greater by one-twentieth than the price agreed upon for the tax, and the sureties shall register the property which they mortgage, in monthly instalments from Dius to . . .'

2. Cf. [56] 14-18 and L. P. 62 [1] 13-[2] 1. Something like τας δε καταγραφας των χρηματων is probably lost there in [1] 16. καταγραφη, M.'s suggestion, is not found in the Revenue Papyrus, but cf. L. P. 62 [6] 12 συγκαταγραφησομενων. On the change of subject in ποιησοιται, cf. note on [32] 10.

5. Διου: the first month of the Macedonian year. The taxes were generally sold for a regnal year, [57] 4 note; but there is not room for the last month Hyperberetaeus in the lacuna, and the payments of the απομοιρα only extended over the summer months, cf. note on line 9 below.

7-8. 'The value of the wine which is received from the tax-farmers for the Treasury shall be credited to the tax-farmers in the instalments due from them.'

7. Cf. [53] 18-[54] 2. The wine εἰς τὸ βασιλικόν was that required for the king and court. As there is no regulation stating the price which the king paid for the wine, probably it was the same as that fixed in [3].

8. The ε of λογει is partly effaced, perhaps intentionally. The use of ὑπολογιζεσθαι, which rather implies a written transaction, and still more the fact that the ἀπομοιρα if paid in money was received by the oeconomus, [31] 16 note, and by him deposited in the royal bank, while if paid in kind it was deposited by the γεωργοι in the official ὑποδοχιον, [31] 19, so that in neither case was the payment really made by the tax-farmers, seem to me irreconcilable with the hypothesis that ἀναφορα means the actual payment. It is only the account of the receipts for the month. Cf. [53] 24, where the same difficulty recurs, and notes on [16] 10 and [34] 9.

[34.] 9-[35]. 'Balancing of accounts. When all the produce has been sold, the oeconomus shall take with him the chief tax-farmer and his associates and the antigrapheus, and shall balance the accounts with the chief tax-farmer and his associates. If there is a surplus left over, he shall pay to the chief tax-farmer and his associates through the royal bank the share of the surplus due to each member of the company. But if there prove to be a deficit, he shall require the chief tax-farmer and his associates and the sureties to pay each his share of it, the payment to be exacted within the first three months of the following year.'

9. διαλογισμος: cf. [18] 9-[19] 4. There is no mention here of a monthly διαλογισμος: cf. [54] 20-[55] 12, where nothing is said about the final διαλογισμος of the oil-contract. It is difficult to say whether much stress is to be laid on the omission in either case. On the whole I think that here it has a meaning, for the accounts of the ἀπομοιρα were kept in money, see [29] 10, [31] 15, [33] 5-8, [34] 6-7, which all deal with τιμαι, cf. L. P. [4] 18 note, and no accurate balancing could be done until the wine was sold, cf. line 10. How often the sale took place is uncertain, owing to the lacuna in [33] 2, but the prices received by the oeconomus varied considerably, see App. ii (5), and note on [31] 4. Moreover the receipts of the tax-farmers in the case of the ἀπομοιρα were limited to the summer months, and were not, like those of the oil-contractors, spread over the whole year. It is quite possible there-

fore that one general διαλογισμος was sufficient, but the term αναφορα, whatever its precise meaning, shows that a certain amount was expected each month (cf. [56] 17) from the tax-farmers, and the regulation concerning the εγγυοι in [34] 4–6 implies that there was a monthly reckoning of some kind.

11. ο ηγορακως, ο εχων, and αρχωνης are here interchangeable; cf. note on [24] 17.

14. επιδιαγραψατω: cf. [19] 4 επιγραψατω where there is no mention of the royal bank, and [32] 10 where διαγραφειν is used in the sense of 'paying through a bank.' Cf. Suidas quoted in Peyron's admirable note on διαγραφειν, Pap. Taur. i. p. 144. There is not room for προσδιαγραψατω which is found in L. P. 62 [5] 5, 16, nor did the tax-farmers receive anything besides the surplus, [12] 13 note. The fact that in one case certainly, in the other probably, διαγραφειν is used in the Revenue Papyrus for payment through a bank, is however, as Wilck. remarked, an accident, for the meaning of διαγραφειν was rightly decided by Peyron to be 'pay' simply, whether through a bank, or, what is much more frequent, to a bank; e.g. P. P. xlvi (c) 13 διαγεγρ(απται) εις την . . . βα(σιλικην) τρ(απεζαν); L. P. 62 [4] 21, [5] 16, &c. Nevertheless the agreement of the Revenue Papyrus with Suidas is remarkable.

18. The tax-farmers therefore as well as the sureties had to make up the deficit, but in what proportions we do not know, since επιβαλλον is quite vague. We should expect that the government would extract what it could from the tax-farmers and force the sureties to pay the rest. But there is no regulation that the farmers' own property was held in mortgage, and in the account of the διαλογισμος in A [16]–[17], the εγγυοι alone seem responsible for making up a deficit, while from the two series of papyri which bear on this subject, we should gather that the sureties were mainly, if not entirely, responsible. In P. P. xlvi the surety apparently has to pay more than half the whole amount which the tax-farmer had promised to the government, though the question is complicated by the occurrence of the obscure term χαλκου προς αργυριον (to adopt Wilcken's reading), on which see App. iii, and by an erasure, which makes it uncertain whether the amount paid by the surety coincided with his liability, or whether it was all that he was able to pay. In the Zois papyri the surety is actually liable for the whole amount promised by the tax-farmer. Unfortunately there are no details

in either case concerning the failure of the tax-farmer to fulfil his contract or of the penalty which he incurred, and presumably the loss to the security in both cases was exceptional. The fact however remains that to be surety for a tax-farmer must have been an extremely burdensome λειτουργία, and it is surprising that any one could have been found to undertake the duty except under compulsion. This I suspect was exercised both in the case of the εγγυοι, and even in the case of the tax-farmers, though not formally admitted either in the Revenue Papyrus or in L. P. 62, in which a large amount of space is devoted to the sureties, [1] 13-[3] 16. The edict of Tiberius Alexander C. I. G. iii. 4957 has a significant passage, line 10 ff. εγγνων γαρ προ παντος ευλογω- τατην ουσαν την εντευξιν υμων υπερ του μη ακοντας ανθρωπους εις τελωνειας η αλλας μισθωσεις ουσιακας παρα το κοινον εθος των επαρχειων προς βιαν αγεσθαι, κ.τ.λ., which shows that the position of the tax-farmers and *a fortiori* that of the εγγυοι had become intolerable. Cf. L. P. 62 [5] 3, which shows the difficulty of finding tax-farmers.

[**35.**] 3. καλεισθωσαν: cf. [8] 3 and [21] 12. οι αδικουμενοι are probably the tax-farmers who had not received the surplus due to them.

With this section the law concerning the απομοιρα comes to an end. The next two columns give the decrees by which the second Ptolemy effected the 'disendowment of the Church' or state religion.

[**36.**] 1-2. The conclusion of a προσταγμα enclosing a προγραμμα [36] 3-[37] 1, which quotes a previous προσταγμα [37] 2-9. This in turn introduces the προγραμμα [37] 10-20. The sequence of these four documents in point of time is therefore the exact reverse of their written order.

[**36.**] 3-19. 'The basilicogrammateis of the nomes throughout the country shall, each for his nome, register both the number of arourae comprised by vineyards and orchards and the amount of the different kinds of produce from them, cultivator by cultivator, beginning with the twenty-second year, and shall separate the land belonging to the temples and the produce from it in order that the rest of the land may (be determined), from which the sixth is to be paid to Philadelphus, and they shall give a written account of the details to the agents of Satyrus. Similarly both the cleruchs who possess vineyards or orchards in the lots which they have received from the king, and all other persons who own vineyards or orchards or hold them in gift or cultivate them on any terms whatever shall, each for himself, register both the extent of his land and the amount of its different kinds of produce, and shall give the sixth part of all the produce to Arsinoe Philadelphus for a sacrifice and libation (to her).'

4. This passage shows clearly that there was one βασιλικος γραμματευς in each nome, though cf. P. P. 138 (a), where the plural is found. But probably the officials of more than the one nome are there meant, cf. [37] 2-5. Though in the Fayoum the oeconomus was undoubtedly an officer of a μερις, not of the whole nome (see P. P. xviii. (1) 2), we do not know that the other nomes were divided into μεριδες, and on the whole the Revenue Papyrus points to the oeconomus being under ordinary circumstances an officer of the whole nome, though it is by no means conclusive, for throughout the papyrus officials are nearly always spoken of in the singular, even when there were many bearing the same title, e. g. the comarch, [40] 3-5.

6. γενηματα : the plural because referring to both αμπελωνες and παραδεισοι, but perhaps with a secondary reference to the different kinds of produce included under the head of παραδεισοι; cf. [24] 12 note.

7. απο του κβL : the meaning is that the προγραμμα is to be retrospective, though issued between Dius and Daisius of the twenty-third year, cf. [37] 9 with [36] 2. The Leyden papyrus Q gives us actual proof that the tax was paid to Arsinoe, not to the temples, on the produce of the twenty-second year, though the transaction recorded by that papyrus, the payment of 20 drachmae for the κεραμιον τηι Φιλαδελφωι by the δοκιμαστης to the πρακτωρ, is dated in the twenty-sixth year, and the payment was therefore some years in arrear, which explains the mention of the πρακτωρ; cf. note on [6] 1.

8. I am indebted to Wilcken for the restoration of this important passage, which shows that the ιερα γη was exempt from the εκτη. It is not surprising that Philadelphus, while diverting the revenue of the older gods to the new goddess Arsinoe, hesitated to demand a tax for the deified Arsinoe upon land actually belonging to the gods. ταυτα is a mistake for τα ; cf. line 6.

10. τηι Φιλαδελφωι: cf. P. P. part I. 70 (2) 1, and note on [37] 19. The date of Arsinoe's death is uncertain ; see Wilck. art. *Arsinoe* in Pauly-Wissowa's Encycl. But as the Pithom stele shows that she was

alive in the twentieth year, it is probable that she was alive in the twenty-third year, though the Revenue Papyrus is equally consistent with the opposite hypothesis. Cf. Introd. p. xxxix.

11. Satyrus: see [37] 11.

12. κληρουχοι: cf. [24] 6 note. Some of them at any rate paid only a tenth after the twenty-seventh year. But nothing can be more precise than this passage; cf. [33] 19, which agrees with it.

15. εν δωρεαις: cf. [43] 11 note. It is clear from the references to this mode of tenure that it was very common, and that holders of land εν δωρεαι were generally to some extent exempt from taxation.

19. Was the sacrifice to be offered by the tax-payers to Arsinoe, or by Arsinoe on their behalf to the gods? M. prefers the latter meaning, arguing that in the other case there would be no article before θυσιαν και σπονδην, cf. Rosetta stone, line 50 συντελουντες θυσιας και σπονδας. But the fact that the tax was called sometimes the εκτη τηι Φιλαδελφωι, sometimes απομοιρα τηι Φιλαδελφωι, see note on [37] 19, is all in favour of the first view.

It is hardly necessary to point out that the εκτη τηι Φιλαδελφωι was collected and paid εις το βασιλικον like any other tax. The θυσια και σπονδη was an ingenious but transparent fiction to cloak the disendowment of the temples.

[37.] 1. αντιγραφον probably refers to the following προσταγμα: see note on [36] 1.

[37.] 2–9. 'King Ptolemy to all strategi, hipparchs, captains, nomarchs, toparchs, oeconomi, antigrapheis, basilicogrammateis, Libyarchs, and chiefs of police, greeting. I have sent you the copies of my proclamation, which ordains the payment of the sixth to (Queen) Philadelphus. Take heed therefore that my instructions are carried into effect. Farewell. The twenty-third year, Dius the twenty . . .'

2. While the strategus already in the third century B.C. combined civil with military duties (see M., P. P. Introd. p. 7 and Wilck. Anmerk. Droysen Kl. Schr. p. 437), the papyri in which he is mentioned either are or may be later than Philadelphus' reign (including even P. P. ii, cf. note on [57] 4); and probably at this period the position of the strategus was still in the main military. At any rate the ηγεμων was a military officer, so that there is a strong probability that the official whose title is lost in

the lacuna, was a military one also, and that the civil officials come afterwards. Neither the ἐπιστρατηγος nor the ὑποστρατηγος has yet been found in the third century B.C., while ιππαρχιαι are frequently found in P. P. There is an unpublished papyrus of that collection which begins Αγαθιδι (sic) στρατηγωι και ιππαρχηι.

3. ηγεμοσι. The hegemones are thus subordinate to the strategi; nevertheless the Romans chose this title as an equivalent for the praefectus. Cf. an inscr. at Alexandria, salle G, Καλλιστρατος ο ηγεμων και οι τεταγμενοι υπ αυτον στρατιωται. This inscription has been asserted by Strack (Mitth. d. K. Deutsch. Arch. Inst. Athen, 1894, p. 237) to be a forgery, but on very inadequate grounds. He adduces four arguments. (1) The writer of the inscription took account of the roughnesses of the stone, leaving a space where there was a hole or excrescence. But this only proves that the writer did not select a very smooth piece of stone, and by itself is no argument for the date. (2) Strack objects that the second title of Ptolemy Epiphanes, Ευχαριστος, is absent. But the second title is omitted on coins, cf. Poole Catalogue, Pl. xxxii. 7, which has Πτολεμαιου Επιφανους, and Epiphanes and Cleopatra are always called θεοι επιφανεις simply. (3) Strack remarks that Callistratus, being a Greek, ought to have his father's name mentioned, an argument which is very far from being conclusive. (4) He says that ηγεμων by itself without επ ανδρων is in a Ptolemaic inscription an anachronism, an argument which is refuted not only by this passage in the Revenue Papyrus, but by L. P. 45 verso line 1, and P. P. xlv, cols. 2 and 3. Cf. pap. 32 in my A. E. F. which has ηγεμων . . . . και οι στρατιωται, like the inscription. Finally the inscription has every appearance of antiquity; and it is not at all likely that a forged Greek inscription should have found its way into the Alexandria Museum, when a forger could spend his time much more profitably by turning his attention to 'twelfth dynasty' stelae, papyri, or scarabs.

νομαρχαις και τοπαρχαις: see [41] 16 note. In P. P. 138 the nomarchs are put after the oeconomi in the list of officials; but cf. [41] 7, which agrees with this passage in giving precedence to the nomarch. There can be no doubt that this is the right order.

4. οικονομοις: see [36] 4 note.

5. Λιβυαρχαις. A Λιβυάρχης τῶν κατὰ Κυρήνην τόπων is mentioned in Polyb. xv. 25. 12, but I agree with M., who thinks that the Libyarchs of

the Rev. Pap. were officials of the nome Libya, which included a wide district. Cf. the terms Αραβαρχης and, in the second century B.C. papyri, Θηβαρχος. This passage shows that the Libyarchs ranked much lower than the nomarchs in the official hierarchy ; cf. [41] 16 note.

The absence of the επιμελητης from not only this list of officials but the whole Revenue Papyrus is remarkable, for he is often mentioned in L. P. 62, 63 with the other financial officials. Cf. Rev. R. E. v. 44, and P. P. 61. 1 (fifth year), and 108. 2 (eighth year). Both papyri may be forty or fifty years later than the Revenue Papyrus, especially the second, in which the drachmae are copper ; see App. iii. There is therefore no direct evidence that the title was used at this time. But the office and title probably existed nevertheless.

6. The θ of καθ, if θ it be, is very irregularly formed and joined to the ο.

7. Cf. P. P. [122] 6, and App. p. 8.

[37.] 10–20. ' Owners of vineyards or orchards, whatever their tenure, shall all give to the agents of Satyrus and the accountants who have been appointed agents of Dionysodorus, nome by nome, a written statement, which statement shall be given by themselves in person or by the agents or tenants of their estates from the eighteenth to the twenty-first year, and shall contain both the amount of the different kinds of produce and the name of the temple to which they used to pay the sixth due, together with the amount of the sixth in each year. Similarly the priests also shall give a written statement of the estates from which they severally derived a revenue, and the amount of the tax in each year, whether paid in wine or in silver. Likewise the basilicogrammateis shall send in a written statement of all these details.'

11. Satyrus : cf. Strabo xvi. 4 ; a general of Philadelphus bearing this name was sent on an expedition to obtain elephants and explore the country of the Troglodytes. But it is not likely that he was the same person as this Satyrus, who must have held a high financial office at Alexandria, and possibly was the dioecetes par excellence, while οι παρα Σατυρου may have been the ordinary dioecetae together with their clerks and subordinates. Cf. [18] 6, where the εκλογιστης is coupled with the διοικητης.

14. The twenty-first year was the last in which the tax was paid to the temples ; cf. note on [36] 7, and [33] 14. The information was

required in order that the tax-farmers might be able to take the average of the four preceding years as their basis in bidding for the tax.

Wilck. suggests δηλουσας at the end of the line, which makes the construction easier, but I am not sure that it is necessary.

17. κτηματος, as Wilck. pointed out to me, refers not to the κτηματα of private persons mentioned in line 14, but to the ιερα γη belonging to the temples; cf. [36] 8, which explains this passage. The government wished to ascertain the number of vineyards and orchards belonging to the priests, in order that they might be exempted from the tax, not in order that they might pay it.

18. While this passage shows that the priests received the rent of their own κτηματα partly in money, partly in kind, it is not stated whether the εκτη which they received from the κτηματα of other persons was paid in the same way. But in exacting the tax on παραδεισοι in money always, and that on αμπελωνες in money under certain conditions, the government was probably continuing the regulations in force when the απομοιρα was paid to the temples.

19. [κ]αι οι: the position of the fragments at the end of this line is doubtful. For no tax of the Ptolemies have we more information than for the απομοιρα, but it is not easy to arrange it chronologically. There is :—(1) Leyden pap. Q (see note on [36] 7), a receipt for the κεραμιον τηι Φιλαδελφωι, dated the twenty-sixth year of Philadelphus. (2) The Revenue Papyrus. (3) Wilck. Ostr. 711, a receipt for the payment of απομοιρα and οινολογια in kind, dated the fifth year, probably of Euergetes', perhaps of Philopator's reign. (4) A papyrus at Dublin, C^b, No. 9 of my A. E. F., &c., dated the eighth year, which mentions the απομοιρα της Φι[λαδελφου. From the close resemblance of the handwriting to that of the wills dated the tenth year of Euergetes in P. P. part I, M. assigns this papyrus to Euergetes' reign. This document and P. P. xlvii. (see below) are conclusive evidence that the απομοιρα of [24]-[35] is identical with the εκτη of [33], [36], and [37]. (5) P. P. part I, xvi. (2), which records the payment of the tax on the produce of παραδεισοι in silver, and is dated the seventeenth year of Euergetes. (6) P. P. xxvii, and (7) xxx (e), which record the payment of the εκτη in kind upon vineyards, and in silver on παραδεισοι, dated the twenty-third year, probably of Euergetes, but possibly of Philadelphus. (8) P. P.

xxx (c), in which the εκτη upon vineyards is assessed partly in kind, partly in silver, that upon παραδεισοι in silver. (9) P. P. xliii (b) εκτη και δεκατη, in which αμπελωνες are assessed partly in kind, partly in silver, and παραδεισοι in silver; cf. note on [24] 13. This papyrus and (8) are before Epiphanes' reign, see App. iii. (10) P. P. xlvi (see note on [34] 18), dated the second and fourth years of Epiphanes, which refers to the απομοιρα τηι Φιλαδελφωι (cf. no. 3) και τοις Φιλοπατορσι θεοις. (11) Wilck. Ostr. 322 = R. E. vi. p. 7, no. 2, a receipt for 2280 drachmae paid to the royal bank in the sixth year of a Ptolemy. Wilck. R. E. l. c. assigned it on palaeographical grounds to Euergetes I, but the fact that the drachmae are copper makes it much more probable that it belongs to Epiphanes' reign; see App. iii. (12) Rosetta stone, lines 13–15, προσεταξε δε και τας προσοδους των ιερων και τας διδομενας εις αυτα κατ ενιαυτον συνταξεις σιτικας τε και αργυρικας ομοιως δε και τας καθηκουσας απομοιρας τοις θεοις απο τε της αμπελιτιδος γης και των παραδεισων και των αλλων των υπαρξαντων τοις θεοις επι του πατρος αυτου μενειν επι χωρας. If τας καθηκουσας απομοιρας τοις θεοις has the meaning which has been generally attributed to it, that the απομοιραι were paid to the temples, the inscription makes two statements, which if true would be of the highest importance, (1) that in the reign of Philopator the temples received the απομοιρα from vineyards and orchards, (2) that they continued to receive them in the ninth year of Epiphanes. But there are grave difficulties in the way of accepting either of these statements. The association of the gods Philopatores with Arsinoe in P. P. xlvi (c), dated the fourth year of Epiphanes, is much more consistent with the supposition that the deified Philopator, far from giving back the απομοιρα to the temples, went a step further than his predecessors, and made himself the recipient of the tax in name as well as in reality. And even if the association of the gods Philopatores with Arsinoe did not take place until the beginning of Epiphanes' reign, it is in any case certain that the tax was paid to the government, not to the temples, within five years, perhaps within three, of the Rosetta stone, and that if Epiphanes gave it back in the ninth year, it was soon appropriated by the government; for the payment of απομοιρα in copper drachmae to the royal bank occurs in numerous ostraca belonging to the second century B.C., see (13) below. But I do not believe that these changes ever took place at all. Though Philopator and Epiphanes owing to the civil war in Egypt found it necessary to conciliate the priests, it is unlikely that either of them, considering the impoverished condition of the exchequer shown by the deterioration of the coinage and the adoption of a copper standard, could afford to give up so profitable a source of income as the απομοιρα: and since the evidence of the papyri and ostraca, while not absolutely irreconcilable with the Rosetta stone, is all in favour of the supposition that the government never renounced the απομοιρα, I think that, if the meaning generally given to this passage of the Rosetta stone be correct, the priests' statements are untrue. But a distinction is carefully drawn in the passage between the προσοδοι and συνταξεις of the temples and the απομοιραι of the gods; and if we suppose that by the 'gods' are meant Arsinoe and the gods Philopatores (cf. P. P. xlvi), the passage only implies that Philopator and Epiphanes maintained the fiction set up by Philadelphus, that the απομοιρα was applied to religious purposes when paid to Arsinoe. In that case we need not find the priests guilty of anything worse than an expression of flattery, not more abject than other phrases in both the Rosetta and Canopus inscriptions.

(13) It is probably not a mere accident that all the receipts for απομοιρα found in the second century B.C. ostraca (see W. Ostr. 332, 354, 1234, 1235, &c.), refer to payment in money, and I conjecture that payment in kind was not allowed after Epiphanes' reign. Moreover an ostracon in Prof. Sayce's collection (no. 1518) deciphered by Wilcken shows that the απομοιρα in the second century was no longer a προς αργυριον ωνη, but an ωνη προς χαλκον ισονομον, i. e. the tax-farmers were allowed to pay in copper without having also to pay the difference of the exchange, cf. L. P. 62 [5] 16 and App. iii. The latest mention of απομοιρα is in a papyrus at the British Museum, from which Wilcken has made the interesting discovery that the tax continued to be paid after the Roman conquest.

[38.] 'The twenty-seventh year, Loius 10th, we will correct this (among?) the agents of Apollonius:' altered by the corrector to 'we corrected this in the office of Apollonius the dioecetes.'

1. Between this and the preceding column are 18 inches of blank papyrus. The writer of it is the same as the writer of [23], the corrector the same as the corrector of [39]-[56], who is in my opinion the writer of the διορθωμα [57] and [58], besides having probably made the few

R

corrections in A and B which are not made by the scribes themselves. His corrections in C fall into two classes, those in which he merely corrects the blunders of the scribes, e. g. [41] 4 and [42] 17, and those in which he alters the meaning of or makes some addition to the original draft of C. The first question which arises in [38] is—to which of these two classes do the corrections here belong? The erasure of παρα and the insertion of του διοικητου obviously belong to the second, the insertion of εν probably to the first. For though a mistake in a note like this is very remarkable, the dative without a preposition is untranslateable. There is less doubt concerning the alteration of the tense in διορθωσομεθα. It is not necessary to suppose a blunder, and therefore it is not legitimate to do so. The meaning of the correction is that the writer of [38], after the first draft, i. e. [39]-[56], was completed, inserted a note saying that he would cause the papyrus to be corrected in Apollonius' office. The papyrus was accordingly sent thither, and the corrector after revising it notified the fact that he had done so by changing the tense from the future to the past. The original draft therefore consisted of [39]-[56], while the corrections in those columns are contemporaneous with [57] and [58], as is also clear from internal evidence, see notes on [41] 20, [53] 18. In what position do [59]-[72], all written by one scribe, stand? [59] and [60] are a repetition with a few variations of [57]-[58], the rest consists of a list of nomes. Now though the original draft [39]-[56] refers in one passage to a list of nomes, that list is certainly not the list which we have, while our list, see notes on [53] 18 and [57] 6, agrees with the corrections in [39]-[56] and the two columns added by the corrector. [59]-[72] were therefore added when the corrections were made, and the explanation of the repetition of [57]-[58] in [59]-[60] is that [59]-[72] originally existed as a separate piece, different from the papyrus of [1]-[58] not only in texture but by at least 3 inches in height, and the corrector probably found it more convenient to join this strip to [58] than to copy out the list of nomes himself, although by doing so he caused the needless repetition of two columns. Whether [59] and [60] were directly copied from [57]-[58] is doubtful, see note on [57] 6, and the cause of the repetition must of course be a matter of pure conjecture; but it concerns us very little whether the list of nomes referred to in [53] 18 was, before the corrections were made, joined to the papyrus at the point where [59] now joins it, and was cut off by the corrector in order that the new list might be substituted, or whether the first draft of the law was incomplete and contained no list of nomes. The important facts are that the official list of nomes referred to in the uncorrected draft of [53] was quite different from the list which we possess, that [59]-[72] originally formed a separate document, and that the corrections in [38]-[56] and the addition of [57]-[72] represent changes introduced into the law concerning the oil contract during the twenty-seventh year, as the date in [38] 1 referring to the corrections shows. The first draft, [39]-[56] without the corrections, is doubtless a copy of the older law on the subject, though how much older we cannot say, except that those parts of it which are διαγραμματα seem to have been revised yearly, [53] 11, and therefore may not be older than the twenty-sixth year.

Since C was written in Loius of the twenty-seventh year, the fact that A and B precede C, even though originally they were probably separate documents, makes it certain that they too were written in the twenty-seventh year. Therefore the date in [24] 2 is the actual year in which the scribe was writing, not as in the case of the dates in [36] and [37] the year in the document which he had before him. On D and E which are contemporary with B see note on [73] 1. As the απομοιρα was only transferred to Arsinoe in the twenty-third year, B cannot be based on much older documents, cf. notes on [24] and [33], but as Soter must have introduced νομοι τελωτικοι, it is quite possible that A is based for the most part on them. Cf. note on [31] 5.

3. του διοικητου: this is the only place in [1]-[72] where this official has the simple title, elsewhere he is called ο επι της διοικησεως τεταγμενος, though see [86] 7. But no stress is to be laid on the variation, cf. note on [24] 17.

M. in P. P. Introd. p. 9, has called attention to the fact that there were local dioecetae as well as the principal dioecetes in Alexandria, and I would go a step further and assert that of the dioecetae mentioned by L. Rec. p. 339, all those quoted from papyri were local dioecetae. It is in any case far more probable that the corrections in [39]-[56] were made in the office of the local dioecetes than that the papyrus was sent to Alexandria to be corrected. And since the whole Revenue Papyrus came from the Fayoum, see note on [73] 1, it is almost certain that the Apollonius in line 2 is the Apollonius mentioned in Cleon's correspondence; see P. P. 6. 2, 8. 1, 9. 8, 33. 3, 34. 3, 10, all either certainly or probably belonging to the thirtieth year of Philadelphus.

The dioecetes, being the chief financial official, controlled not only the oeconomus, [18] 6–8, but the nomarch, [41] 12, [46] 5. Prisoners were sent to him, L. P. 62 [8] 17, and P. P. 34 [3] 10. He was not permanently resident in a nome, [18] 6 note, cf. P. P. 122. 5, 9, a letter written from some one in the Nile valley, perhaps at Memphis, to the Fayoum ; and it is clear that the district under the care of the dioecetes included more than a single nome.

[**39.**] 1–12. 'The contractors shall pay the cultivators for an artaba of sesame containing 30 choenices prepared for grinding 8 drachmae, for an artaba of croton containing 30 choenices prepared for grinding 4 drachmae, for an artaba of cnecus prepared for grinding 1 drachma 2 obols, for an artaba of colocynth 4 obols, for linseed 3 obols. If the cultivator will not give the contractors produce prepared for grinding, he shall measure it out from the store, having cleaned it with a sieve, and shall measure out in addition for completing the preparation of the produce for grinding 7 artabae of sesame for every 100, of croton the same amount, and of cnecus 8 artabae.'

1. This section is a διαγραμμα, see 16 and [53] 11, a term used in C to express those sections of the papyrus which are concerned with values or prices : e.g. [40] 9–16, [43] 11–19, and [53]. Cf. [73] 1 note, and L. P. 62 [8] 5.

2. Cf. [25] 8 note. An artaba of 28 choenices is mentioned in my A. E. F. pap. 18. The difficult question of the various artabae in the Ptolemaic period is fully discussed by Wilck. in his forthcoming Corpus Ostracorum. The choenix, he tells me, is approximately a litre.

3. Cf. [53] 16, where this proportion of 8 : 4 : 1⅓ is found between the value of an artaba of sesame, croton, and cnecus; and [41] 10 and 17, [43] 17–18, where the same or nearly the same proportion is observed. Cf. also the tax on sesame and croton, [39] 14–15, [57] 12. The prices here are probably προs χαλκον, see [40] 10 and [43] 16, i.e. payment was made in copper; cf. line 17 below, where αργυριον is probably opposed to payment in copper as well as to payment in kind, and see App. iii.

I am indebted to Dr. E. P. Wright of Dublin for the following notes on the oil-producing plants. ' Sesame oil is extracted from the seeds of

Sesamum orientale and Sesamum indicum. When the seeds are in good
condition, from 49 to 51 per cent. by weight of oil will be taken from
them. 'Croton' oil is extracted from the seeds of Ricinus communis,
the castor-oil plant; the seeds under favourable circumstances yield
about 25 per cent. by weight of oil. Cnecus oil was almost certainly
made from the seeds of some composite plant, possibly an artichoke.
The sunflower yields 15 per cent. by weight of oil, but oils from such
a source are inferior. As to colocynth oil, the seeds of Citrullus colo-
cynthis yield oil, but are not apparently used at present for such purposes.'

As Dr. Wright suggests, the fact that sesame yields 50 per cent. by
weight, and croton 25 per cent., helps to explain the proportion of 2 : 1
in their prices, but to what extent depends on the respective weights of
an artaba of sesame and an artaba of croton. In speaking of 'croton,'
I should explain that I mean throughout what the ancients meant by
it, the castor-oil plant, not the plant which is now by a misnomer called
'croton.' This does indeed produce an oil, but it is only useful as
a very powerful drug.

The most remarkable point in the list is the absence of olive-oil (see
Introd. p. xxxv), the place of which for cooking purposes was clearly taken
at this time by sesame oil. For the uses of castor-oil, see Strabo xvii.
824 εἰς μὲν λύχνον τοῖς ἀπὸ τῆς χώρας σχεδόν τι πᾶσιν, εἰς ἄλειμμα δὲ τοῖς
πενεστέροις καὶ ἐργατικωτέροις. Cf. Herod. ii. 94 and Wiedemann's note,
Herodot's zweites Buch, p. 382. Probably it was occasionally used then
even for cooking by the poorest inhabitants, a practice which has not yet
died out in Nubia. Dr. Wright tells me that castor-oil is still used in
China for cooking purposes, but the Chinese have some method of
depriving it of its purgative principle. Verily *de gustibus non est dis-
putandum.*

6. κολοκυνθίνου: elsewhere this is used for the oil, not the plant; but
cf. [55] 6, and the ambiguity of του εκ κ.τ.λ. in the next line.

7. In the enumeration of the oils, [40] 9–13 and [55] 7–9, in the place
of linseed oil we have το επελλυχνιον 'oil for wicks,' but see [57] 19 το
απο του λινου σπερματος where the oil is meant, not the seeds, so that
there is little doubt about the identity of το επελλυχνιον with linseed oil,
and it is improbable that this επελλυχνιον was a less valuable quality of
some of the other oils. σπερματος is governed by εκ, although the seeds
are meant here, not the oil.

8. The γεωργοι in [39]-[60], like the γεωργοι in [24]-[37], are private cultivators. Though the cultivation of sesame and croton was strictly regulated by the government, the land was not βασιλικη γη, nor is there any system of corvée such as that described in L. P. 63. Cf. a demotic contract with Greek subscription in Revillout's Nouv. Chrest. Dém. p. 155, in which Phib the son of Phib agrees, pledging himself by a βασιλικος ορκος, to plant 20 arourae of land belonging to the temples with sesame : and P. P. xxxix (*a*), where the κληροι of private individuals are to be planted with croton.

9. παραμετρειτω : 'measure *out*,' publicly, in the presence of some one, cf. [43] 2, 12. αλω : the place where the produce was kept, cf. [41] 19, and P. P. 121. 23 των δε αλων ουσων θηκων. The oil was manufactured in an ελαιουργιον or εργαστηριον, see [44], [45].

καθαρας : cf. πυρος ρυπαρος in Wilck. Ostr. 768, and a papyrus at Alexandria, M. Bull. de Corr. Hell. xviii. p. 145, line 13 . . .]ματα απο της αλω συν τωι κονιορτωι αρ ιε, and line 17 αποκαθαρσις του σιτου.

11. The 'sign' for αρταβα is to be explained as αρ with a stroke over it to mark the abbreviation, the top of the ρ being added separately : cf. [46] 17 where the same sign occurs, but without a stroke over it. In [53] 16 the loop of the ρ is joined to the α, while the tail has almost disappeared. In [60] 25 and the succeeding columns the sign is drawn without lifting the pen from the papyrus, the form found most commonly in the Petrie papyri. The addition of a curved line above, i. e. υ, transforms it into the 'sign' for αρουρα, as is clearly shown by pap. 33 of my A. E. F. Cf. also [57] 12 and [59] 13, where artaba is represented by α with a stroke after it, which may be ρ or a sign of abbreviation.

[**39.**] 13-18. 'The contractors shall receive from the cultivators, for the tax of 2 drachmae payable on the sesame and the tax of 1 drachma on the croton, sesame and croton at the value decreed in the legal tariff, and shall not exact payment in silver.'

13. That the contractors are the persons meant throughout [39] and [40] is evident from numerous passages in the following columns. Cf. [39] 13 with [41] 10 and [54] 23 ; and [40] 9 with [49] 18 ; and see [53] 16 note.

14. The tax was levied on each artaba, see [41] 10 and [57] 12 = [59] 13, and thus amounted to one-fourth of the value in the case of sesame and croton. No tax was levied on cnecus, colocynth, and flax,

the growth of which was not regulated by the central government, though the distribution of all crops was supervised by the nomarch, see note on [41] 16. On the other hand the precise amount of sesame and croton to be grown throughout the country is fixed in [60]-[72].

Since the contractors paid the cultivator 8 drachmae for an artaba of sesame but received 2 drachmae back in sesame, why is there not one regulation that they should pay the cultivator 6 drachmae, instead of two regulations, one that they should pay him 8 drachmae, the other that he should pay them two? It is quite certain that the contractors were the same in both cases, see [41] 10-11. Yet there is no mention of the tax in the διαλογισμος [54] 20-[55] 12, and since the sesame and croton collected as the tax must have been made into oil, like the sesame and oil bought by the contractors, it is impossible that the account of the tax should have been kept separate from the other accounts, and administered according to the regulations laid down in A for farming the taxes. As the effect of the tax on sesame and croton was to reduce one element in the cost of making oil, the price of the seeds, by one-fourth, probably the tax was ignored in the accounts, and the price of sesame and croton treated as 6 and 3 drachmae for an artaba.

The only explanation of the circumlocution which I can suggest is that the government wished to draw a nominal distinction between the υποτελεις here and the ατελεις in [43] 11, though in reality the ατελεις received scarcely anything more for their produce than the υποτελεις.

The position of οι πριαμενοι την ελαικην differs considerably from that of οι πριαμενοι in A and B. The latter contracted to pay a fixed sum for a tax the amount of which was uncertain. If the tax produced more than what they had agreed to pay, the surplus went to them; if it produced less, they had to bear the loss. On the other hand the contractors of the oil monopoly agreed to pay the government a fixed sum for the profits arising from the sale of oil [45] 2 and [55] 2, and here there seems little room for a deficit or a surplus such as that mentioned in A and B. The precise cost of manufacturing a metretes of oil was fixed beforehand, [55] 2-12, as was the retail price, [40] 9-16, and since the amount of sesame and croton to be made into oil in each nome was fixed in [59]-[72], the number of metretae that could be sold was also limited. The only elements of uncertainty were (1) the price received by the contractors from the retailers, which was fixed by auction, [48] 14. (2) The amount of oil produced from a given amount of seed could not be anticipated with absolute precision, but apparently there was a fixed amount of oil expected from each artaba, and if the amount of oil actually produced was above the average, this surplus belonged not to the contractors, but to the Treasury [58] 8. (3) The number of metretae sold might fall short of the contractors' expectations, and they received less for oil remaining over when the contract expired than for the oil which they had sold, [53] 14. (4) The duty on foreign oil brought into the country was paid to the contractors, [52] 20, and the amount of this would be uncertain. But the margin for either profit or loss, so far as the contractors were concerned, was extremely narrow, and the absence of any regulation like that in [18] 9 and [34] 9-21 might be thought to show that there was no margin at all. Still, as the actual profit made by the sale of the oil must have had a definite relation to the sum promised by the contractors, it is probable that any surplus or deficit on the whole contract was treated in the usual way.

On the other hand there are good reasons for supposing that such a surplus was likely to be very unimportant. These are: (1) the absence of any regulation providing for the contingency ; (2) the use of ἐπιγένημα in C, not for the surplus above the total amount which the contractors had agreed to pay, but for the profit on the sale of each metretes of oil, i.e. the difference between the cost and the selling price, [41] 11 ; (3) the fact that the contractors received a portion of this ἐπιγένημα as their μισθός or pay, [45] 6, [55] 13-16, while in A and B there is no hint of a μισθός for the tax-farmers, [31] 14 note. In A and B the government by farming out the taxes secured a fixed revenue, while the tax-farmers were allowed the opportunity of making a surplus. In C the government farmed out the oil-monopoly, not in the least to secure a fixed revenue, for the revenue from it was fixed already, but to ensure the economical manufacture of the oil, while the tax-farmers received a definite reward for their labour in superintending the manufacture and sale of the oil instead of an indefinite surplus.

It is in their capacity of manufacturers far more than in their capacity of tax-farmers that οἱ πριαμενοι την ελαικην were necessary to the government, and for that reason throughout C I have translated οἱ πριαμενοι ‘contractors.’

17. See notes on lines 1 and 3.

[**39.**] 19-[**40**] 8. 'The cultivators shall not be allowed to sell either sesame or croton to any persons other than the contractors . . . and the contractors shall give the comarch a sealed receipt for what they have received from each cultivator; if they do not give him the receipt, the comarch shall not allow the produce to leave the village. If he disobeys this rule, he shall pay 1000 drachmae to the Treasury, and five times the amount of the loss which his action may have caused, to the contractors.'

[**40.**] 3. See note on [39] 13; line 7 also shows that the contractors are meant. αποσφραγισμα: cf. [31] 17.

5. προιεσθω: cf. [27] 11.

[**40.**] 9-20. 'The contractors shall sell the oil in the country at the rate of 48 dr. for a metretes of sesame oil containing 12 choes and for a metretes of cnecus-oil, accepting payment in copper, and at the rate of 30 dr. for a metretes of cici, colocynth oil, and lamp oil' (altered to 'The contractors shall sell the oil·in the country, both sesame oil, cnecus oil, cici, colocynth oil, and lamp oil at the rate of 48 dr. for a metretes of 12 choes, accepting payment in copper, and 2 obols for a cotyle'). In Alexandria and the whole of Libya they shall sell it at the rate of 48 dr. for a metretes of sesame oil, and 48 dr. for a metretes of cici (altered to '. . . 48 dr. for a metretes of sesame oil and cici, and 2 obols for a cotyle'), and they shall provide an amount sufficient to meet the demands of buyers, selling it throughout the country in all the towns and villages, (measuring it) by measures which have been tested by the oeconomus and antigrapheus.'

9. That the government were able to suddenly raise the price of the inferior oils more than 50 per cent., making them equal in value to the superior oils, shows the gulf which separates ancient from modern political economy. It is difficult to see why any one should have bought e.g. oil of colocynth, when he could get sesame oil at the same price. As M. suggests, it was probably with the object of maintaining the demand for sesame oil that the government levelled up the price of cici, colocynth, and lamp oil to that of sesame and cnecus oil.

10. προς χαλκον: see App. iii. To anticipate, this passage means that 288 of the large copper coins which represent the obol (or an equivalent amount of the smaller ones) would be accepted as the equivalent of 48 silver drachmae, although in reality 48 drachmae thus

paid in copper were worth about 10 per cent. less than 48 drachmae paid in silver. Since however the contractors of the oil monopoly not only received payments in copper but made them in copper to the government, [58] 6, the loss by the exchange fell on the government, not on them. The ελαικη ωνη was in fact an ωνη προς χαλκον ισονομον, cf. L. P. 62 [5] 19. Literally προς χαλκον means 'against copper,' cf. χαλκου προς αργυριον, and my explanation of it in App. iii p. 204.

The Petrie papyri have as yet yielded no information concerning the price of oil in the third century B.C., which, as the correction here shows, varied largely from year to year. The Sakkakini papyrus however, of the third century B.C. (Rev. R. E. iii. 89), mentions frequently the payment of 1 obol for cici. M. Revillout suggests that the amount was 2 cotulae, which would make the price of a metretes 12 drachmae. This suits his conclusions about the price of oil in the next century, but is hardly compatible with the 30 dr., still less with the 48 dr., which the Revenue Papyrus states to be the price of a metretes of cici. I should therefore suggest that the obol was the price of ½ cotyle or at most of 1 cotyle. On the price of oil in the second century B.C. see note on [51] 12.

επελλυχνιον : see note on [39] 7. While the retail price of oil is here fixed at 48 dr. προς χαλκον, the contractors did not receive 48 drachmae, as most of the selling, if not the whole, was done by small traders, [47] 10 sqq., to whom the contractors sold the oil by auction.

11. On the metretes of 12 choes see notes on [25] 8, [31] 6, and [55] 8.

14. πασηι : i. e. including the αφωρισμενη, the produce of which was reserved for Alexandria, [60] 10 and [61] 3. It is obvious that the nome Libya had no very clearly defined boundary. Cf. [37] 5 note.

15. Cnecus, colocynth, and linseed oil are omitted, though they must have been required in Alexandria, cf. [53] 22, and [58] 1 note. Probably they were sold at the same price as sesame oil and cici ; cf. [42] 4 note.

16. την written above μη means that την δε κοτυλην, written in line 15, comes in here. Cf. [41] 27 and [43] 25, where, a note having been inserted, the next few letters of the following sentence are written in order to fix the place of the note.

19. Cf. the similar precaution in [25] 10.

[41.] 3-13. 'They shall exhibit the land sown to the contractor in conjunction with the oeconomus and antigrapheus, and if, after surveying it, they find that the right number of arourae has not been sown, both the nomarch and the toparch and the oeconomus and the antigrapheus shall, each of them who is responsible, pay a fine of two talents to the Treasury, and to the contractors for each artaba of sesame which they ought to have received 2 dr., and for each artaba of croton 1 dr., together with the surplus of the oil and the cici. The dioecetes shall exact the payment from them.'

3. αποδειξατωσαν: i. e. the nomarch and toparch; cf. [43] 3.

5. το πληθος: the number decreed in [60]-[72]. Only sesame and croton are meant in this column.

10. The reference is to [39] 13-18.

11. το επιγενημα του ελαιου is the whole difference between the cost price and the selling price of sesame oil, not merely the share of this surplus which the contractors received as pay for their trouble in superintending the manufacture, cf. [45] 2 note, and [55] 9. It was this surplus which the contractors had agreed to pay to the Treasury, and they are here completely secured against loss from a deficiency in the crop, cf. note on [39] 14. ελαιον, when coupled with κικι, means sesame oil here, as in [51] 21, 24, [53] 20, [57] 16, and [60] 16; cf. B. M. pap. xxi. 24. In [47] 14 and [48] 4, however, ελαιον appears to include all the oils except cici, for cnecus, colocynth, and lamp oil must have been distributed to the καπηλοι like sesame oil and cici. This argument is not conclusive, since in several places cnecus, colocynth, and lamp oil are ignored, and we are left to assume the arrangements concerning them from the regulations concerning sesame and cici; see [42] 4 note. But [47] 7 εκαστου γενους, not εκατερου, is strongly in favour of more than two oils being meant; cf. [42] 12 εκαστα κατα γενος, where at least three kinds of produce are referred to, and [54] 23, where εκαστου γενους means all the five kinds of produce mentioned in [39] 1-7. That the phrase το ελαιον και κικι was felt even at the time to be ambiguous, is shown by [49] 18, where το ελαιον ought from the context to include cnecus oil as well as sesame, and it is more probable that the first hand intended it to do so than that he omitted cnecus oil by mistake. But the corrector was not satisfied with the clearness of the phrase, for after το ελαιον he inserted το σησαμινον η το κνηκινον.

S 2

It follows from this frequent use of ελαιον for sesame oil that where ελαιον is found in papyri of this period, meaning one kind of oil, the presumption is that sesame oil is meant: e. g. P. P. part I, 78. 7.

13. On the dioecetes see note on [38] 3. εξω ορα at the end of the line, 'look outside,' calls attention to the fact that a note on the *verso* is to be inserted at this point: cf. [43] 2.

[41.] 20–27. 'The contractor shall give orders with respect to the sesame and croton to be grown for other nomes, and (if the due amount is not sown) the dioecetes shall exact the amount from the officials who have received the orders, and shall pay it to those nomes which ought to have received the sesame and croton'. (Added by the corrector.)

20. Though the lacunae are too great to be filled up with any certainty, this section clearly supplements the foregoing one, and provides for the case in which the deficiency affected the sesame and croton to be grown for other nomes. Since some nomes did not grow enough sesame for their own consumption, e. g. the Heracleopolite, [70] 13, while many of them did not grow enough, or even any, croton, e. g. Libya [61] 7, and the Nitriote nome, [61] 22, the deficiency was made good by making other nomes grow more than was required for their own consumption. It is noticeable that the case of sesame and croton being thus transferred from one nome to another is not provided for in the original draft of [39]–[56], but is frequently mentioned in the διορθωματα, as here, [43] 21, and [57] 8–13, where the general regulation concerning it is laid down.

The use of εδει and εισπραξας and the mention of the dioecetes, all agreeing with 3–13, show that 20–27 refer only to the case in which the proper number of arourae had not been sown, and are not a general statement.

21. The letters at the end of the line do not suit προσ; the papyrus is deeply stained here, and I am not certain that the piece containing the end of this line is in its correct place.

27. Cf. note on [40] 16.

[41.] 14–19. 'Before the season comes for sowing the sesame and croton, the oeconomus shall give the official in charge of the distribution of crops, be he nomarch or toparch, if he desires it, for the seed sufficient for sowing an aroura of sesame 4 drachmae, and for the seed sufficient for an aroura of croton 2 drachmae, and he shall transport the seed from the store instead of . . .'

16. νομος I consider is here equivalent to νομη in the sense of 'distribution,' as it is in the sense of 'pasture,' cf. Hesych. Νομόν, νομήν ; and [43] 3, where των αρουρων probably goes with νομου, not σπορου ; and P. P. xxx (d), a list made out by a nomarch of various crops sown in the Fayoum. The Fayoum was for this purpose divided into several νομαρχιαι, called after their respective nomarchs; e. g. there is the νομαρχια Νικωνος in P. P. part I. 62 (2) 4 ; Διογενους in part II. 46. 8 ; Αχολπιος, Φιλιππου, and Μαιμαχου in xxxix. Not until the second century B.C. do we find the nomarch often identified with the strategus, and therefore chief of the 'nome.' I am fully aware of the boldness of taking νομου here in any other sense than that of 'nome,' though 'nome' itself of course originally meant a 'division.' But the difficulty of taking προεστηκως του νομου here as 'chief of the nome' appears to me overwhelming. The absence of an article before τοπαρχηι shows that the phrase τωι προεστηκοτι του νομου applies as much to the toparch as to the nomarch, i. e. the 'chief of the nome' could be either a nomarch or a toparch, cf. [43] 3, where the nomarch need not be 'chief of the nome,' and [24] 6 note. Now, since we know from the Petrie papyri that there were several nomarchs in a nome, the phrase ο προεστηκως του νομου would mean that one of these nomarchs occupied a superior position to the others, and that he is the person referred to here and in [43] 3, while in the other passages the ordinary nomarchs are meant. This draws an artificial distinction between two kinds of nomarchs, which does not in the least suit the passages where they are mentioned in this papyrus or elsewhere. On the other hand, if this difficulty is avoided by taking the phrase 'chief of the nome' as applicable to all nomarchs, the phrase becomes purely otiose in this passage, except in so far as it applies to the toparch, and the papyrus is self-contradictory, for in [43] 3 it is stated that the 'chief of the nome' is not always the nomarch. But if the difficulty of the phrase 'chief of the nome,' even as applied to the nomarch, is great, the difficulty of applying it equally to the toparch, a consequence which necessarily follows from the absence of the article before τοπαρχηι, is much greater. There are only two possible conditions under which a toparch could be 'chief of the nome.' Either there were some nomes in which there were no nomarchs at all, and

their functions were performed by toparchs, or the nomarchs might all be away on leave and hence a toparch might become for a time 'chief of the nome.' For, as has been shown, there were several nomarchs at any rate in the Fayoum, and if only one went away, his place would obviously be filled by another nomarch, not by a toparch who was necessarily subordinate to a nomarch. But both of these suppositions are equally unsatisfactory. So far from it being probable that certain nomes had no nomarchs, all the evidence we have points to their being universal, while we know for certain that in some nomes there are no toparchs, see Strabo 787 εἰς γὰρ τοπαρχίας οἱ πλεῖστοι (νομοὶ) διῄρηντο. Nor can [42] 5–6 be taken as an argument for the non-existence of nomarchs in certain nomes, for (1) ου in line 6 refers to places, not to whole nomes, and (2) that passage implies that where there were no nomarchs there were also no toparchs, cf. νομαρχαι η τοπαρχαι in line 6 with τωι νομαρχηι και τωι τοπαρχηι in line 5. As for the alternative supposition that the nomarchs were for a time absent, we are forced to believe not only that all the nomarchs could be away at once, which is very unlikely, but that their absence was a matter of frequent occurrence, since it was necessary to provide for the contingency, and further that, when a toparch was acting for a nomarch under these circumstances, he could be called 'chief of the nome.' But it is hardly credible that the toparch should have thus usurped the title of the nomarch; moreover, if the writer of the papyrus had meant that the toparch was for the moment acting-nomarch, he would have used ο παρα or some such phrase. On the other hand, all these difficulties are avoided by supposing that νομου is here and in [43] 3 equivalent to νομη, a meaning which not only suits the context in both cases, but is perfectly consistent with the duties of nomarchs, so far as they can be gathered from the Petrie papyri. The phrase 'chief of the nome' would apply with much greater propriety to the strategus.

17. I have taken σπορου here as equivalent to σπερμα, cf. [43] 4, and perhaps [42] 16. Elsewhere it means the 'crop': e.g. [41] 3. It is not clear why the nomarch should receive this money, or who is the subject of κομιζεσθω, which may mean simply 'receive.' If it is ο προεστηκως, cf. [32] 10 note. In [43] 3 it is the nomarch who distributes the seed to the cultivators: cf. App. ii (3). The first few letters of lines 17 and 18 have now disappeared.

19. αλω: see note on [39] 9.

[42.] 3-[43] 2. 'When the season comes for gathering the sesame, croton, and cnecus, the cultivators shall give notice to the nomarch and the toparch, or where there are no nomarchs or toparchs to the oecconomus; and these officials shall summon the contractor, and he shall go with them to the fields and assess the crop. The peasants and the other cultivators shall have their different kinds of produce assessed before they gather it, and shall make a double contract, sealed, with the contractor, and every peasant shall enter on oath the amount of land which he has sown with seed of each kind, and the amount of his assessment, and shall seal the contract, which shall also be sealed by the representative of the nomarch or toparch.'

3. Cf. [24] 15, the parallel regulation for cultivators of vineyards.

4. This passage and line 16 show that cnecus, whatever it was, did not grow wild, but was cultivated like sesame and croton. The omission of colocynth and linseed is a difficulty which arises in several places, cf. line 12, [40] 15, [43] 18, [44] 6, [46] 17, [49] 17, [53] 10, 15. But the inference to be drawn is not that the regulations were inapplicable to colocynth and linseed, but that the regulations for them were parallel to those for sesame, croton, and cnecus. See [43] 14 τα λοιπα φορτια, while only cnecus is mentioned in 18; and [57] 18, where cnecus oil is unaccountably omitted; and cf. notes on [41] 11, [57] 16.

6. This class of places where there were no nomarchs or toparchs, included, as L. suggests, besides Alexandria, the cities with a Greek constitution (e. g. Naucratis which was distinct from the Saite nome, [60] 18, and Ptolemais in the Thebaid), and possibly the places ruled by Libyarchs, [37] 5. The Thebaid, the government of which was peculiar to itself, being ruled by a Θηβαρχος (Lumb. Rec. p. 239), contained τοπαρχιαι in the next century, Wilck. Observ. pp. 24-30. Cf. the passage in Strabo quoted in note on [41] 16.

8. There is no difference intended between ο εχων and ο διοικων την ωνην: see [24] 17 note.

9. αρουρας, 'fields': cf. Rev. Proc. Soc. Bibl. Arch. December, 1891, p. 65.

11. λαοι are the fellaheen: cf. L. P. 63. 100 των εν ταις κωμαις κατοικουντων λαων, and P. P. 14. 4. τιμασθωσαν is probably passive, as in line 17. The method of assessment resembles that for cultivators of vineyards [25] 1-2, rather than that for cultivators of orchards [29] 6.

13. η is omitted by mistake after προτερον: on the uncorrected blunders of this scribe see note on [48] 9.

15. διπλην: see [27] 5 note.

17. ορκου: sc. βασιλικου; cf. the demotic contract quoted in note on [39] 8.

20. συναποσταλεις: this does not imply that the nomarch was there: see note on [27] 13.

[43.] 2. εξω ορα: see [41] 13 note.

[43.] 20-25. 'The crop of sesame and croton assigned to the cultivators to be grown for other nomes shall be assessed by the oeconomus and antigrapheus, who shall receive the sesame and croton from the cultivators' (added by the corrector).

20. διαγραφεντος: i.e. in [60]–[72]; cf. [41] 20 note. The tax on sesame and croton grown for other nomes belonged to the contractors of the nome to which the produce was transferred, [57] 7–13. Hence it was not allowed to pass through the hands of the contractors in the nome where it was grown. Cf. [60] 11, where the oeconomus, not the contractor, receives the produce grown εν τηι αφωρισμενηι.

25. Cf. [40] 16 note.

[43.] 3-10. 'The nomarch or official in charge of the distribution of crops shall give out the seed to each cultivator sixty days before the crop is gathered. If he fails to do so or to show the cultivators who have sown the assigned number of arourae, he shall pay the contractor the fine which has been decreed, and shall recover his loss by exacting it from the disobedient cultivators.'

3. Cf. [41] 16 note. δοτω does not imply that it was more than a loan: see App. ii (3) 2–4.

5. The sixty days do not apply to croton, which takes a long time to grow, or to cnecus, colocynth and flax, the amount of which was not fixed, cf. note on [39] 14. It is remarkable that sesame and croton are treated throughout the papyrus as precisely parallel, although the one had to be sown every year, and the other lasted several years.

6. παρασχηται: cf. [51] 8, where too the middle is (probably) found in place of the active.

7. διαγραφεν: i.e. in [60]–[72], though the list of nomes to which the scribe was referring before the corrections took place was different; see note on [38] 1 and [57] 6. γεγραμμενα: see [41] 9–12.

[**43.**] 11-19. 'All persons throughout the country who are exempt from taxation, or hold villages and land in gift, or receive the revenues therefrom as income, shall measure out all the sesame and croton assigned to them, and the other kinds of produce included in the oil-monopoly, leaving a sufficient amount for next year's seed ; and they shall be paid the value of it in copper coin, at the rate of 6 dr. for an artaba of sesame, 3 dr. 2 obols for an artaba of croton, 1 dr. for an artaba of cnecus.'

11. ἀτελεις: e.g. the Fayoum was exempt, so far as the produce which it grew for the Memphite nome was concerned : see note on [69] 1.

ἐν δωρεαι: cf. note on [36] 15. ἐν συνταξει: συνταξις means a 'contribution,' especially for religious purposes ; see the Serapeum papyri, Ros. stone 15, and Rev. R. E. I. 59. L. suggests that the difference between villages ἐν δωρεαι and villages ἐν συνταξει was that in the latter case only the revenues were assigned to a person (cf. the case of Themistocles who received the revenues of five cities, Athen. i. 30), while in the former, besides the revenues, the whole village was made over, including the duty of administering it. Cf. [44] 3, where it is stated that no oil factories are to be set up in villages ἐν δωρεαι. This shows that the administration of villages ἐν δωρεαι was not quite the same as that of ordinary villages, from which villages ἐν συνταξει are not there distinguished ; and I prefer Lumbraso's explanation to those suggested by M. Introd. p. xxxviii. In any case the holders of land ἐν συνταξει were no doubt mainly, if not wholly, the priests, cf. [50] 20, while holders of land ἐν δωρεαι were court favourites.

13. γενομενον: there is no reason to think that the ἀτελεις were allowed greater freedom in the choice of crops than other cultivators. For this use of γενομενον as 'due' cf. [30] 21, [37] 16, [56] 19, but in all these cases the present participle is used, and perhaps γενομενον here merely means what they have grown.

16. προς χαλκον: cf. note on [40] 10, and App. iii pp. 194-198.

17. In the case of sesame, since the ἀτελεις only received 6 dr. instead of 8 paid to the ordinary cultivators, [39] 3, who had, [39] 18, to give back 2 dr. as tax, their ἀτελεια was purely nominal ; cf. note on [39] 14. With regard to croton they were slightly better off than the ordinary cultivators, receiving 3 dr. 2 obols instead of 3 drachmae net. On

T

the other hand, in the case of cnecus they were actually worse off, receiving only 1 dr. instead of 1 dr. 2 obols. Colocynth and linseed are as usual omitted, cf. note on [42] 4, though they must have been included in τα λοιπα φορτια. Probably the ατελεις received the same amount for these as the υποτελεις, since there was no tax on them ; but the case of cnecus is remarkable.

19. The apodosis is probably 'they shall pay the deficiency'; cf. line 10. It is unlikely that there is here a reference to their keeping back sesame and croton and so violating the monopoly, for that is discussed in [49] 16 sqq.

[44.] 'The oeconomus and antigrapheus shall appoint . . . to be a factory and shall seal their choice by stamping it. But in villages which are held as a gift from the Crown they shall not set up an oil factory. They shall deposit in each factory the requisite amount of sesame, croton, and cnecus. They shall not allow the workmen appointed in each nome to cross over into another nome ; any workman who crosses over shall be subject to arrest by the contractor and the oeconomus and antigrapheus. No one shall harbour workmen from another nome ; if any one does so knowingly or fails to send back workmen when he has been ordered to restore them, he shall pay a fine of 3000 dr. for each workman, and the workman shall be subject to arrest.'

1. A comparison of [45] 7 and 13 with [44] 4 shows that the oeconomus and antigrapheus are the subject.

3. See note on [43] 11.

5. Cf. an ostracon in Prof. Sayce's collection published by Wilck. Akt. p. 59, dated the thirty-fifth year of Euergetes II, in which Asclepiades, probably ο προς τηι ελαιουργιαι, i. e., if the law was still the same, the chief contractor, gives a receipt to Heracleides, probably a γεωργος, but possibly the oeconomus, for κροτων[ος] β, as Wilck. now reads, the sign for artaba being omitted.

16. επισταλευτος : Wilck. Cf. the frequent use of βουλομενου in [25] 1, [28] 10 et al. αναγαγη : cf. [22] 2, note.

[45.] 1–12. '. . . and from the surplus of the oil that is sold (altered to 'manufactured'), the oeconomus shall divide among the workmen for every metretes containing 12 choes 3 dr. (altered to '2 dr. 3 obols.')

Of this sum the workmen and the men who cut the crop shall receive
2 dr. (altered to ' 1 dr. 4 obols'), and the contractors 1 dr. (altered
to '5 obols'). But if the oeconomus or his representative fails to pay
the workmen their wages, or their share in the profits from the sale
of the oil, he shall pay a fine of 3000 dr. to the Treasury, and to the
workmen their pay, and to the contractors twice the amount of the
loss which they may have incurred on account of the workmen.'

2. There is not room for του επιγενηματος: probably the first scribe
wrote γενηματος by mistake, and επι was added by the corrector, for
γεννηματος is meaningless and in [55] 9 and 13, which clearly refer back
to this passage, επιγενημα is found. As the phrase in line 9, το μεμερισμενον απο της πρασεως (cf. [55] 9 το συντεταγμενον μεριζεσθαι απο του
επιγενηματος) shows, the surplus here was the profit on every metretes
of oil sold after the expenses of production had been deducted, cf.
[41] 11, and [39] 14, note, and is quite different from the επιγενημα
of A and B.

3. κατεργαζομενου: cf. [56] 19–21, a regulation which ought to have
come in here to the effect that no share of the profit was to be paid
to the workmen for the oil that was stored, on which see note on
[53] 5.

5. The construction is not very logical. The contractors are mentioned here without having been mentioned in line 3, and nothing is
said in lines 7–12 of the compensation which they are to receive, if
the oeconomus does not pay them, for line 11 refers only to compensation
for loss inflicted on them through the workmen not being paid. The
reason is that here the payment of the workmen is the subject and
the payment of the contractors incidental. The salary of the latter
is discussed in [55].

It is interesting to note that in this, one of the earliest examples
of profit-sharing, the workmen received more than the 'entrepreneurs.'
The author of this law, whether Soter or Philadelphus, certainly favoured
the fellaheen at the expense of the richer classes or the foreign settlers,
who in most cases farmed the taxes.

κοπεις: a new sense of this word; cf. Herodotus' description of the
manufacture of cici, ii. 94 τουτον επεαν συλλεξωνται, οἱ μεν κοψαντες
ἀπιποῦσι, οἱ δὲ καὶ φρύξαντες ἀπέψουσι. The Revenue Papyrus gives no
details about roasting the seeds.

T 2

8. κατεργου: wages for piece work, cf. [46] 18–20, while μισθος is a general term, 'pay.' Cf. line 11 where μισθου includes both κατεργου and the share of the profits; [55] 14–15, where it differs from κατεργου as 'salary' from 'wages'; [46] 2, note; and LXX Exod. 30. 16, and 35. 21 τὸ κάτεργον τῆς σκηνῆς. From the way in which the κατεργου is mentioned here, we should expect that it had been fixed in the lost top of [45]; but see [46] 18, note.

[45.] 13–18. 'If the oeconomus and antigrapheus fail to set up oil factories in accordance with these regulations, or to deposit a sufficient quantity of produce, thus inflicting a loss on the contractors, both the oeconomus and antigrapheus shall be fined the amount of the deficit which results, and shall pay the contractors twice the amount of the loss incurred.'

14. παραθωνται: cf. [44] 5.

16. την εγδειαν: sc. εις το βασιλικον, cf. [40] 7, and [41] 9.

[45.] 19–[46] 20. 'The oeconomus and antigrapheus shall provide tools for each factory, ... when the oeconomus visits the factory in order to pay the wages(?), he shall not interfere with the work in any way to the damage of the contractors. If he fails to provide tools, or damages the interests of the contractors in any way, he shall be judged before the dioecetes, and if he is found guilty, he shall pay (to the Treasury) a fine of two talents of silver, and (to the contractors) twice the amount of the damage which he has caused. The contractors and the clerk appointed by the oeconomus and antigrapheus shall have joint authority over all the workmen in the nome, and over the factories and the plant, and they shall seal up the tools during the time when there is no work. They shall compel the workmen to work every day, and shall supervise them in person, and they shall every day make into oil not less than 1½ artabae of sesame (altered to '1 artaba') in each mortar, and 4 artabae of croton, and 1 of cnecus, and they shall pay the workmen as wages for making 4 artabae of sesame, into oil . . ., for . . artabae of croton 4 drachmae, and for . . artabae of cnecus 8 drachmae.'

[45.] 19. The fragment containing]κονομ[and]ασ[has disappeared. Cf. [46] 4 and 11, χορηγηι and κατασκευης.

[46.] 2. If κατιων is right and goes with κατεργου, it is difficult to

take κατεργον in its ordinary sense, cf. [45] 8 note. M. suggests that
it here means the 'work,' i. e. if the oeconomus visited the factory while
the work was proceeding, he was not to interfere, and compares P. P.
7. 8 εγραψα σοι ο δει δοθηναι εις εκαστον αργου και το κατεργον, which
he thinks means 'working time' as opposed to 'time when there is
no work,' cf. [46] 12. But the ordinary meaning, 'wages' is equally
possible there, and therefore I hesitate to depart here from the ascertained
meaning of κατεργον.

6. The mention of silver here and in [47] 8 does not imply that other
fines were προς χαλκου.

10. τ]οπωι is an equally possible reading.

11. παρασφραγιζεσθωσαν: see note on [26] 7.

14. κατεργαζεσθωσαν: the subject may be the workmen, cf. note on
[32] 10; but κατεργαζεσθαι is not applied to the workmen only, see
[57] 19.

18. κατεργον might be expected in the lacuna, since κατεργαζεσθωσαν
has just been mentioned, but there is not room for it, and against the
hypothesis that the sums here represent the wages of the workmen
is to be set the fact that κατεργον is spoken of in [45] 8 as if it had
been already fixed, and that the wages were paid by the oeconomus,
not the contractors, [45] 7, while the subject of αποδιδοτωσαν is apparently
the contractors and the clerk. But see [53] 25 note. Colocynth oil
and lamp oil are once more ignored; in fact in [44]-[47] 9, the section
dealing with the manufacture of oil, they are never mentioned. But
it is hardly possible that the conditions of their manufacture were different;
cf. note on [42] 4, and [54] 23-[55] 1, where the manufacture of all
five kinds is implied.

[47.] 1-9. 'No arrangement with the workmen regarding the flow
of the oil shall be made either by the oeconomus or the contractor
under any pretext whatever, nor shall the tools in the factories be
left unsealed during the time when there is no work. If they make
an arrangement with any of the workmen, or leave the tools unsealed,
each of the guilty parties shall pay a fine of 1 talent to the Treasury,
and to the contractors the amount of their loss if the contract results
in a deficit.'

1. ρυσις: cf. [60] 15, which probably refers to this passage. It is
there stated that, if the flow resulted in a surplus, this surplus belonged

to the Treasury. But it is not clear whether that section alters, or whether it merely supplements, the previously existing law. There is nothing in [39]-[56], so far as they are preserved, to show what was to be done with a surplus resulting from the 'flow of the oil.' The case does not seem to have been contemplated, though if it went to the contractors it is perhaps covered by [53] 12-15, since, if there was an unexpectedly large amount of oil, there would be the more left over when the term of the contract expired. But in that case I do not understand the anxiety of the government to prevent the contractors from coming to terms with the workmen about the amount of oil to be made from the seed provided; for it would be to the contractor's interest that the output should be as large as possible. On the other hand, if this surplus went to the Treasury in accordance with [60] 15, and the object of that passage is only to make the point clear, not to alter the law, the anxiety of the government to prevent a limit being placed on the output of oil is intelligible. Then however the difficulty arises that this passage, if taken by itself, rather implies the absence of any fixed ratio of oil expected from the seed, while on the other hand πλειον in [60] 15 implies that there was a fixed ratio (cf. note on [60] 25), and if the ratio was mentioned anywhere it must have been mentioned at the top of this column, since it was certainly not mentioned in the διορθωμα. On the whole it seems to me least difficult to suppose the ratio was fixed here at the top of the column, but the question of the surplus was left open, i. e. it was not separated from the other oil manufactured, and that [60] 15 is a real correction, altering the previous law.

9. Cf. [17] 1 εαν δε ο επανω χρονος εγδειαν ηι πεποιηκως, and note on [22] 2.

[47.] 10-[48] 2. 'The clerk appointed by the oeconomus and antigrapheus shall register the names of the dealers in each city and of the retailers, and shall arrange with them in conjunction with the contractors how much oil and cici they are to take and sell from day to day. In Alexandria they shall come to an arrangement with the traders, and they shall make a contract with each of them, with those in the country every month, with those in Alexandria . . .'

11. The difference between καπηλοι and μεταβολοι on the one hand, and παλιμπρατουντες on the other, depends on the place where they

carried on their trade, the καπηλοι and μεταβολοι trading in the πολεις and κωμαι throughout the country, and the παλιμπρατουντες, who were no doubt as M. suggests large shop-keepers, in Alexandria. Whether the distinction between the καπηλοι and the μεταβολοι is on the same lines, is somewhat doubtful. For though from a comparison of [47] 10, 11 with [48] 3, 4, we might conclude that the καπηλοι traded in the πολεις, and the μεταβολοι in the villages, the mention of κωμη in [48] 6 referring to both καπηλοι and μεταβολοι is against this supposition. The objection however is far from being fatal; the language of the Revenue Papyrus is often inexact, as is shown by the frequent omission of the less important oils; and since the πολεις are mentioned in [47] 12 they must in any case be understood in [48] 6, though not expressed. M. suggests that the μεταβολοι sold by barter, but we have no evidence of selling by barter in the papyri of this period.

15. καθ ημεραν: perhaps by the same writer as the rest of the column.

17. Between the συνταξις and the συγγραφη, at any rate in the case of the καπηλοι and μετοβολοι, intervened an auction, [48] 13–18.

18. That the agreement with οι εν τηι χωραι was for a month is shown by [48] 5: probably that with οι εν Αλεξανδρειαι was for a longer period; see note on [48] 13.

[48.] 2. This probably refers to the money paid by the παλιμπρατουντες at Alexandria to the oeconomus and antigrapheus, and credited by them to the account of the contractors at the royal bank. Cf. [48] 10 and [31] 14 note. καταχωριζεσθω is probably passive, as there is no instance in the papyrus of this verb in the middle voice. ο καθεστηκως, cf. [47] 10, is therefore inadmissible.

[48.] 3-[49] 4. 'The amount of oil and cici which the dealers and retailers in each village agree to dispose of, shall be conveyed by the oeconomus and antigrapheus before the month arrives to each village, each kind of oil being conveyed; and they shall there measure it out to the dealers and retailers every five days, and shall receive payment, if possible, on the same day, but if not, they shall exact payment before the five days have elapsed, and pay the money to the royal bank, the expenses of the transport of the oil being defrayed at the cost of the contractors. The oil which it has been arranged that each of the dealers and retailers shall take, shall be put up to auction ten days before the month arrives, and they shall write out and publish the highest bid for each day during ten days in both the metropolis of the nome and the village, and shall make a contract with the highest bidder.'

5. διαθησεσθαι: cf. the phrase frequently recurring in [60]-[72] εις την εν Αλεξανδρειαι διαθεσιν, and Hdt. i. 1 διατίθεσθαι τὰ φορτία. ελαιον: see note on [41] 11: here it includes all the oils except cici.

9. εξελθουσων was deciphered by Wilck. There can be little doubt that M. is right in supposing that ει δη μη is a mistake for ει δε μη μη. The text as it stands gives just the opposite of the sense required. Though as a rule it is very unsafe to attribute blunders to the text, there is ample justification for doing so here, since in this column οικονος is left uncorrected in line 5, and there is certainly a mistake in line 17. Cf. [43] 8, [49] 18, [51] 8, [55] 23, where the corrector has left blunders uncorrected, or made mistakes himself.

11. το αιηλωμα: the singular is used in the papyrus where we should expect the plural, cf. [53] 25.

13. These six lines probably refer only to the καπηλοι and μεταβολοι, cf. 15 with 6, unless the contract with the παλιμπρατουντες was also for a month. But in [47] 18 a contrast is drawn between οι εν τηι χωραι and οι εν Αλεξανδρειαι, probably in reference to the length of the contract. Moreover εν τε τηι μητροπολει και τηι κωμηι suits the nomes, not Alexandria, and if there was no auction in the case of the παλιμπρατουντες at Alexandria, it is intelligible why this section is placed at the end, and not between the συνταξις and the συγγραφη in [47] 17. See also [55] 15, which shows that there were at Alexandria προπωληται between the contractors and the παλιμπρατουντες.

14. επικηρυσσετωσαν: cf. pap. Zois i. [2] 2: the scribe first wrote επικηρυσσατωσαν.

16. το ευρισκον: cf. pap. Zois i. [2] 1 and L. P. 62 [6] 9, του ευρισκοντος.

17. The simplest change is to read κυρωθεντος; for the genitive cf. the passages just quoted.

On the price at which the ελαιοκαπηλοι bought the oil from the contractors see P. P. xxviii and App. iii p. 197. If my theory is correct, at the date of that papyrus they were buying it at 42 drachmae προς χαλκον for a metretes.

[49.] 1. There are 11 inches of blank papyrus between this and the preceding column, and a new hand begins here, but it is not clear whether these four lines are connected with what precedes or with what follows. The writing of [49]-[51] is slightly different from that of [52]-[56], but I think that all these columns were written by the same scribe, who is probably different from the writer of [24]-[35], though there are many points of similarity between [24]-[35] and [49]-[56].

If the word in the first line be intended for ελαιοκαπηλοι, the sentence may run, as M. suggests, παραλαμβανοντες το ελαιον πωλησουσι τιμης της γεγραμμενης εν τωι διαγραμματι και μη πλειονος, cf. P. P. 122, a letter from Horus, apparently an agent of the dioecetes, to Harmais about oil being sold at a higher price than the προσταγμα allowed. In that case this section would be connected with the preceding columns. ελαιοκα[πηλοι however is certainly not what the scribe wrote, and though he has in any case made a blunder and the letters are too much rubbed for any certainty, ελαιουργοι seems to be the word meant. Moreover the gap between this column and the preceding one and the fact that the rest of this column is concerned with a new subject, possible violations of the monopoly, are all in favour of joining lines 1-4 with what follows, especially as οι ελαιουργοι are in any case the probable subject of the verb in line 5.

[49.] 5-[50] 5. 'Nor shall they . . . mortars or presses or any other implements used in the manufacture of oil on any pretext whatever, under pain of paying a fine of 5 talents to the Treasury, and to the contractors five times the amount of the loss incurred by them. Those persons who already possess any of these implements, shall register themselves before the contractor and the agent of the oeconomus and antigrapheus within thirty days, and shall produce their mortars and presses for inspection. The contractors and the agent of the oeconomus and antigrapheus shall transfer these to the royal oil-factories. If any one is discovered manufacturing oil from sesame, croton, or cnecus under any circumstances, or buying oil and cici (altered to 'sesame oil, cnecus oil, or cici') from any persons other than the contractors, the king shall decide his punishment, and he shall pay the contractors 3000 dr. and be deprived of the oil and the produce; the payment of the fine shall be exacted by the oeconomus and antigrapheus, who, if the offender is unable to pay, shall send him to (prison?).'

U

5. [49]–[53] 3 deal with possible violations of the monopoly granted
to the contractors, (1) by manufacture of oil by private individuals,
[49]–[50] 5: (2) by importation of foreign oil into Alexandria(?),
[50] 6–13: (3) by adulteration, [50] 14–19: (4) by the action of the
priests, who were allowed within certain limits to manufacture oil,
[50] 20–[52] 2: (5) by importation of foreign oil into the country,
[52] 7–[53] 3.

18. η before αλλοθεμ should come before το ελαιον. On the correction
see note on [41] 11, and on the mistake τη for η note on [48] 9.

[**50.**] 6–13. 'They shall not be allowed (to sell) the oil on any
pretext, nor even to bring it into Alexandria beyond the Crown repository. If any persons introduce more oil than they will use up in three
days for their own consumption, they shall be deprived of both the
freight and the means of transport, and shall in addition pay a fine of
100 dr. for each metretes, and for more or less in proportion.'

6. The subject of this section appears to be foreign oil brought by
sea to Alexandria to be consumed there: cf. [52] 26 and [54] 17. The
oil brought to Alexandria or Pelusium, which was to enter the country,
is discussed in [52], where its importation for sale is absolutely forbidden,
though it might be imported for personal use on payment of a duty.
There is hardly any doubt however that oil brought to Alexandria to
be consumed there paid no duty, [52] 26 note. On the other hand the
merchants who brought the oil were not allowed to sell it; the oil was
placed in official υποδοχια, [54] 18, which is the meaning of το βασιλικον
in line 8 here (cf. note on [28] 14), and the contractors superintended its
sale, [54] 19.

10. φορτιων is here clearly opposed to πορειων, and is not, as elsewhere, the raw material, i. e. the seeds as contrasted with the manufactured product: πορειων refers, as L. suggests, to ships in the first
instance. For the regulation that oil brought overland to Alexandria
should be duty-free occurs in a correction, [52] 25–29, and therefore was
probably not contemplated by the writer of the first draft. But in the
light of the correction πορειων is general.

[**50.**] 14–19. 'The cooks shall use up the lard every day in the
presence of the contractor, and shall neither sell it as lard to any one on
any pretext, nor melt it down, nor make a store of it. If they disobey,

each of them shall pay the oil-contractor for every day that he keeps the lard, 50 drachmae' (altered to 'each person who either sells or buys it shall pay the oil contractor for every piece that is bought, 50 drachmae').

14. Like οι ελαιουργουντες εν τοις ιεροις in line 20, the cooks are probably a distinct class, but it is difficult to see how this remarkable regulation was to be enforced, except in kitchens where cooking was done for a large number of people, e. g. for a regiment or at an inn. It is impossible that the kitchens in private houses were subject to the invasion of the tax-farmer.

17. The enormous profit made by the government from the sale of oil, see [53] 16 note, must account for the adulteration of oil with animal fat. Nowadays it is the lard which is often adulterated with (cotton-seed) oil; cf. a paragraph in the Daily News for May 8, 1895, which was pointed out to me by Dr. Wright, on 'The adulteration of lard.'

[50.] 20–[52] 3. 'Those who make oil in the temples throughout the country shall declare to the contractor and the agent of the oeconomus and antigrapheus the number of oil-factories in each temple and the number of mortars and presses in each workshop, and they shall exhibit the workshops for inspection, and bring their mortars and presses to be sealed up . . . If they fail to declare the numbers, or to exhibit the work-shops, or to bring the mortars and presses to be sealed up, the officials in charge of the temples shall, each of them who is guilty, pay 3 talents to the Treasury, and to the contractors five times the amount of their loss according to the contractors' estimate of it. When they wish to manufacture sesame oil in the temples, they shall take with them the contractor and the agent of the oeconomus and antigrapheus, and shall make the oil in their presence. They shall manufacture in two months the amount which they declared that they would consume in a year; but the cici which they consume they shall receive from the contractors at the fixed price. The oeconomus and antigrapheus shall send to the king a written account of both the cici and the oil required for the consumption of each temple, and shall also give a similar written account to the dioecetes. It shall be unlawful to sell to any one the oil which is manufactured for the use of the temples; any person who disobeys this law shall be deprived of the oil, and shall in addition pay a fine of 100 dr. for every metretes, and for more or less in proportion.'

[51.] 8. παρασφραγιζμον: see notes on [48] 9 and [26] 7.

[**51.**] 9. οι επι των ιερων τεταγμενοι: cf. Canop. Inscr. line 73 ο δ εν εκαστωι των ιερων καθεστηκως επιστατης και αρχιερευς, and the επισταται των ιερων (L. P. 26. 23, and B. M. pap. xxxv. 24), who were responsible for paying the Twins their συνταξις.

12. If the present regulations remained in force under Philometor, a possible explanation is suggested for the substitution of one metretes of sesame oil for two of cici in B. M. pap. xvii. 54. It would have been much cheaper for the επισταται of the temple to supply sesame oil, which they manufactured themselves, than cici, which they had to buy from the contractors. In any case, if the temples retained the right of making sesame oil in the second century B.C., the value of sesame oil in relation to cici in the temples may well have differed from its value in the rest of Egypt. On the other hand, if the temples had lost the right, which M. thinks probable, as there is no mention of oil manufactured in the temples to be found in any of the Serapeum papyri, it is still quite doubtful whether the substitution of one metretes of sesame oil for two of cici was due to their being of equal value, as has been often assumed. The Revenue Papyrus does not favour the idea that cici was half the value of sesame, and the oft-quoted passage from B. M. pap. xvii. 54 is a very uncertain basis for generalizations. Cf. Rev. R. E. 1882, pp. 162–5. He there attempts to show that the price of cici in the second century varied between 1800 and 1300 copper drachmae, so that if the ratio of exchange was 120 : 1 (cf. App. iii), the price had fallen considerably. But none of the instances which he quotes give a definite number of drachmae as the price of a definite amount of oil, and they are therefore not very convincing. The inferior oils together with cnecus are ignored ; see note on [42] 4. Probably they are to be classed here with the cici, not with the sesame oil.

18. The final ι of κικι is repeated by mistake.

19. καθισταμενης: in [40] 9 sqq.

23. διδοτωσαν: usually αποστελλειν is used in reference to the dioe-cetes ; cf. [18] 6 note.

[**52.**] 4–6. This probably refers to some oil which the contractors took over when they entered on the contract. Cf. [53] 3.

[**52.**] 7–[**53**] 3. 'No one shall be allowed to introduce foreign oil into the country for sale, whether from Alexandria or Pelusium or any other place. Offenders against this law shall both be deprived of the oil, and in addition pay a fine of 100 dr. for each metretes, and for less or more in proportion. If any persons bring with them foreign oil for their private use, those who enter the country from Alexandria shall register themselves at Alexandria, and pay a duty of 12 dr. for a metretes, and for less in proportion, and shall obtain a receipt for it before they bring it into the country. Those who enter the country from Pelusium shall pay the duty at Pelusium, and obtain a voucher for it. Those who collect the duties at Alexandria and Pelusium shall place the tax to the credit of the nome to which the oil is brought. If any persons, when bringing oil with them for their personal use, fail to pay the duty or to carry with them the voucher, they shall both be deprived of the oil, and pay in addition a fine of 100 dr. for each metretes.' (Added by the corrector: 'Those merchants who transport foreign or Syrian oil from Pelusium across the country to Alexandria shall be exempt from the duty, but shall carry a voucher from the tax-collector appointed at Pelusium and the oeconomus, as the law requires . . . If they fail to carry the voucher, they shall be deprived of the oil.')

8. Though foreign oil was necessary to supply the wants of Alexandria, [50] 6 and [54] 18, the rest of the country was protected against foreign competition. But it is doubtful how long the country remained self-sufficing, for in a papyrus published by Egger (Compt. Rend. de l'Acad. d. Inscr. N. S. iii. p. 314) Asclepiades, superintendent of the oil manufacture at Thebes, gives a receipt to the royal bank for 800 drachmae received for the carriage of 80 metretae ελαιου ξενικου. It is hardly likely that this oil was destined for Alexandria, and if it had been brought into the country εις ιδιαν χρειαν, the expenses of transport would not have been paid by the royal bank.

15. The price of a metretes being 48 dr., the duty was 25 per cent., which confirms the passage in Arrian regarding the duty of 25 per cent. levied at Leuce Come on imports, quoted by L. Rec. p. 306. But Wilcken is right in objecting to L.'s explanation of the tax τεταρτη in L. P. 67 as an import duty. For an unpublished Petrie papyrus, in the same handwriting as P. P. xliii, has the heading τεταρτη followed by a list of names with sums of money, and the payment of the τεταρτη in the Fayoum is consistent with W.'s theory that it was τεταρτη αλιεων, but hardly with the theory that it was a duty on imports.

18. It is noticeable that none of the Red Sea ports are mentioned, nor is Sebennytus, which is coupled with Pelusium in [93] 1. Most of the foreign oil came from Syria, where sesame is largely cultivated to this day: cf. line 26 and [54] 17. Olive oil probably formed a large part of the ξενικον ελαιον distinguished from Syrian oil in line 26. As a commercial port Pelusium appears in this column and elsewhere to be no less important than Alexandria owing to the amount of the Syrian trade : cf. [54] 17 note.

21. The tax was paid to the contractors in the nome to which the oil was brought, as compensation for the diminished amount of oil sold in the nome.

24. See note on [9] 3.

26. παρακομιζωσιν : i.e. through the country by land, or by canal, not by sea. This διορθωμα is appended to the regulations concerning the introduction of oil into the χωρα, and meets the case of merchants who were bringing oil to Alexandria, as they were entitled to do, and who, if they brought it by sea direct would be exempt, but, if they wished to take it by land, might, according to the foregoing regulations, either be forbidden or be forced to pay the duty. The διορθωμα therefore decrees that these persons shall be ατελεις, i.e. like those who brought the oil direct to Alexandria. If παρακομιζωσι be taken as 'transport by sea,' we have to admit that for some reason those who took oil to Alexandria via Pelusium were favoured beyond those who brought it direct, and that the διορθωμα is misplaced, for this column has to do with oil introduced into the χωρα. The other explanation, which gives a much better meaning, is based on the assumption that at Alexandria there was no duty upon oil imported direct from Syria or elsewhere for the consumption of the capital. This is not stated in [50], but neither is the reverse stated ; and, if the oil imported to Alexandria via Pelusium, whether by land or sea, was duty-free, the presumption is in favour of oil imported direct being also exempt. Moreover the persons appointed to watch over the importation of Syrian oil at Alexandria and Pelusium were αντιγραφεις, not λογευται, [54] 16.

27. The λογευτης was the representative of the contractors, see [13] 1.

28. εν τωι νομωι : i.e. in 18–19 : cf. note on [21] 10. The merchants had to carry the voucher, although they had not paid the duty.

[53.] 4-17. 'The contractors shall receive the sesame and croton, of which a store (?) has been ordered for each nome, within three days from the day on which they take over the contract, paying for it at the rate of . . . for sesame, . . . for a metretes of sesame oil, for croton . . . for cici . . . (altered to '17 dr.') . . . But if, when they give up the contract, they leave behind them more oil (than they were ordered to store?) they shall receive from the oeconomus as the value of the sesame oil 31 dr. 4¼ obols (altered to '28 dr. 3 obols') for a metretes, of cici 21 dr. 2 obols (altered to '20 dr.') for a metretes, of cnecus oil 18 dr. 4 obols (altered to '17 dr. 1 obol') for a metretes, and as the value of the sesame 8 drachmae for an artaba, of the croton 4 dr., and of the cnecus 1 dr. 3 obols (altered to '1 dr. 2 obols').

4. The lacunae are too great for any certainty, but I conjecture that this section refers to the produce and oil of which a store had to be kept by the predecessors of the contractors, and was bought by the incoming contractors within three days of their entering on the ωνη, 7-11 being the prices which the contractors paid for it, 12-17 the prices they received on giving up the contract for any surplus above the amount which they had been ordered to store for their successors. The price which they received for what they were ordered to store is partly lost in the lacuna, partly given by 9-11. For the construction of 4-8 παρα-ληψονται . . . σησαμον του σησαμου του με ⊢ ., cf. 18-21 οσον δ αν ελαιον υποκηρυξωμεν . . . ληψομεθα . . . του μεν ελαιου του με ⊢ . .

παραληψονται: cf. [9] 1.

5. αποτιθεσθαι: cf. [56] 21, where του αποτιθεμενου sc. ελαιου is, I think, certain. There is no place where the regulations about the oil stored can come except here, and this section cannot refer to the ordinary sesame and croton required from each nome, because (1) that has been discussed in [39]; (2) it is impossible that it should have been received within three days of any fixed time, cf. [42] 3; (3) the contractors are to receive not only sesame and croton but sesame oil and cici, line 8. Nor can this section refer to oil required for Alexandria or the king, for that is mentioned in the following sections, while the sesame and croton to be grown for other nomes, [41] 20, would be obviously irrelevant here.

9. Possibly της εν εκαστωι νομωι καθισταμενης τιμης; cf. [51] 19.

11. The reference is to [39]. As the διαγραμμα is fixed *for*, not *in*,

the twenty-seventh year, probably the διαγραμματα were revised every year: cf. note on [38] 1.

Since the corrector says that the contractors are to receive for the produce the prices mentioned in [39], and his corrections in the next sections are all to the disadvantage of the contractors, probably the original draft ordained that the contractors should receive more.

16. The corrected prices here are the same as the prices in [39]; therefore on the produce the contractors only recovered what they had themselves paid: cf. 10–11. I suspect that this is approximately the case with the oils also, and that the corrected prices in 14–15 nearly represent the cost price of the oils, or a little more; see note on 20. In any case it is practically certain that the contractors did not receive less for this oil than what the production of it had cost them. The profit on the inferior oils was much greater than on the superior, since there was no difference in the (corrected) retail price of any of the oils, [40] 9–16. Cf. [53] 22 for colocynth which is omitted here.

[53.] 17–26. 'The oil which we hereinafter proclaim our intention of taking from each nome for disposal at Alexandria, we will take from the contractors in the nome, paying for it at the rate of 31 dr. 4¼ obols for a metretes of sesame oil containing 12 choes without jars, and 21 dr. 2 obols for cici, 18 dr. 4 obols for cnecus oil, and 12 dr. for colocynth oil. (Altered to '18 dr. 2 obols for a metretes of cici.') This price shall be credited to the contractors in the instalments due from them, but the price of the produce, the wages of manufacture, and the miscellaneous expenses shall first be paid by the oeconomus.'

18. υποκηρυξωμεν: i. e. in the list of nomes. The original list, as this passage shows, contained not only the amounts of sesame oil and cici required from each nome for Alexandria but the amounts of cnecus and colocynth oil; see notes on [57] 6, [58] 1, and [41] 20. The corrector, however, substituting only one oil, cici, for the four, intended υποκηρυ-ξωμεν to refer to [60]–[72], and in fact the produce εις τας εν Αλεξανδρειαι διαθεσεις is in those columns always croton, except in two instances, [60] 24 and [62] 5, of sesame. Hence his omission of the price of sesame oil, about which there is no doubt, is a mistake, to which however little importance is to be attached.

Who is meant by the first person in υποκηρυξωμεν and ληψομεθα? Cf. [53] 27 εχωμεν; [54] 1 [προκηρυξ]ομεν; [57] 3 = [59] 2 πωλουμεν;

[58] 6 = [60] 13 πωλουμεν, and frequent instances in [57]–[72] ; together with L. P. [1] 1, where πωλουμεν is probable ; or, to put the question in another form, who is the author of the Revenue Laws? Both the general probabilities of the case and these instances, which all imply that the person speaking lays down rules for the whole country, require as the answer—the king. The only other person who could possibly be meant is the dioecetes at Alexandria, or the chief financial minister, whoever he was. Against the king being the author may be urged the fact that in many places ο βασιλευς is spoken of in the third person, while the dioecetes at Alexandria is not mentioned. But this is no real objection, for in [36] 13 του βασιλεως, not εμου, occurs in a προγραμμα undoubtedly issued by the king himself, and the difficulty of supposing that under an autocratic government the law of the country should be issued in any other name than that of the king is overwhelming. With regard to L. P. 62, the official title of which is uncertain, see note on [1] 6 of that papyrus. The general similarity between it and the Revenue Papyrus is so close that, even apart from my conjecture πωλουμεν and the evident parallelism between L. P. [1] 1–3 and [57] 3–5, cf. notes ad loc., it is not easy to separate the rank of the author in the two documents. The ingenious argument by which Lumb. Rec. p. 342 tries to show that L. P. 62 was written by a υποδιοικητης cuts both ways, and is not in the least inconsistent with that papyrus, like the Revenue Papyrus, having been issued in the king's name.

19. διαθεσεις : see note on [48] 4.

20. εν τωι νομωι : the Crown paid the cost of the carriage to Alexandria, and also supplied the jars, cf. [55] 4 ; on the other hand, the oeconomus paid for the produce, the wages of manufacture, and the miscellaneous expenses, presumably entering what he paid in the contractors' accounts against the sums credited to them. There is no question therefore that all these expenses were more than covered by the sums written by the first hand in 20–22, but the profit on the sale of a metretes was even greater than the difference between these prices and the selling price, cf. note on line 16 and the corrected price of cici here, 18 dr. 2 obols, which covered the expenses in lines 24–25.

There is no mention here of the share of the surplus which, according to the corrected reading in [45] 3, was to be paid to the workmen and contractors on the oil that was manufactured. Cf. [45] 9 το μεμερισμενον

x

απο της πρασεως, which is left uncorrected, though πωλουμενου in [45] 3 was altered. It is possible that oil εις τας εν Αλεξανδρειαι διαθεσεις was not included in the oil 'sold,' but in any case according to the correction the share ought to have been distributed from the profits of the oil manufactured for Alexandria.

23. Cf. [34] 6, a similar regulation for wine required εις το βασιλικον. αναφορα : see note on [16] 10, [34] 8, and [56] 15.

25. The oeconomus here pays for the produce, which was usually paid for by the contractors ([39] 13), and for the ανηλωμα, which also under ordinary circumstances was paid for by them, cf. [54] 4. Was his payment of the κατεργον also exceptional? The answer to the question depends on the meaning of [46] 18, which owing to the lacuna is uncertain. [55] 15 however is an argument in favour of supposing that the κατεργον was paid by the government, not the contractors, for it is coupled there with μισθοι. But the conditions of making oil at Alexandria may have been different from those in the country, and owing to the lacuna in [55] 3 it is not clear whether the wages were included in the διαλογισμος. If the contractors had nothing to do with paying the κατεργον, it must have been paid out of the profits, and therefore the sum paid by the contractors to the government did not represent the net profits of the government, since the government would have to subtract the κατεργον. On the whole, however, it seems more probable that the contractors paid the ελαιουργοι as well as the γεωργοι than that the account of the κατεργον was kept separate. The question does not affect the general position of the contractors to the government, cf. note on [39] 13, for if they did not pay the κατεργον, they would bid a correspondingly higher sum for the ωνη.

[53.] 27–[54] 14. 'The amount of sesame oil or cici which we require in Alexandria, we will proclaim at the time of the sale, and we will pay for it (?) at the rate of 48 dr. a metretes. (Bracketed by the corrector) . . . they shall not be allowed to introduce the oil into Alexandria on any pretext (added by the corrector "if they are discovered doing so they shall be deprived of the oil"). If they fail to render account of it, or if they introduce the oil into Alexandria without declaring all of it ("or are discovered introducing oil into the loads," bracketed by the corrector), they shall both be deprived of the oil and in addition each of those who have contracted for the village, shall pay a fine to the Treasury of 3 talents. (Altered by the corrector to 'they shall both be fined the value of the oil which they have introduced into Alexandria without declaring it . . .' The corrector in the next sentence omits 'to the Treasury,' and adds a new section over one which he has effaced, 'The fine shall belong to the Treasury and shall be put down to the oil-contractors in the country.')

[**53.**] 27. This section is one of the most obscure in the whole papyrus. In the first place there is the question whether [53] 27–[54] 2 forms a complete section or whether it is connected with what follows. The fact that it is bracketed and no new regulation added perhaps shows that [54] 2–14 could stand alone, but as this section is clearly concerned with oil required in Alexandria, it was probably connected by the original scribe with [53] 27–[54] 3. On the other hand it is quite possible that the corrector intended by bracketing [53] 27–[54] 3 to connect [54] 3–14 with [53] 17–26. Next, what was this oil required in Alexandria? It cannot be oil for sale there, for that subject has been disposed of in the preceding section, 17–26, but if I am right in supposing that the king is the subject of εχωμεν (see note on [53] 18), this oil was perhaps required for the consumption of the court; cf. [34] 6, which however only mentions wine taken εις το βασιλικον and does not specify Alexandria. It is possible that the oil referred to here was to be exported, but as Egypt produced hardly enough oil for its own use, that is not likely. Another difficulty is the high price, 48 dr., apparently paid by the king for this oil. If he received oil εις τας εν Αλεξανδρειαι διαθεσεις at a reduced rate, we should expect him to pay still less for oil which he required himself. A possible explanation is that as the profit on the sale of each metretes ultimately came back to the government, the king recovered the difference between the cost price which he might have paid, and the price which he did pay, because the contractors who knew beforehand the amount which the king would take (see [54] 2), made for the contract a bid greater by the sum which they would receive for this oil taken by the king; cf. note on [53] 25.

3. The bracket after μη is very irregularly formed and apparently turned the wrong way.

4. If ημιολιν is right, cf. the not infrequent omission of the ο in αργυριον at this period, e. g. Wilck. Ostr 329, see App. iii. p. 200.

12. The farming of the taxes, which were sold collectively to a

company for a whole nome, was sub-divided by the tax-farmers among themselves, sometimes each contracting to collect the taxes of a particular district, e. g. P. P. xlvi, where Philip is stated to have bought the right of collecting the αποµοιρα των περι Φιλαδελφειαν και Βουβαστον τοπων, sometimes, as the plural µεµισθωµενοι here shows, several of them combining to collect the revenues of a particular place. In this case the ελαικη ωνη of the nome was sub-divided into the smaller ωναι of the villages, and those who had contracted to make oil at certain villages were apparently responsible for sending this oil required for Alexandria. Whether they had a particular interest in introducing oil into Alexandria without declaring it is not clear, and the corrections are very difficult. From the analogy of the other places in which καταχωριζειν is used, we should expect the meaning of line 14 to be that the fine was put down to the credit of the oil contractors, though the emphatic manner in which it is stated that the fine was to belong to the Treasury makes the opposite meaning 'put down against' quite possible. But as the insertion of εν τηι χωραι implies a contrast with the contractors at Alexandria, i. e. although the fine was exacted at Alexandria, it affected only the contractors of the nome to which οι µεµισθωµενοι την κωµην belonged, and as the contractors in Alexandria had obviously done nothing to incur a penalty, there is more point in the contrast if καταχωριζεσθω has its usual meaning. Then the explanation of the fine being credited to the contractors of the nome from which the oil was brought to Alexandria, must be that their interests had been somehow damaged by the action of οι µεµισθωµενοι in not declaring all the oil. Perhaps οι µεµισθωµενοι had sold some of it secretly without entering it in the accounts, see line 8 δωσιν τον λογον.

[54.] 15–19. 'The contractors shall appoint also clerks to act as their agents at Alexandria and Pelusium for the oil imported from Syria to Pelusium and Alexandria, and these clerks shall seal the repositories and follow up the disposal of the oil.'

16. αντιγραφεις : see note on [3] 2, and cf. L. P. 62 [8] 15.

17. εκ Συριας : see note on [52] 18. As the oil mentioned in this section is to be consumed at the port to which it is brought (cf. [52] 26 for oil brought to Pelusium on its way to Alexandria), and there was no duty at Alexandria on the oil mentioned here, [52] 26 note, probably there was no duty on it at Pelusium also.

18. αποδοχια : cf. [31] 19, and see note on [50] 6. On the abrupt change of subject see note on [32] 10.

[54.] 20-[55] 16. 'The clerk of the oil-contract appointed by the oeconomus shall hold a balancing of accounts every month with the chief contractor in the presence of the antigrapheus, and he shall write down in his books both the amount of the different kinds of produce which he has received, with the amount of oil which he has manufactured and sold ('at the price written in the legal tariff' added by the corrector), except the oil which is set apart, and the price of the produce written in the legal tariff, together with the price of the jars and miscellaneous expenses, which shall be calculated at the rate of 1 dr. for an artaba of sesame, · obols for croton, 2 obols for cnecus, ... for colocynth, ... for linseed, for .. metretae of sesame oil ..., for 5 metretae of cici 1 dr. 1 obol, for 9 metretae of cnecus oil ..., for 7 metretae of lamp oil 1 dr., for 12 metretae of colocynth oil 1 dr. 1 obol, and that share of the surplus of which the division between the workmen and the contractors has been ordered, and the expenses, whatever they may be, of transport of the produce. The contractors shall receive their pay from their share of the surplus.' (' But in Alexandria the wages for the manufacture of the sesame oil, the brokerage, and the pay of the contractors shall be given in accordance with the proclamation which shall be made at the time of the sale.' Added by the corrector.)

[54.] 20. Cf. [46] 8, [47] 10, &c., where an antigrapheus appointed by both the oeconomus and antigrapheus acts in conjunction with the contractors. But this person is appointed only by the oeconomus and is called an antigrapheus της ωνης, so that he is probably different. Cf. [3] 2 note.

21. διαλογιζεσθω : cf. [16]-[19] and [34] 9-21. There is nothing said in this διαλογισμος of the final balancing of accounts, but see note on [53] 25.

23. εκαστου γενους : see note on [41] 11. The τε after φορτια is contrasted with the τε after τιμην. [54] 23-[55] 2 αφαιρετον, are the amounts for which the contractors were responsible, [55] 2-12, the sums which they were allowed to deduct. The difference between the two was due to the Treasury.

[55.] 1. διαγραμματι: i.e. [40]. If χωρις is right, cf. [61] 1 χωρις της αφωρισμεινς. το αφαιρετον perhaps refers to το αποτιθεμενον, [53] 5, or to the oil required in Alexandria, [53] 27. It cannot refer to the oil required εις τας εν Αλεξανδρειαι διαθεσεις, for that was included in the αναφοραι, [53] 23.

2. τιμην: see [39]. Whether a reference to the κατεργον is lost in the lacuna in the next line is doubtful, [53] 25 note.

4. κεραμιον: cf. [53] 21. Apparently the contractors received an allowance in the account for pottery and the miscellaneous expenses.

5. The proportion of two to one is that nearly always found between the prices of sesame and croton, cf. note on [39] 3, and it is probable that the allowance for the αυηλωματα of croton was 3 obols.

6. The insertion of this line is very doubtful. If colocynth and linseed were mentioned the αυηλωματα must have been excessively small, see [39] 3–7.

8. The abbreviation which elsewhere means artaba, see note on [39] 11, is here found with the oils: if the artaba and metretes had the same capacity (Rev. R. E. ii. 159), it is here perhaps equivalent to metretes. But which artaba was equivalent in capacity to which metretes? The papyrus elsewhere uses the ordinary sign for μετρητης, με, and there is no parallel in any papyrus for the sign meaning artaba as the equivalent of metretes. If however the abbreviation here really means artaba, it would seem to be a mistake.

10. συντεταγμενον: i.e. in [45] 1–6. The επιγενημα here is the difference between the cost and the selling price of oil so far as the contractors were concerned. Cf. notes on [41] 11 and [45] 2.

13. μισθοι: see [45] 2 note.

15. κατεργον: see note on [45] 8. το προπωλητικον: in the case of Alexandria there were middlemen between the tax-farmers and retail traders. In the rest of the country the oil was sold by auction direct to the retailers, [48] 13 note.

[55.] 17–[56] 13. 'Search. If the contractors or their subordinates wish to make a search, on the ground that some persons have concealed oil or oil-presses, they shall hold a search in the presence of the agent of the oeconomus and antigrapheus (altered to 'or the agent of the antigrapheus'). If the agent of the oeconomus or antigrapheus when summoned fails to accompany the contractors, or to remain present until the search is made, he shall pay the contractors twice the amount of the oil supposed to be concealed, at their assessment of it, and the contractors shall be allowed to make the search within . . days . . . If the contractor fails to find what he declared himself to be in search of, he may be compelled by the person whose property is searched to take an oath, and swear that his search was made for absolutely no other than its declared purpose, which strictly concerned the oil contract. If he fails to take the oath on the day on which he is required to take it or on the one following, he shall pay the person who requires him to take it twice the value of the oil supposed to be concealed, as it was estimated before the search took place.'

[55.] 17. ὑπηρεται : see note on [13] 2.

20. καρπιμον : though the general sense of the passage is clear, we have been·unable to make any satisfactory suggestion for this word. The second letter may be λ, in which case κλοπιμον is the only word possible, and that can hardly be used in a passive sense. In line 19 the a of ελ]αιον may possibly be ε, but it is more like a. Wilck. suggests ελαιουρμον (γι and μ are practically indistinguishable in this hand), i.e. a mistake for ελαιουργιμον, and thinks it is contrasted with καρπιμον, but the correction of the singular to the plural seems to me in favour of ελαιουργιον.

22. οικον(ομ)ον. As the corrector has corrected και in line 21 to η, this person is yet another antigrapheus ; see [3] 2 note.

23. αποτινετωσαν ought to have been altered to the singular as only one person is meant, even if the original reading και in line 21 had not been a mere blunder.

25. δε ought probably to have been erased when μη was altered to και, cf. note on [48] 9.

[56.] 5. The letters above η μη are more like ουραν, which may be a mistake for ωραν.

8. η μην : cf. Wilck. Akt. xi. 2. The temples had an official whose duty it was to superintend the taking of oaths : see Rev. Chrest. Dém. p. 45. The object of forcing the searcher to take this oath must, as M. suggests, have been to clear the character of the person whose house was searched.

[56.] 14–18. 'The contractors shall appoint sureties for a sum greater by one-twentieth than that which they have contracted to pay, and shall pay up the taxes collected every day to the bank, while the monthly instalment shall be paid up before the middle of the month following.'

14. Cf. [34] 2.

15. λογευμα, λογευτης, and λογευειν are the regular words for collecting a tax, cf. [10] 1, [12] 13 (?), [16] 11, [52] 20, 27. Hence the λογευματα here have nothing to do with the ordinary payments for oil sold by the contractors, i. e. the αναφορα with which λογευματα are contrasted. Moreover neither διορθωσονται nor καθ ημεραν is consistent with the supposition that ordinary payments are meant, cf. [48] 4–13. The only λογευματα mentioned in C are the duties on foreign oil in [52], and these I think are meant here, but both διορθωσονται and καθ ημεραν as applied even to them are extremely difficult. The last part of the regulation is clear; an instalment (αναφορα) amounting to one-twelfth part of the year's revenue which the contractors had agreed to pay the government was expected from them every month, and if the actual instalment did not reach the required amount, the contractors had to make up the deficiency (διορθουσθαι), either themselves or through their sureties, before the middle of the next month. If καθ ημεραν is opposed to προ της διχομηνιας there is no alternative but to suppose that a certain proportion of the λογευματα was expected every day and the contractors had to pay it, whether the λογευματα received each day reached the required amount or not, unless indeed we admit that διορθωσονται does not mean, when applied to λογευματα, what it means when applied to αναφοραν, which is very unlikely. But it is hardly conceivable that the contractors should be required every day to make up any deficiency in the λογευματα, whether these are the duties on foreign oil or no; and therefore I think that καθ ημεραν is to be closely connected with λογευματα, τα being omitted by a very natural error, and is opposed to την επιβαλλουσαν τωι μηνι. The meaning then is that the contractors or their sureties had to make up the deficiency first on the λογευματα received every day, and secondly on the monthly instalment, in both cases before the middle of the next month. This gives a satisfactory sense, but is open to the objection that if εν τωι εχομενωι προ της διχομηνιας applies to both halves of the section we should expect τε ... και, not μεν ... δε, and that as καθ ημεραν stands in the Greek, it is unquestionably opposed to εν τωι εχομενωι, not to την επιβαλλουσαν τωι μηνι.

16. επι την τραπεζαν in any case applies to both halves of the section; cf. [48] 11 and note on [75] 1.

[56.] 19–21. 'The oil-workmen shall receive their due from the oil that is manufactured, not from the oil that is stored.'

19. το γινομενον is the share of the surplus (see [45] 2, where this regulation ought to have been placed), for the ordinary κατεργον seems to have been paid in money, [46] 20.

κατεργαζομενον is here passive.

[57.] 1–5=[59.] 1–5. 'Revision of the law concerning the oil-contract. We offer for sale the oil-contract for the country from the month Gorpiaeus, which is in the Egyptian calendar Mesore, for a period of two years in accordance with the proclamation which has been issued.'

1. On the relation of [57]–[72] to [39]–[56] see note on [38] 1. διορθωμα: cf. L. P. 62 [1] 7. επι τηι ελαικηι: cf. [53] 4 το προκηρυχθεν εφ εκαστωι νομωι. The 'law' here is [39]–[56].

3. πωλουμεν: see note on [53] 18, and cf. L. P. 62 [1] 1. την χωραν: Alexandria is therefore excluded, the conditions of the ωνη there being different, since oil required for the capital came partly from abroad, [54] 15, partly from the various nomes, [53] 19, partly from the αφωρισμενη in Libya, [58] 5. Cf. [47] 18 and [55] 15.

4. Though no formula of the extant double dates helps to fill up the lacuna, it is clear that no day was mentioned and therefore Gorpiaeus coincided with Mesore in this the twenty-seventh year. This is quite consistent with a double date in a papyrus at Leyden, B 379, of the twenty-ninth year of Philadelphus in which Peritius 28 = Tybi 2. If the two calendars had coincided during the two years' interval, Peritius 2 would have fallen on Tybi 2. Therefore, between Gorpiaeus of the twenty-seventh and Peritius of the twenty-ninth year, the Macedonian calendar had gained nearly a month on the Egyptian. Other instances of double dates in the third century B.C. are (1) P. P. 3, the twenty-fifth year, Apellaeus 10 = Pharmouthi 6; (2) the Canopus inscr. ninth year of Euergetes, 7 Apellaeus = 17 Tybi; and (3) P. P. part I. 67 (1), Daisius 23 = Thoth 2, the year not being mentioned. M. assigns P. P. 3 to the twenty-fifth year of Philadelphus, not Euergetes, but, as I think, wrongly. For if Apellaeus 10 = Pharmouthi 6, Xandicus would approximately have corresponded to Mesore in the twenty-fifth year, and since Gorpiaeus

Y

corresponded to Mesore in the twenty-seventh year, we must conclude that the Macedonian calendar gained no less than five months or lost seven on the Egyptian between Apellaeus of the twenty-fifth year and Gorpiaeus of the twenty-seventh, which is scarcely credible. Leaving that papyrus aside for the moment, the Canopus inscription, in which the 7th Apellaeus corresponded to the 17th Tybi and therefore the 28th Peritius to about the 8th Pharmouthi, shows that between the twenty-ninth year of Philadelphus and the ninth of Euergetes, a period of seventeen years, the Macedonian calendar had lost a little over three months compared to the Egyptian, unless indeed it had gained nearly nine months, in which case the confusion between the regnal years of the king according to the two calendars must have been quite inextricable. But if we suppose that P. P. 3 is the twenty-fifth year of Euergetes, the following result is obtained. In the ninth year of Euergetes, Apellaeus 7 corresponded to Tybi 17, and therefore, if in the twenty-fifth year, Apellaeus 10 corresponded to Pharmouthi 6, the Macedonian calendar had in sixteen years either lost nearly three months compared to the Egyptian, or gained a little more than nine. This is approximately the same as the amount which it lost or gained in the seventeen years preceding the Canopus inscription. Therefore, since there is nothing in the correspondence of Diophanes, P. P. 2–4, which points to Philadelphus rather than Euergetes being the reigning king, (for the twenty-sixth year mentioned on page 2 may belong to Euergetes just as well as to Philadelphus), and since, in opposition to M., I think that there is no more reason to attribute undated or insufficiently dated papyri in the Petrie collection to Philadelphus' or the early part of Euergetes' reign than to the later part of Euergetes' reign, Philopator's, or in some cases even to Epiphanes', the balance of probability seems to me in favour of the twenty-fifth year in P. P. 3 referring to Euergetes. From the twenty-ninth year of Philadelphus to the twenty-fifth of Euergetes the Egyptian calendar was, as has been shown, gaining upon the Macedonian; but between the twenty-fifth year of Euergetes and the ninth year of Epiphanes, a period of twenty-six years, a reaction took place; for in the Rosetta Stone the 4th Xandicus = 18th Mecheir, and therefore the 10th Apellaeus corresponded to about Phaophi 24, and Pharmouthi 6 to about Artemisius 22, i.e. the Macedonian calendar had either gained six months and a half on the Egyptian or lost five and a half. In the one case it had got back nearly to its original relation in the twenty-seventh year of Philadelphus, in the other it had lost a whole year, which is very unlikely. Such being the irregularity of the two calendars it is impossible to fix the year of P. P. part I. 67 within any approach to precision: but of the three double dates known for the third century B.C., it comes nearest to P. P. 3. On the superiority of the Egyptian calendar to the Greek cf. a passage in the astronomical treatise of Eudoxus, L. P. 1. 62–80, pointed out to me by M., διο ου συμφωνουσιν τοις αστρολογοις αι ημεραι ουδε οι Ελληνικοι μηνες . . . οι δε αστρολογοι και οι ιερογραμματεις . . . τα καταχυτηρια και κυνος ανατολην . . . αναλεγομενοι τας ημερας εκ των Αιγυπτιων αυται γαρ ουτε υπεξαιρουνται ουτε παρεμβαλλονται.

5. It is curious that the term of the contract began in the last month of the Egyptian year, Mesore, for απο cannot exclude the month mentioned. But both the commencement in Mesore and the fact that the contract was sold for two years are, as Wilck. remarks, probably due to exceptional causes, for elsewhere we find the ωναι sold only for one year and that a regnal year; e. g. Leyd. pap. F; pap. Zois i; Jos. A. J. 12. 4. 3; papyrus in Introd. to P. P. part ii. p. 29 line 3, and P. P. xlvi (*b*) 2. L. P. 62, where also by a strange coincidence Mesore, not Thoth, is the starting-point, has several difficulties of its own (see App. i), but the exceptional character of the starting-point is obvious.

[**57**.] 6–23=[**59**] 6–[**60**] 2. '(Where the number of arourae sown exceeds the number decreed), the tax on the additional sesame and croton shall belong to the contractors for the coming term. But wherever it appears from the following list that fewer arourae have been sown than the number previously decreed, we will make up the deficiency both in sesame and croton from other nomes; and the tax on this sesame and croton which we shall supply, being 2 drachmae for sesame and 1 drachma for croton, shall belong to the contractors of the nome to which the produce is supplied. But in the nome from which we take away the sesame and croton in excess of the amount previously decreed, the tax on sesame and croton shall not be exacted upon the produce which we take away. But the colocynth and linseed oil, which we do not take to fill up the deficiencies of other nomes in sesame and sesame oil, we will manufacture through the agency of the oeconomi and then measure it, and the contractors shall receive a surplus from this oil equal to the surplus which they used to receive from sesame oil and sesame ; and the colocynth and linseed oil, which we do not take to fill up deficiencies of other nomes in cici, we will manufacture through the agency of the oeconomi and then measure it, and from it the contractors shall receive a surplus equal to that which they used to receive from cici and croton. The contractors shall superintend the manufacture by the oeconomus, and shall seal the oil.'

[**57.**] 6. First as to the differences of reading between the two columns, (1) in [57] 6 [ση]σαμου is not enough to fill the lacuna, and I therefore conjecture τε which is absent in [59] 7. (2) In [57] 12 the sign following τελος is quite different from that in [59] 13, but both can be resolved into α with a stroke after it, i. e. αρ(ταβη) : see note on [39] 11. Artaba is required by the sense, and it is confirmed by the blunder of the scribe in [59] 14, where της αρταβης is a mistake for του σησαμου, showing that he had artaba in his mind when writing that passage. (3) In [59] 16 εξαγωμεν of [57] 15 has been changed for the worse into εισαγωμεν. (4) [57] 17 has το επιγενημα, [59] 19 inserts και before το. (5) [57] 18 has και απο του σησαμου, while [59] 21 omits απο or του. (6) In [57] 18 there is no room for το before κολοκυντινον which is found in [59] 21. The difference is of little importance whether the passage be right or not, see note on [57] 16. (7) In [59] 21 we have κ[. . κ]ατεργασμενοι, probably και, or else κα was written twice over by mistake. κατεργασαμενοι without και [57] 19 is correct. (8) In [59] 23 αφ is omitted, cf. [57] 20. Minor differences are [57] 8 τωμ = [59] 9 των : [57] 10 ελλειποντα = [59] 11 ευλειποντα : [57] 17 λ[ηψον]ται = [59] λημψονται, cf. [57] 21 = [59] 24, and [58] 5 = [60] 11, for the same difference of spelling : [57] 18 κολοκυντινον = [59] 21 κολοκυνθινον. The changes of reading introduced by the writer of [59] are thus for the most part mere variations, in no case improvements, except perhaps (6), and it may be argued that [59]–[60] were directly copied from [57]–[58] by a rather careless scribe. But the number of differences in [59]–[60] especially those which are mere variations, neither better nor worse than [57]–[58], makes me incline to the belief that they are independent copies of a common archetype which the scribes may have had before them, or which may have been dictated to them simultaneously.

The meaning of this difficult column depends on the sense of των προκηρυχθεισων [57] 8 and προκηρυχθεντος [57] 13. The reference is, I contend, not to the following list of nomes, [60]-[72], but to a previous list, with which [60]-[72], referred to by αποδειξωμεν, are contrasted. Since the original draft of the law concerning the oil monopoly contained a direct reference to a list of nomes, different from the list which we have, [53] 18 note, and [60]-[72] were not part of the original document, [38] 1 note, the list referred to by προκηρυχθεισων is probably that referred to by υποκηρυξωμεν in [53]. Assuming the correctness of this identification, in what way did the original list, which no doubt contained the law for the twenty-sixth and possibly earlier years, differ from the list in [60]-[72] which represented the law for the twenty-seventh year? In the first place the number of arourae to be sown with sesame and croton in the nomes was different in the two lists, for the section beginning οσας δ αν αρουρας ελασσους, [57] 7, is clearly opposed to the preceding one which in that case may have begun οσας δ αν πλειους, and the two lines which are left confirm this view. The revised list therefore assigned in some cases more, in others fewer arourae to the nomes, and where the revised amount was smaller the deficiency was made up from other nomes, a contingency which, as has been shown, see note on [41] 20, was not contemplated in the original draft of [39]-[56], for under the old regulations each nome grew enough for its own consumption. The difference however between the two lists is not limited to sesame and croton. The original list contained also the amounts of cnecus oil, colocynth oil, and perhaps lamp oil required for Alexandria, [53] 22. In the revised list, in accordance with the correction of [53] 20, only croton is required for Alexandria, except in the two cases where sesame is required, [60] 24 and [62] 5, and there is no mention of the other oils, though see [58] 1 note. ·

6. τελος: cf. [39] 13-15. By εισιοντα χρονον the two years mentioned in line 4 are meant. It is possible that the alterations in the law were made between the time of the sale and the collection of the tax, cf. προκηρυχθεισων in line 9 with [55] 16 and probably [54] 1, and that although the contractors for the different nomes had bought the tax under the old regulations, in which the numbers of arourae to be sown were different, the government nevertheless allowed them to gain where the change in the law was in their favour, just as it secured them against

loss when the change injured them, see 8–10. But the phrase τοις τον εισιοντα χρονον πριαμενοις rather implies that the contract had not yet been bought, and so I think does πωλουμεν in [57] 3 and [58] 6. Hence it is more probable that the alterations were made prior to the sale of the contract and represent the terms under which it was to be bought.

It is impossible of course to fix in which nomes the amounts of sesame and croton to be grown for the nome itself were increased. Many nomes in [60]–[72] have to grow croton (and two have to grow sesame) for Alexandria, but as no tax was paid on this in the nome where the produce was grown, see 13–15, this increase did not affect the contractors who had bought the tax. The nomes meant in 6–7 are those in which the number of arourae was increased without the surplus thus produced being taken away, and this section decides what was to be done with the increase of the tax on sesame and croton. What was to be done with the oil produced from this increased amount of sesame and croton is perhaps laid down in 15–23, but see note on line 16.

8. ελασσους: e.g. the Heliopolite nome, [64] 1–18, which only grew 500 arourae of sesame and therefore had to be supplemented by 2000 artabae from other nomes, while it grew no croton at all: cf. [63] 17, [64] 22, &c.

11. υπαρξει: cf. [61] 11, [62] 1, &c. There are however two apparent exceptions to this rule [69] 5–7 and [72] 15–18.

13. εξ ου: e.g. the Tanite nome [66] 18, the Mendesian [62] 19, &c.

16. The construction and meaning of this section have given us more trouble than any passage in the papyrus, nor have we been successful in finding a satisfactory solution. The general outline of lines 16–22 is certain in so far that they consist of two parallel sections, neither of which is written out in full, but the great difficulty is to decide how far the parallelism is to be carried. Assuming there are no mistakes in [57] 16–22 and putting aside for the moment the variations in [59] 18–25, the construction seems to be οσον δ αν μη δωμεν εις το ελλειπον σησαμον και ελαιον (κολοκυντινον ελαιον και το απο του λινου σπερματος, κατεργασαμενοι δια των οικονομων μετρησομεν), αφ ου το επιγενημα το ισον ληψονται οσον απο του σησαμινου ελαιου και απο του σησαμου (ελαμβανον· οσον δ αν μη δωμεν) εις το (ελλειπον) κικι κολοκυντινον

ελαιον και το απο του λινου σπερματος, κατεργασαμενοι δια των οικονομων μετρησομεν, αφ ου το επιγενημα το ισον ληψονται οσον απο τε του κικιος και απο του κροτωνος ελαμβανον.

The variations in [59] 18-25 do not affect the sense, the only one of any importance being the insertion of το before κολοκυντινον. But if, as I think, κολοκυντινον ελαιον is the object of both δωμεν and μετρησομεν, it makes no difference to the meaning that in 57 κολοκυντινον ελαιον και το απο του λινου σπερματος is grammatically the object of δωμεν and the whole clause οσον—σπερματος is the object of μετρησομεν, while in [59] το κολοκυντινον—σπερματος is the object of μετρησομεν and is qualified by οσον μη δωμεν. The meaning then will be that colocynth oil and linseed oil, when not required to fill up deficiencies in sesame oil and cici in the other nomes (cf. line 10 ελλειποντα), are to be manufactured by the oeconomi, and the tax-farmers are to receive an επιγενημα equal to that which they received from sesame oil and sesame or cici and croton. It might be thought that this explains the absence of colocynth and linseed in [44]-[47] which are concerned with the manufacture of oil. But there is no reference in C either to the substitution of colocynth and linseed oil for sesame oil and cici or to the adulteration of sesame oil and cici with colocynth and linseed oil, which M. suggested was the meaning of this passage. The oils are invariably kept distinct, cf. [40] 10, [53] 14, 21, moreover in line 10 it has been already stated that the deficiency in sesame and croton would be made up by sesame and croton from other nomes. There is also the objection, why should the επιγενημα on the colocynth oil not given εις το ελλειπον σησαμον be different from the επιγενημα on the colocynth oil not given εις το (ελλειπον) κικι? This επιγενημα is itself one of the most obscure points in the whole section. The only επιγενημα mentioned in C is the difference between the cost and selling price of oil, a part of which was paid to the contractors, cf. [45] 2 and [55] 14. This suits απο του σησαμινου ελαιου, but is no explanation of the επιγενημα απο του σησαμου in [57] 18, for which phrase C offers no parallel. Other alternatives are either to take επιγενημα as the surplus on the whole account of the tax-farmers, which neither suits το ισον, nor yields a satisfactory meaning, or to consider it equivalent to πλειον in [53] 13, in which case the επιγενημα on the sesame oil as well as the επιγενημα on the sesame must refer to the prices in that passage. But it is very difficult to see how the prices there could be called an επιγενημα since they are much less than the selling price, [53] 16 note.

If the explanation suggested is very unsatisfactory, it is less so than several other explanations which may seem possible. (1) If οσον in [57] 15 refers not to colocynth and linseed oil but to sesame oil, the construction becomes still more complicated and the old difficulty of colocynth oil and linseed being used to supplement cici still remains. (2) If οσον—εκ του λινου σπερματος be taken as one sentence, i. e. what we do not give εις το ελλειπον σησαμον but what we do give εις το κικι, αφ ου — απο του σησαμου in 16-18 is left unaccounted for. (3) We may suppose that και has been omitted between κικι and το κολοκυντινον, in which case [59] 21 is nearer to the correct reading than [57] 18, and the section will refer to the sesame and croton which is in excess of the previously decreed amount, but is not required for other nomes. Then in line 18 we ought to supply οσον δ αν μη δωμεν κικι η το κολοκυντινον η το απο του λινου σπερματος εις το κικι κ.τ.λ. But the amount of colocynth and linseed to be grown was not fixed, cf. [39] 14, note, and therefore it could not be in excess των προκηρυχθεισων, and why is nothing said of the επιγενημα on colocynth and linseed or the oils produced from them? (4) If in line 18 we only supply κικι, we avoid the last difficulties, but why should the deficiency in colocynth and linseed oil be supplied by cici and not by colocynth and linseed oil?

The omission of cnecus oil here, cf. [58] 2 note, is in any case remarkable. If the explanation of the passage which I have suggested is near the truth, and we have here a regulation concerning the manufacture of colocynth and linseed oil, the reason may be that the regulations for the manufacture of cnecus have already been given and that a deficiency in its supply was not likely to occur. But it is more likely the omission is a mere accident, cf. notes on [41] 11, [42] 4.

19. το απο του λινου σπερματος: cf note on [39] 7. In [39]-[56] it is called το επελλυχνιον.

[58.] 1-4 = [60] 3-9.

1. Two facts are clear concerning the sesame and croton mentioned in this paragraph, (1) that they are taken away (εξ) from each nome, and (2) that no tax is to be levied on them by οι πριαμενοι την ελαικην

εξ....; either of these facts is sufficient to prove that the sesame and croton mentioned here cannot be the ordinary sesame and croton required for the nome itself, while εκαστον, if correct, shows that the sesame and croton cannot be that required εις αλλους νομους, even if that subject had not been already discussed in [57] 7-15. The only other classes of sesame and croton are that εις τας εν Αλεξανδρειαι διαθεσεις [53] 18 and that required εν Αλεξανδρειαι [53] 27. Against the latter class being meant here are the bracketing of the section [53] 27-[54] 2 and the absence of any mention of this class in the list of nomes. On the other hand croton εις τας εν Αλεξανδρειαι διαθεσεις, on which no tax was to be levied in the nome, is frequently mentioned in [60]-[72], and in two cases, [60] 24 and [62] 5, sesame εις τας εν Αλεξανδρειαι διαθεσεις. Since we should expect a general regulation in these two columns concerning the tax on this class of sesame and croton parallel to that concerning the tax on sesame and croton εις αλλους νομους, and εις Αλεξανδρειαν is possible in [58] 2, it is extremely probable that this section refers to the oil 'for disposal at Alexandria.' The only difficulty is the mention of colocynth oil in [58] 2, cf. [53] 22 where colocynth oil is bracketed by the corrector. But as sesame oil is also bracketed by the corrector, the inconsistency need not trouble us.

In [60] 8 σησ]αμων is impossible, as is ν]ομου, though the a and ν are extremely doubtful. We should expect 'the nome from which we take away the sesame and croton,' cf. [57] 14 and [61] 17.

[58.] 4-6 = [60] 9-13. 'The sesame and croton sown in the district which is set apart shall be received by the oeconomus from the cultivators, and he shall forward it to the oil factory in Alexandria.'

5. η αφωρισμενη was part of the Libyan nome, [61] 3 (cf. [40] 14), the produce of which was reserved for Alexandria. Hence as in the case of sesame and croton grown εις αλλους νομους, [43] 22-24, the oeconomus, not the contractors, received the produce, and no tax was paid on it to the contractors of the Libyan nome, [61] 4-6, and note [on 61] 1. In [60] 10 the a of κροτωνα is elided.

[58.] 6-8 = [60] 13-15. 'We offer the contract for sale accepting payment in copper coin, and we will take 24 obols for the stater.'

6. πωλουμεν reverts to πωλουμεν in [57] 3 and refers to the whole contract for the χωρα, not to the αφωρισμενη only.

z

7. On this all important passage see App. iii. p. 195. To anticipate my conclusions, this passage means that the government would not only accept copper coin from the contractors as payment of the sum which they had promised, but would take it at par, demanding no exchange and counting 24 copper obols as the full equivalent of a silver stater or tetradrachm ; i. e. copper was legal tender not merely for the fractions of a drachma, as it always was, but for the whole amount. In the case of most other taxes, e. g. the απομοιρα, the government insisted on payment in silver, and if the tax-farmer was allowed to pay in copper at all he had also to pay the difference of the exchange which seems to have been fixed in all cases by the government. Cf. [76] 2–5.

[**58.**] 8–9 = [**60**] 15–17. 'If the flow of the oil produces a surplus, this surplus of oil and cici shall belong to the Treasury.'

8. ρυσις : see note on [47] 1, to which, as L. remarked, this passage probably refers. It seems that the reading differs in [58] 9 from [60] 16, the first having το πλειον, the other το ελαιον και κικι, but there may be an error in my restoration of 8–9 and in any case the sense is the same in both passages.

[**60.**] 18–25. 'In the Saite nome with Naucratis, of sesame 10,000 arourae, of croton 11,433⅔ arourae, and likewise for disposal at Alexandria, of croton, on which no tax shall be levied by the contractor of the Saite nome, 10,666⅓ arourae, and of sesame for disposal at Alexandria 3000 artabae.'

18. The mention of Naucratis here though its importance was rapidly decreasing, coupled with the absence of it from the list in [31], is somewhat in favour of the view suggested in note on [31] 5, that the list in [60]–[72] is much the older classification. Ptolemais της Θηβαιδος is not mentioned in either list.

20 β'. The sign for ⅔ is common in P. P. Cf. also B. M. pap. cxix. 42, of the second century A.D., by which time the β had degenerated into o. This passage and line 23 settle the question whether the aroura was ever divided into thirds at this period, but Wilck. tells me that he adheres to the opinion he has expressed that in the case of fractions smaller than ⅓, the other series, ¼, ⅛, 1/16 and so on, is always used for arourae.

21. ωστε : cf. App. ii. (4) saep. ; P. P. 49 (1 c) 4, πλινθουλκοι οι

εξειληφοτες ελκυσαι [πλινθου] M^β ωστε εις την συντελουμενην εν Πτολεμαιδι βασι[λικην] καταλυσιν ; and Wilck. Akt. vi. 15 τα ειθισμενα συμβολα επισταληναι ωστε τοις μετακειμενοις. In all these cases it is followed by the dative or εις.

24. σησαμου : see note on [53] 20 and cf. [62] 5.

25. After the lacuna is what looks like the tip of a σ, but as διαθεσιν is elsewhere followed immediately by the amount I do not think anything is lost. διαθεσιν : cf. note on [48] 5. The amounts of sesame and croton required for Alexandria are given here and in [61] 19 in artabae, in other places, where there is not a lacuna, they are given in arourae. The fact that arourae and artabae are used indifferently shows that there was a fixed amount of seed expected from each aroura. The enormous quantity of croton to be grown in the Saite nome includes of course the croton already planted. Probably only a very small amount was sown in each year, cf. note on [43] 5, while the figures in the case of sesame meant the quantity to be actually sown. There is no proportion between the relative amount of sesame and croton to be grown in the various nomes, nor is there any between the amounts to be grown for the nome itself and those to be grown for Alexandria or other nomes. The figures exhibit the utmost variety throughout the list.

[61.] 1–12. 'In all Libya, except the district set apart, of sesame 5700 arourae, and in the district set apart, of sesame which must be supplied to Alexandria for disposal there, and on which no tax shall be levied by the contractor of the Libyan nome, . . arourae. Of croton which must be made into oil in the nome we will provide from other nomes . . artabae, the tax on which shall belong to the contractor of the Libyan nome.'

1. See [58] 5, note. It does not seem that any croton was grown in the αφωρισμενη, for there is hardly room for another line.

8. ωνηι : i.e. the nome of which the tax was farmed. Cf. note on [29] 7.

As the same formulae are repeated in each column, it is unnecessary to translate the rest of the list.

[61.] 20. See note on [31] 6 and Introd. p. xlviii.

[62.] 5. Though the lines are often very uneven, there is not room for την εν τοις αλλοις νομοις διαθεσιν, even if that had been the usual order, and not την διαθεσιν την εν τοις αλλοις νομοις.

[**63.**] 9. Perhaps την εν Αλεξανδρειαι, but from the Mendesian nome to the Fayoum, [71], the formula, where preserved, is εις τους αλλους νομους.

[**67.**] 12. πραξετα(ι). Other mistakes in spelling occur in [68] 1, 19, [72] 18.

[**69.**] 1–2. Cf. [61] 3 and [72] 11–12. The Memphite nome as well as Memphis was supplied from the Fayoum.

5. Cf. [72] 15–17, and [71] 8–11. From these two passages it appears that the produce of the Fayoum sent to the Memphite nome and Memphis was exempt altogether from the tax and is therefore an exception to the rule decreed in [57] 13–15, unless, as is quite possible, the scribe has written εν Μεμφει and εν τωι Μεμφιτηι for εν τηι λιμνηι or εν τωι λιμνιτηι. For the position of the Memphite nome in the list see M. Introd. p. xlviii. But I am inclined to think that the separation of the Memphite nome from Memphis is due to want of precision in the drafting of the law rather than to any sacredness attaching to the number twenty-four, and that the agreement between the two lists in point of number is accidental. Cf. note on [31] 5.

18. The figure after 'B is 900: so [71] 12.

[**71.**] 10. Λιμνιτην: cf. App. ii. (2) 13, which proves the existence of the word and probably refers to the Fayoum. The note added at the side in a very minute hand appears to refer to some amount which had been omitted, and does not affect the construction of the principal sentence. But it is possible that we ought to read εις τον Μεμφιτην και Μεμφιν in lines 8–9 and [Μεμφι]την in line 11, cf. [69] 2 and [72] 12.

[**72.**] 1. There is hardly any doubt that the nome lost is the Cynopolite which is wanting to complete the list in [31].

8. The fragment containing part of lines 8–10 is perhaps incorrectly placed here, though no other place suits it. In any case there is a variation in it from the usual formula. I conjecture that the scribe wrote και τον κροτωνα ου δει κατεργασθηναι, which elsewhere is used only of the croton supplied from other nomes, in place of κροτωνος, i. e. the croton to be grown in the Cynopolite nome. Where arourae are mentioned, they

naturally refer to the sesame and croton grown in the nome, and where sesame and croton are supplied from other nomes, the amount is given in artabae.

11. See note on [69] 5.

18. Considering the size of the Thebaid compared to other nomes, the amounts are not large, being less than those assigned to the Saite nome [60] 19–20. The Thebaid was bounded by the Hermopolite nome on the north and by the first cataract on the south.

[73.] The roll bought from a dealer in Cairo by Prof. Petrie in Dec. 1893 ends with [72]; the pieces which constitute D and E were bought by me in 1895 from the same dealer, with the exception of [100] and part of [103] on the *verso* of [100]. This piece and the fragments printed after [107] I obtained in the Fayoum in December, 1894. For any one who has studied [1]–[72] a mere glance at D and E and the fragments is sufficient to convince him that they all belong to the same series of documents as [1]–[72], and it is hardly necessary to call attention to the close similarity in colour and texture of the papyrus, the obvious parallelism of the subjects treated, and the identity of the writer of [87]–[91] with the writer of [24]–[35]. The roll containing [1]–[72] probably consisted originally of four separate documents, cf. note on [38] 1, so that the question whether [73]–[107] were ever actually joined to [1]–[72] is of little importance. Since [1] is the beginning of a section, it is probable that D and E were not actually joined, but as the distance between the folds in [73]–[107], so far as it can be ascertained, shows that these columns formed the outside of a roll, the core of which had been separated from it, and the distance between the outside folds of [1]–[72] is perfectly consistent with the view that [1]–[72] are the missing core of [73]–[107], it is probable that [73]–[107] were folded round [1]–[72] but not joined to them, and hence were separated from [1]–[72] by the finders of the papyrus. Whether this hypothesis be correct or not, [73]–[107] must have been found at the same place as [1]–[72], and as it is quite certain that [73]–[107] were found in the Fayoum, it follows that [1]–[72] were found there also ; cf. note on [38] 3.

[73]–[78] form a section by themselves, and some folds may have been lost between [78] and [79], but probably not many.

[73.] 1. διαγραμμα: see note on [39] 1. At first sight the word appears to be used here in a wider sense than there, for D appears to fix the relations of the royal banks towards the government officials, cf. note on [3] 2. But such a section as [76] is a διαγραμμα in the sense of [39], and as other sections of a similar character may have been lost, e. g. one fixing the rate of interest (cf. [78] 1), the meaning of διαγραμμα may be the usual one. In line 4]ιβικην is perhaps for βασ]ιλικην. M.

[74.] 2. οι καταβαλλοντες are the tax-payers, not the tax-farmers, cf. [52] 15, 18.

[75.] 1. The acute conjecture of Wilcken from P. P. xxvi (G. G. A. 1895, no. 2, p. 156), that there were royal banks in the villages as well as in the large towns, is thus completely established. No one however had suspected the surprising piece of information afforded by line 4 and [76] 3, that the royal banks were farmed, and this fact produces important modifications in the current view concerning the position of the banks in this and the next century ; cf. Wilcken's Ostraca.

2. The subject of αναφερετωσαν is probably not αι τραπεζαι. The exact breadth of all of the columns in D is uncertain. The number of letters lost at the beginnings and ends of lines here is calculated on the supposition that 3-4 αποτινετωσαν τωι την is correct, in [76] on the supposition that συνταξηται προς τον ηγορακοτα (cf. [47] 5 and 13) is right, in [74] on the supposition that πρασσοντες τι (cf. [15] 4) is right. The length of [73], [77] and [78] depends on the correctness of the previous conjectures combined.

5. M. suggests αντι] των καταβαλλομενων χρηματω]ν.

[76.] 4. No lacuna is more deplorable than that at the beginning of line 5, which would have given us the discount on copper when paid in place of silver by the farmers of a προς αργυριον ωνη. Cf. App. ii (5) and L. P. 62 [5] 16, which gives the discount at some period of the second century B.C., and App. iii. pp. 198–200 and 214–216.

7. If τωι την τραπεζαν ηγορακοτι, the lacuna is longer than I have supposed.

[77.] 1. παντα χαλκον διδοναι : e. g. the farmers of the ελαικη ωνη, who paid in copper without any discount, cf. [58] 6 and App. iii. p. 195.

[78.] 1. Probably επι τ[οκωι] ; so in line 4.

[80.] 1. αν[τιγραφον?

2. Probably ΔΕΚΑΤ[ΗΣ or ΔΕΚΑΤ[ΩΝ.

[84.] 10. Perhaps ΖΙΙ]ΤΗΣΙΣ, cf. [55] 17.

[85.] 6. ναυτεια: cf. Rosetta stone 17, προσεταξεν δε και την συλληψιν των εις την ναυτειαν μη ποιεισθαι.

[86.] 6. διοικητου: see note on [38] 3.

10. ομνυω: this would seem to be the beginning of a βασιλικος ορκος, cf. [27] 6 and App. ii (2). But its occurrence here is very strange.

[87.] From this point to [107] the subject is a tax connected with clothes; cf. Rosetta stone 17, των τ εις το βασιλικον συντελουμενων εν τοις ιεροις βυσσινων οθονιων απελυσεν τα δυο μερη with the mention of βυσσινων in [103] 1 and οθονια in [98] 9 and [99] 5; and Rosetta stone 29, ωσαυτως δε και τας τιμας των μη συντελεσμενων εις το βασιλικον βυσσινων οθ[ονι]ων και των συντετελεσμειων τα προς τον δειγματισμον διαφορα (απελυσεν) with the παραδειγμα in [89] 3 and [102] 4. λινος, ιστος and υφανται are frequently mentioned, and there are two references to the priests, [106] 3 and [107] 4.

9. There does not seem to be room for αποτι]νετω. Perhaps the right-hand strip belongs to a different column.

[90.] There is a break between this and the preceding column.

[94.] 3. τριηραρχημα: cf. P. P. 129. 8.

[95.] 6. i. e. 2 drachmae, 1½ obols.

[96.] 1. Probably χρειαν εχωμεν, cf. [53] 27 and note on [53] 18.

3. τρηραν: ηρα seems to be the termination of a word expressing the tax on some article, cf. ζυτηρα the tax on ζυτος, and επι τηι οθο[νιηραι? [103] 3.

4. Cf. note on [12] 1.

[98.] 1. ε̂: the curved line above ε and ιη in lines 2 and 3 represents π, i. e. πηχυς: cf. B. M. pap. l. 7.

αν(α) means 'at' or 'multiplied by,' cf. App. ii (5) passim.

[103.] 2. στυππεινων: cf. LXX. Lev. 13. 47, where B has στυππυινων.

3. Cf. [96] 3 note.

[104.] 4. Cf. [7] 3.

[107.] 1. Cf. [9] 2 note.

[Frag. 1.] I do not feel very confident that all the columns which

I have assigned to the tenth scribe are by him, [73]–[86], [99]–[107], except [99] 8–9, and the fragments. It is easy to select two columns which, when put side by side, appear to be written by different persons, e. g. [76] and [82], but there are several columns in which the writer's hand changes gradually from one style to another, and after trying in vain to distinguish more than one hand I have come to the conclusion that these columns were all written by him. His change from a rather formal to a much more cursive hand is clearly exhibited in [73]–[78].

That Fragments 1 and 2 do not belong to the parts of [73]–[102] written by the tenth hand is quite certain; Frag. 3 is more doubtful. Fragments 4, 5, and 6 might belong to [73]–[102], but so far as can be ascertained they belong to 1 and 2, for all of them seem to be concerned with the ευνομιον or pasture-tax. The fragments grouped together under one number come at corresponding folds and therefore at corresponding intervals, most probably of about 8 inches, so that each one belongs to a different column. But the order in which they are placed under each number is in some cases doubtful. Frag. 1 (*a*) and (*b*) go together, and are in the right order, and so are (*c*)–(*g*), but whether (*a*)-(*b*) come before or after (*c*)–(*g*) and whether there are any corresponding fragments lost between (*a*)–(*b*) and (*c*)–(*g*) is unknown. Similarly in Frag. 2, (*a*) and (*b*) go together, and so do (*c*)–(*f*) and (*g*)–(*i*), but the position of these three subdivisions to each other is unknown. In Frag. 4, (*a*)-(*e*), (*g*)–(*l*), (*m*)–(*n*) go together, (*f*) is by itself. In Frag. 5, (*a*) and (*b*) are by themselves, (*c*) and (*d*) go together. In Frag. 6, (*a*)-(*c*) go together, so do (*a*)-(*f*), and (*g*)-(*h*).

APPENDIX I.

PAPYRUS 62 OF THE LOUVRE, NOTICES ET EXTRAITS DES
MANUSCRITS, VOL. XVIII, PART II, 1866.

[Col. 1. [πωλουμεν τας εν τ]ωι Οξυρυγχιτηι ωνας εις το αL
[. . . . . απο μην]ος Μεσορη εις δωδεκαμηνον
[και τας επαγομενας] ημερας ē α'γ]ορα ζετε δε
[τας ωνας . . . . . και] μελλετε μη[θ]ενα συκοφαντησειν
5 [. . . . . μηδε] δ[ια]βαλλειν αλλ απο του βελτιστου
[. . . . .]ς κατα τους νομους και τα δια
[γραμματα και τα πρ]οσταγματα και τα διορθωμεθα
[τα . . . .]ησομενα εφ εκαστης ωνης
[τας δ ωνας ανα]πληρωσειν ουθεια υπολογον
10 [. . . . . το] βασιλικον παρευρεσει ητιν[ι]ουν
[. . . . .]εισθαι ως και τας εγδειας πραχθη
[σονται . . . . οι] τα τελη λαμβανοντες οσα και
[. . . . . εγγ]υους δε καταστησουσιν οι εγλα
                                                    τωι
[βοντες τωι οικο]νομωι και βασι['λικωι] γραμματει
15 [. . . . . τω]ν επιδ[εκατω]ν
[. . . . .]τω[. αφ ης αν ημερας]

Col. 2. παρομολογηθηι [επι της] πρασεως εν ημεραις λ̄ κατα
πενθημ[ε]ρον [του επι]βαλλοντος τουτων δε τα συμβ[ολα]
τεθησετα[ι αφ ης αν ημ]ερας ληφθηι ε[ν] ημεραις [.]
επι της βασιλικης τραπεζης μετ αναγραφης εσφρα
5 γισμενα υπο [των . . . .]ων και του τραπεζιτου ουτος δ[ε]
προσθη[σε]ται ε[ν τοις μη]νι[ε]ιοις το καθεν των συμβ[ολων]
ευσημως [ο]σα [επι των υ]ποθηκων εστιν και την . . [. .

A a

βεβαιωτ[.. και οσας εκασ]τοι εις την βεβαιωσιν
υποθηκας [.........] δεδωκασιν και των ει[λ]ηφο[των]
10 τα διεγγυημ[ατα τας ...]γραφας οτι επεσκεμμεν[αι]
εισιν κα[ι] εισιν αξ[.......]θους ως εαν τι απ[ολι]πωσ[ι....]
κ.. η καθηκον τ[.........]ωσιν [.....]τεισον[τ..]
τοις δ] αναπλ[ηρουσι τας] ωρ[ας................]
[.......] συμβολα [.....]ν[.....
15 επιμελ[ητης και ο....]κα[...... γρα]μματευ[ς]
και ανοισ[ουσιν επι την βασιλικην τραπεζαν]
[ο]ς δ αν αλλ[ως οικονομησηι η.............]
[·] περι ταυτα κα[.......... αποτεισει]

Col. 3. εις το βασιλικον καθ εκαστον αδικημα ⚹ ε
και προς τον διοικητην καταποσταλησεται μετα φυλακης
εαν δε τινες ανευ της των προγεγραμμενων γνωμης
διεγγυησωσιν τα ληφθεντα υπαρξει εις την εγληψιν
5 και αναγκασθησεται προσδιεγγυαν του παρομολογηθεντος
εαν δε οι λαβοντες τα συμβολα της διεγγυησεως μη
[επαν]ενεγκωσιν επι την τραπεζαν αποτεισουσιν
[εκα]στου συμβολου ε[κ]αστος αυτων ⚹ α
κ[αι ουθ]εν ησσον αναγκ[α]σθησονται αποκαταστησαι
10 τα συμβολα εις την [τ]ραπεζαν
εαν δε τινες των κατασχοντων τας ωνας μη διεγγυη
σωσιν εν τωι ωρισμενωι χρονωι επαναπραθησονται
⟨·⟩ντων αι ωναι κ[αι ε]αν τι αφευρεμα γενηται πραχθησονται
παραχρημα τοις δε βουλομενοις υπερβαλλειν μετα το τον
15 θαλλον δοθηναι εξεσται εν αυτωι τωι πρατηριωι ουκ ε
[λασ]σονος δε των [ε]πιδεκατων
[οι δ] εγλαβοντες τας ωνας ποιησονται τα αποπραματα
[με]τα του [οικονομου] και του βασιλικου γραμματεως
[και] οι παρα [τουτων] κατασχοντες εγγυους καταστησουσιν

Col. 4. τοις προγεγραμμενοις α ου λογισθησεται τοις τελωναις
εις τα δι αυτων κατασταθησομενα διεγγυηματα
οικονομηθησεται δε και τα τουτων συμβολα τον αυτον
τροπον αι δ αναφοραι μερισθησονται της μεν ζυτηρας
5 της χειμερινης εξαμηνου λογιζομενου του μηνος

εξ ημερων λ̄ε̄ της δε θερινης εξ ημερων κ̄ε̄
των δ αλλων ωνων εκ του κατα λογον των υπαρχουσων
μεχρι του αΓ εαν μη επι τινων αλλο τι λυσιτελεστερον
συνχωρηθηι επι της πρασεως τοις δ εγλαμβανουσιν
10 τας ωνας μεταδοθησεται υπο των προπραγματευ
ομενων τα γενηματα των προεληλυ⟨θυ⟩θυιων ημερων
μετα χειρογραφιας ορκου βασιλικου

ο δε διαλογισμος της εγληψεως συαταθησεται προς αυτους
κατα μηνα εκ των πιπτουντων επι την τραπεζαν

15 των δε προς γενηματα διοικουμενων ο μεν χειρισμος
εσται δια των παρα των βασιλικων γραμματεων συνχειρι
ουσιν δε και οι παρα των οικονομων και οι τελωναι
ο δε λογος της προσοδου γραφησεται προς τους τελωνας
προς τραπεζαν και τα διεγγυηματα ενε[χ]υρασθησεται
20 προς τα οφειληθησομενα προς τον χειρισμον των γενη
ματων τα δε συναχθησομενα διαγραφησετα[ι] εις το βασιλικον

Col. 5. ακολουθως τοις υπαρχουσι περι τουτων προσταγμασι
και χρηματισμοις

τοις δ αναπληρωσουσιν τας ωνας δοθησεται οψωνια
εανπερ εκπληρωσωσιν και καθεστακοτες τα διομολο
διεγγυηματα
5 γηθεντα του × Γ χ ο προσδιαγραψουσιν εκτος της
ε[γ]ληψεως οι δε παρα των τοπογραμματεων καθεστα
μενοι προς τε τουτοις και τοις αλλοις χειρισμοις κριθη
και
σονται υπο των βασιλικων γραμματεων εις χερα δε
ουθενι ουθεν δωσουσιν ει δε μη ου παραδεχθησεται
10 αυτοις τοις δ εγλαβουσι εξακολουθησει τα υποκειμενα
προστιμα

των δε καταβολων συμβολα λαμβανετωσαν παρα του
τραπεζιτου υπογραφας εχοντα παρα των επακολου
θουντων εαν δ α[λλ]ως οικονομωσιν ακυροι αυτοις εσονται
15 αι δοσεις

των δε προς αργυ[ρ]ιον ωνων προσδιαγραψουσιν αλαγην
ως της μνας ι = [C] και καταγωγιον ʃ και τιμην

σπυριδων και ταλλ ανηλωματα α ∫ ϲ ωστ ειναι ιβ ∫
και των προς χαλκον ισονομ[ον] ζυτηρας μεν χωρις της
20 υποκειμενης εις την επισκευην δραχμης α και εις το
καταγωγιον αλλας [   ]β   ωστ ειναι   γ

Col. θ. των δε λοιπων ωνων των πρ[ος χαλκον ισονομον]
χωρις των απο του χειρισμου [...............]
και εις τιμην σπυριδων και ταλλ ανηλ[ωματα Ⱶ ·]
εαν δε τινες των τελωνων πλειους ων[ας εγλαβωσι]
5 και εν τισιν μεν επιγενημα ποιωσιν εν [τισιν δ ελλι]
πωσιν αντιλογισθησεται τα επιγενημα[τα ....]
χωρις του εγκυκλιου οσοι αν ..... ι και αποι[.......]
μη προσδιεγγυησωσιν του οφειληματος του[..........]
αι ωναι επαναπραθησονται του ευρισκοντος κ[αι το οφει]
10 λημα και το αφευρεμα πραχθησονται τοις δ αν[απληρουσι]·
τας ωνας ου[θ]εις μεθεξει πλην των επι τη[.......]
συνκαταγραφησομενων εαν δε παρα ταυτα π[οιησωσιν]
ο τε μεταδους αποτεισει επιτιμον ⊃ κ και ο [......]
           θεων
λαβων ⊃ κ εαν δε τινες προς τας εγληψεις οφε[ιλωσιν]
15 η πραξις εσται εξ ενος και εκ παντων ατελη δ[......]
εως του αL εαν δε τινε[ς ατ]ελειαι διδω[ντ]αι υπο[......]
χωρις των υπαρχουσων το καθηκον τελος παραδε[χθησεται]
εκ των ανενηνεγμενων γενηματων εως του α[L]
εαν δε τις απο των υπαρχουσων αναληφθη πρ[ο]σαχθ[ησεται]
20 τα καθηκοντα τελη τηι εγληψει και αν[..........]
παραγενομενου η δυναμεις απ[οστ]ειλαντο[ς ....]
κρινηται επαναπω[λ]εισθαι τας ωνας η[..............]

Col. 7.   ]νεικος
                               ]μενα εν αυτοις
                               ]ωσονται
                               ]θησονται
5   ε]ληλυθοτος
                               υ]παρχουσαν
                               ] εν τοις μετα
                               ]ται εις τα
                               ]νες μη οφει
10   οι την ων]ην εγλαβοντες

```
                              ]ρες ησαν
                              ]γμενων
                              ] εν τηι τουτων
                          υπα]ρχουσιν εν τοις
   15                         ]κια κατα τους
                              ] εγλαβωσι
                              ] υπερ
                              ]
                              ]εντα
   10                         ]ται
```

Col. 8. εφ ημερας δ[εκα . . . . τ]ων τιμησεων [κατα το δια]
γραμμα ποι[ησον]ται καθ [ημε]ραν τας εκθεσε[ις εν τοις]
τελωνιοις [ομοιως] δε και [προς τ]ους αντιγρ[αφεας . . . . .]
[ο]υκ εμφανιζοντες του [ηγορ]ακοτος το ονομα και δια [των]
5 τραπεζιτων προς τηι τ[ρα]πεζηι επι τας δια του δια
γραμματος δηλουμενας [ημ]ερας δεκα και αει τηι δεκα[τηι]
ημεραι παραμενουσι εως της εσχατης ωρ[α]ς της ημερα[ς]
εαν δ υπερβολιον ενεστηκη[ι] εως του λυθ[ηνα]ι οι δε τρα[πε]
ζιται ανοισουσιν εμ μεν ταις [κ]αθ ημεραν εφ[η]μερισιν
10 επι της διαγραφης του τελου[ς οτ]ι εκκειται εις υπερβο[λιον]
εν δε τοις μηνιειοις το καθεν [των] επι τας δεκα ημερα[ς]
εκκειμενων εαν δ επι . εν[. . . μ]η εκτεθηι μηδε τ[ωι]
διοικητηι και τωι επιμελη[τηι] παραχρημ[α] ανενε[γ]
κωσιν πραχθησονται εκαστου [. . . .]ματος τ[ο . . . .]
15 μενον τελος πενταπλου[ν εαν δ] οι τελω[ναι κ]αι οι αυτ[ι]
[γρα]φεις μη ποιωσιν κ[αθως] προγεγραπται καταποσταλη
[σον]ται προς τον διο[ικ]ητ[ην με]τα φυλακης και τα ιδια
[αυτ]ων ανα[λ]ηφθη[σε]ται εις το βασιλικον ουτως γαρ τωι τε
[βασιλ]ει το δε[ον] εσται οι τε βουλομενοι κτησασθαι τι των καιως
20 [. . . . . ου] στερηθησονται του τοιουτου.

At Professor Lumbroso's suggestion I revised the text of this
papyrus in Notices et Extraits by a study of the original in September,
1894. Several corrections of the numerous inaccuracies found in the
Paris editors' text have already been published by Lumbroso, Revillout,
and Wilcken in various books or articles, and the last-named in August
1895 most generously placed at my disposal his unpublished copy of

the text made several years ago. Where I have adopted his readings in preference to my previous ones, I have recorded the fact in the notes. Most of the papyrus has been explained by Lumbroso in the eighteenth chapter of his admirable *Recherches*. I confine my notes to points on which we have new suggestions to make, or on which the Revenue Papyrus throws light.

[1.] 1. Cf. Rev. Pap. [57] 3 and note on [53] 18. Whether πωλουμεν be right or not, I think this papyrus was issued in the king's name.

το αL is a great puzzle. The universal practice of the Ptolemies, so far as we know, was to count the period between their accession and the beginning of the civil year, Thoth 1st, as their first year. Therefore if εις το αL coincides with εις δωδεκαμηνον και τας επαγομενας ημερας, not only is the first year of this sovereign a full year, but the papyrus seems to be written before the first year had begun. Revillout (R. E. vi. 154) has tried to solve the difficulty by supposing that the first year applies to the second Cleopatra, ἡ ἀδελφή, who on his theory ousted Euergetes II in the fortieth year of his reign, but decided not to begin the computation of her own reign before the next Thoth 1st. The difficulty however of supposing that the sovereign did not begin his or her reign at once is equally great whether the preceding sovereign was dead or whether he was only exiled, and with regard to the particular year suggested by Revillout there is the further difficulty that a Theban papyrus (A. E. F. pap. 19) and an inscription (Strack. Mitth. K. Deutsch. A. I. in Ath. 1894, p. 230) are dated in the forty-first year of Euergetes II. I am inclined therefore to doubt whether εις το αL really coincides with εις δωδεκαμηνον, especially as the starting-point of the tax is not, in accordance with the conjecture of the Paris editors, accepted by Revillout, απο Θωθ εω]ς Μεσορη, but probably απο μην]ος Μεσορη, cf. Rev. Pap. [57] 4; and I would suggest that by 'the first year' is meant only Mesore and the επαγομεναι ημεραι, the rest of the δωδεκαμηνον falling in the second year. It is not impossible that a reference to the second year is lost in the lacuna at the beginning of line 2. In any case there must have been an exceptional cause for Mesore being the starting-point, as Wilcken remarks; cf. note on Rev. Pap. l. c.

4. Possibly δικαιως, cf. [8] 19.

6. Perhaps πραγματευσεσθα]ι. νομους: cf. note on Rev. Pap. [21] 11. διαγραμματα: cf. notes on Rev. Pap. [39] 1 and [73] 1. διορθωμεθα: i. e.

διορθωματα, cf. Rev. Pap. [57] 1. From the way in which these classes are mentioned, it would seem that the papyrus is not included in any one of them, and if so, I should suggest it is a προγραμμα, cf. Rev. Pap. [37] 6. But in [8] 5 there seems to be a cross-reference to another passage in the papyrus as a διαγραμμα, though that would not show that the whole document was a διαγραμμα, for διαγραμματα are scattered up and down the νομος επι τηι ελαικηι, cf. Rev. Pap. 39. 1 note.

9. The meaning appears to be, as M. suggests, that the tax-farmers were to fill up the list of μετοχοι, not passing over any person who was liable (υπολογος) to be called upon to serve as τελωνης, cf. [5] 3 where οι αναπληρουντες receive a special οψωνιον, and note on Rev. Pap. [34] 4.

13. Cf. Rev. Pap. [34] 2, [56] 14-15, where the security has to be only one-twentieth greater.

14. In this papyrus we find the βασιλικος γραμματευς associated with the oeconomus, no longer the αντιγραφευς, as in the Rev. Pap., cf. [3] 18, [4] 16-17. The antigrapheus is not mentioned in L. P. 62, though αντιγραφεις are associated with the tax-farmers in [8] 15. Cf. [8] 3, where I conjecture αντιγραφεας, though it is not clear whether these are the same persons as those mentioned in [8] 15, and see note on Rev. Pap. [3] 2.

16. The Paris editors read πεπτω[κεν . . . . αλλων (sic), but there is nothing to justify πεπ or αλλων in the facsimile, so that if these letters ever existed here, they disappeared long ago. But αφ ης αν ημερας is required by παρομολογηθηι . . . εν ημεραις λ, cf. [2] 3, Rev. Pap. [34] 3 and [53] 6, and following [34] 4 I should suggest some phrase like τας δε καταγραφας ποιησονται των χρημα]τω[ν.

[2.] 5. Perhaps [εγγυ]ων.

6. μηνιειοις: cf. [8] 11.

7. I was unable to decipher the mutilated letters after την. Wilck. reads them εσ°, i. e. εσο[μενην], accepting the reading βεβαιωσ[ιν in the next line. The papyrus however seemed to me to have βεβαιωτ[.

The Paris editors read επ]ι των υποθηκων, but there is no trace of ι των in the facsimile.

9. ειληφοτων: cf. [3] 6. M. suggests των ουσιων for the lacuna.

10. Perhaps καταγραφας, cf. Rev. Pap. [34] 4.

11. απολιπωσι, cf. pap. Zois i, το απολειπον.

12. ωσιν I owe to Wilcken; the meaning is clearly that the sureties are to be men of substance able to make up any deficiency left by the tax-farmers.

13. Cf. [1] 9 and note on [5] 3.

14-16. Probably δωσουσι]ν, cf. [3] 6-7 εαν δε οι λαβοντες τα συμβολα μη [επαν]ενεγκωσιν επι την τραπεζαν. The conjectural restoration of 16 occurred to me since I had seen the original, and I do not know whether τραπεζαν suits the vestiges of letters visible at the end of the line which in the facsimile may be almost anything.

17. οικονομησηι: cf. [5] 14.

18. Probably κατα το προγραμμα or whatever the title of the papyrus was.

[3.] 9. ϛ[αι: Wilcken.

11. κατασχοντων: cf. Jos. A. J. xii. 4. 10 εἴκοσιν ἔτη καὶ δύο τὰ τῆς Συρίας τέλη . . . κατασχών.

14. Cf. Rev. Pap. [2] 1 note.

17. αποπραμα: cf. Rev. Pap. [18] 16.

[4.] 1. τοις προγεγραμμενοις: i.e. the oeconomus and basilicogrammateus, [3] 18; cf. [1] 14.

7. M. suggests καταλογον as one word.

8. The number of the year here might be δ, δ and α often resembling each other closely, but in the other cases it is certainly α.

15. προς γεινηματα was seen by Wilcken and Mahaffy to be two words, and opposed to των προς αργυριον ωνων and των προς χαλκον ισονομον in [5] 16-19. The απομοιρα was in the third century B.C. partly a προς γεινηματα ωνη, but subsequently became an ωνη προς χαλκον ισονομον, cf. note on Rev. Pap. [37] 19, and App. iii.

19. προς τραπεζαν implies, as M. suggests, that the receipts of the tax-farmers were to be credited to them in money, and that the securities would be held in trust pending the 'handling of the crops.' Cf. Rev. Pap. [34] 10 note.

21. διαγραφησεται: cf. note on Rev. Pap. [34] 14.

[5.] 3. As M. suggests, οι αναπληρουντες are those who offer to fill up the list of farmers or undertake to obtain τελωναι and εγγυοι. If they were successful, they were to receive a commission of 10 per cent., but they were not allowed to offer a person money if he would join in the ωνη (εις χερα ουθενι ουθεν δωσουσι). If they offered money, their recom-

mendation was rejected. This is more satisfactory than taking οι αναπληρουντες as equivalent to οι εγλαβοντες, meaning the tax-farmers who
fulfilled the terms of the contract. For in that case we should have to
suppose that all τελωναι might receive an οψωνιον besides the επιγειημα,
but cf. Rev. Pap. [12] 13, [31] 14, and [39] 14 notes. These passages
show that the payment of anything besides the επιγενημα was then quite
exceptional, and it is unlikely that the tax-farmers would obtain more
favourable terms in the second century B.C. than in the third. If M.'s
explanation is correct, the difficulty of obtaining tax-farmers and sureties
had become serious. Cf. note on Rev. Pap. [34] 4.

16. The premium on silver at this period was therefore $10\frac{8}{13}$ per cent.,
100 drachmae in silver being equivalent to $110\frac{8}{13}$ drachmae προς χαλκον,
cf. App. ii (5), where the rate of exchange is not very different, and
App. iii pp. 198–200 and 214–216.

[6.] 6. Wilcken suggests αυτοις. Cf. Rev. Pap. [17].

7. αν : Wilcken.

11. ουθεις : Mahaffy. At the end of the line Wilcken suggests επι
τη[ς πρασεως.

13. Perhaps [παρα]λαβων.

14. θεων in another hand seems to have no reference to the subject
of the papyrus.

15. There are here three regulations concerning exemptions from
taxation ; (1) ατελη δ (εστω or μενετω?) εως του αL, stating that the
existing ατελειαι would continue as before : (2) 16–18, stating that if any
new exemptions were granted υπο [του βα(σιλεως)?, an equivalent allowance would be made to the tax-farmers from the produce already
collected : (3) 19–20, stating that if any of the existing ατελειαι were
confiscated, the tax would be added to the sum which the tax-farmers
had contracted to pay. 20–22 are obscure, but apparently refer to the
tax being put up to auction again under certain circumstances.

[8.] 1. The Paris editors read δεκα [το] υπερβο[λιον τω]ν τιμησεων.
There is no trace of περβο in the facsimile, and there is not room for
υπερβολιον and των. Perhaps υ[περ τω]ν.

2. The subject of ποιησονται is probably the oeconomus and basilicogrammateus, cf. [1] 14 note, and Rev. Pap. [14] 4 note. Perhaps προς
τοις τελωνιοις, cf. line 5 προς τηι τραπεζηι, but in line 3 προς has the
accusative not dative, and the accusative is the natural construction.

5. The 'ten days mentioned in the διαγραμμα' may be a reference to the ten days in line 1 ; cf. note on [1] 6.

14. [ονο]ματος, i. e. 'item,' suggested by the Paris editors, hardly fills the lacuna. There is not room for [αδικη]ματος, cf. [3] 1.

19. If βασιλ]ει is correct, it is another argument against Revillout's theory that the 'first year' refers to Cleopatra, cf. [1] 1 note. καιως seems to be a mistake for δικαιως.

20. Possibly αγοραζοντων, cf. [1] 3.

APPENDIX II.

SOME NEW PETRIE PAPYRI.

1.

Σιμαριστου δ′	δια γραμματε[ω .]
/Φαρμουθι ιβ̄	᾿ΕΣ.θγ′ιβ′
Παχωνς κ̄ζ	᾿Δυξεβ′
Παυνι κ̄θ	᾿ΔΣμαβ′
5 Επειφ γ̄	χλθβ′
[. . . . . .]αλλα	᾿ΓΣκηγ′ιβ′
κ	᾿Ατοεβ′
Αμμων[. . .	.]ψ. γ′ιβ′

1. See note on [24] 9.

2. (xx).

[βασιλευοντος Πτολεμαιου] του Πτολεμαιου σωτηρ[ος]
[ετους . . εφ ιερεως . . . . . .] του Λαι̣στου . .
[Αλεξανδρου και θεων α]δελφων κανηφορου Αρσ[ινοης]
                                υ
[Φιλαδελφου . . . . μη]υ̣α Διο κδ δου . .[. . . . .]
         ]ς   φιλωνι⟩
5 [. . . . .]⟨. . . . . .[. . .⟩] Σωσιφανει απ[. . . . .]
[ομνυω . . . .]ς βασιλεα Πτολεμαιον κα[ι β]α[σι]
[λισσαν Αρσινοην θ]εους αδελφου⁵ τους τ[. . . . .]
[. . . . .]εις υπο του προς τηι αυ[. . . . .]
[. . . . . .μ]εριδος τα χωματικα πραγμα
10 [τα . . . . ομωμο]κα ουτε αυτος νοσφειουσθ̣αι [. . .]
                          ε
[. . . . .] παρευρεσι⟨ν⟩ ηιτινιουν εαν [. . .]
[. . . . . συ]ντελειν σοι αυθημερον η τηι [υστε]

$$\theta$$
[ραιαι . . . .]εν τωι λιμνιτηι γραψεσαι [. .]ν
[. . . . .]κα των πραγμα[τ]ων εις το βασ[ιλι]
15 [κον . . . .]ζεσθαι τωι βασιλει ορκ[. . . . .]
$$o$$
[. . . . . πραγμ]ατευμενους τον αυ[. . . . . . .]
$$\epsilon\iota \ . . .$$
[. . . . .] . . . μαιενου . as τωι ορ[κωι . . . .]

1. The formula shows that this papyrus cannot be older than the twenty-seventh year, cf. Rev. Pap. [1] 1 and Introd. pp. xix sqq.

2. After -του are two letters like ηι.

3. The number of letters which may be lost at the end of the line is not quite certain. The writing is extremely faint throughout.

6. Cf. Wilck. Akt. xi, and P. P. xlvi (*b*). There is not much doubt that this papyrus is a written βασιλικος ορκος; see lines 15, 17, and cf. [27] 6 note.

10. Apparently νοσφιεισθαι is intended. Cf. [27] 11.

13. εν τωι λιμνιτηι: perhaps the Fayoum, cf. [31] 12, note and [71] 11 note. The subject of the papyrus is connected with the building of the dykes for reclaiming land from the lake, cf. Cleon's correspondence in P. P.

3.

Ηρακλειδης . . . . . ει χαιρειν
μετρησαι τοις υπογεγραμμενοις γεωργοις
δια των κωμαρχων και κωμογραμματεων
δανειον εις τον σπορον του κροτωνος
5 εν τωι κϛL αμα τοις εκφοριοις κροτωνος
εκ του κδL εις δε τουτο επι . . . . . .
πληθος και συμβολον παρασχ . . . προς . . .
        ερρωσο L κε Αθυρ α (or λ)
εις Βερενικιδα δια κωμαρχων κροτωνος . . . . . παρα
10 Φρ . εσθεουτος και των αλλων κροτωνος . . . .
εφ . . . . καρπωνθιου κροτωνος . . . .

1. The papyrus was covered with a thick coating of plaster and

the ink is extremely faint; the ends of the lines are for the most part illegible. Cf. the regulation concerning the distribution of seed in [43] 3 note.

7. Perhaps παρασχες προς εμε.

8. The twenty-fifth year belongs to Philadelphus or Euergetes.

4. (Ε″).

```
      [. . . . . . . . . . . . . . . . . . . φυλ]ακιτων
      [. . . . . . . . . . . . . επισ]τατου φυλακιτων
      [. . . . .]του Χοιαχ και Τυβι του ηL
      [ως του] μηνος χα τ ┼ χ και ωστε Αρ . . . ιωι
    5 [φυλα]κιτηι της Πολεμωνος μεριδος ως του μηνος π
      [χα ]ρξ και ωστε Αμ . . . . . ιωι της Θεμιστου
      [ως του μη]νος υ χα ρ και ωστε Βιωνι της Ηρακλειδου
      [μεριδος] ως του μηνος μ χαλ π και ωστε
      [. . . . . . .]ι της μικρας λιμνης ως του μηνος λ̄ χα ξ
   10 [. . . . . .] και ωστε εφοδοις τοις ακολουθουσι τωι
      [. . . . . . . .] τουτων φ[υλ]ακιτων ουσι λ̄ οψωνιον
      [. . . . . . .] εκαστον[. . .] χα ξ και ωστε τοις
      [. . . . . . . . . . . . . . . . .] μηνος ουσι κ̄ε̄ ιη
      [. . . . . . . . . . . . . . . . .] και ωστε τοις ακολου
      [θουσι . . . . . . . . . . . . .] και ωστε τοις ακολου
   15 [θουσι. . . . . . . . . . . . . . .] αυτου τκ και
      [. . . . . . . . . . . . . . . . . . . . . . . .] τοις Αγηνορι
```

3. The eighth year may belong to either the third, fourth or fifth Ptolemy.

4. Judging by the comparatively low numbers of the drachmae, they are probably on the silver standard but προς χαλκον, cf. Rev. Pap. [40] and App. iii pp. 196–8. If μεριδος after Θεμιστου is understood, not written out, about five or six letters are lost at the beginning of lines 3–10. ωστε: cf. Rev. Pap. [60] 21 note.

5. ως του μηνος: cf. Rev. Pap. [12] 15.

9. λιμνης: M. Cf. P. P. xiii (5) 3, where a μικρα λιμνη is mentioned.

10. εφοδοις: cf. Rev. Pap. [10] 1 note. Here they are probably the inspectors of the dykes.

5.

(*a*) Col. 1.   Col. 2.

```
              ]ωπ
              ]'Ανοβ                    μϛ[
              ]ιγβ′                        /με ωιβίβ′[
              !Σκβίβ′                   και προς χαλκον κδ [α]ν η/ Σδ
   5          ]βL                        ο        ανα η        φξ
              )/ΣκγLγ′ίβ′          5 λε       ανα [ζ/]      Σξβϛ
                                         κγ       ανα ε       ρλα
              ]  Ση                       /με ρνβ        ⊢'Αρνζϛ
              ]  Σν                       αι αργυριου 'Αμγϛ
   [γινεται   ]υνη
10 [λδLγ′    ]αν ϛ Σθ            γινεται με 'Αμδίβ′ ϗα'Ατκθϛ
   [κϛβ′     ]     ρξ            10 συν δε τοις προς αργυριον ϗα
                                         'Ανοζϛ=
   [γινεται αργ]υριου τλβϛ—        και οινου περιειναι φϥϛγ′
```

(*b*)

```
   μηί[        ανα            . . .
   λη[         ανα            . . .
   νϛβ′[       ανα            . . .
   ρκγϛ′[      ανα            . . .
5  ϛ           [α]να ϛ        λϛ
   γινετ ̄αι    με] τπεϛ′      'Γυκθc
   αι αργυ[ριου]              'Γϥα—c
                ωι
   γινετ[αι με] 'ΔψπεLδ′      ϗϛ 'Ετξδϛ—
   συ[ν] δε [τοις] προς αργυριον  ϗιδ 'ΑΤβϛ—
10 [και περιειναι] οινου     ψλβδ′
   ]τοις Αθιασυλου            υμβγ′
   ] ρλα                      καLδ′
```

(*c*)

```
   [   . . ]      ανα    ι     ν[. .
   [ρπϛLίβ′μ′δ′]  ανα    η     'Ανϥβϛ=
   [ιθLίβ′    ]   ανα    θ     ροϛ
```

```
        [ι        ]    ανα    ια    ρι
  5     [ιθ       ]    ανα    θϛ    ρπϛ
        [ιϛ       ]    ανα    θ=    ρμθ=
        [λβ.      ]    ανα    ϛ—c   τλϛ[.
        [α        ]    ανα    ϛϛ    ϛϛ
        [ιL       ]    ανα    ϛ     ογϛ
  10    [β′       ]    ανα    η—c   εϛ
        [ϛγ′      ]    ανα    ε     λαϛ—
        [ιη       ]    ανα    ϛ=    ρλε=
        [ε        ]    ανα    ϛ     λ
        [/ με . . . . . ]′Γψϲα—c
  15    [αι αργυριου  ]′Γτqθϛ—c
        [γινεται      ]με  φοδβ′  'Δυξβϛ
```

(d)

```
      ———————
      και ων τριτη[
            /  'Β[
      κεραμου ροεL
      εψηματος ιθγ′
  5   αφ ων πεπρα[ται
      προς αργυριον με [
      ιγγ′        ανα      ι      ρλγ=
      δ          [ανα]     θ      λϛ
      υιηLγ′ιβ′  [ανα]     η      'Γτνα=
  10  κδL        [ανα]     ϛ=     ροθϛ
      λδ         [ανα[     ϛ      Σλη
      ιϛ         [ανα]     ϛϛ—c   ριδϛ—c
```

(a). 1. These fragments which all belong to a papyrus of the third century B.C., are probably accounts of an oeconomus or antigrapheus. They relate to metretae of wine received as taxes and sold, cf. [34] 10 note, payment being made in copper or silver. They are for the most part in three columns, the first containing the number of the metretae, the second the rate at which the metretae were sold, the third the total amounts. The sums are added up at the bottom of each list, and where the payments had been made in copper, the sum is converted into the equivalent amount of silver.

Dismissing for the moment col. 1 which is too fragmentary for any conclusion to be drawn from it alone, I proceed to col. 2 about which there is no doubt. The account in lines 3–8 is as follows—

24 metretae	at	8 dr. 3 obols (προς χαλκου)	204 drachmae
70 „	„	8 dr.	560 „
35 „	,,	7 dr. 3 obols	262 dr. 3 obols.
23 „	„	5 dr.	131 dr.
152 metretae			1157 dr. 3 obols
which are in silver			1043 dr. 3 obols.

It will be noticed that in line 6 the multiplication is incorrect, since the number of drachmae should be 115, but the addition is correct. 1157 dr. 3 obols in copper were therefore equivalent to 1043 dr. 3 obols in silver. On this use of αι meaning 'which are equivalent to' cf. Leipzig pap. 8 F 32, and on the importance of this for the coinage question see App. iii. The average price of these metretae was a little under 7 silver drachmae each, cf. [31] 4 note. The average in line 9, $1044\frac{1}{12}$ metretae for 7328 dr. 3 obols, is a little over 7 dr. for each metretes. In lines 5, 6, &c. L means $\frac{1}{2}$.

(*b*) is a similar list of metretae sold προς χαλκου, the total in lines 6–7 being $385\frac{1}{3}$ metretae for 3428 dr. $\frac{1}{2}$ obol, which is in silver 3091 dr. $1\frac{1}{2}$ obols. The grand total in line 8 is $4785\frac{3}{4}$ (corrected to 4810) metretae for 41964 dr. 4 obols, i. e. about 8 dr. 4 obols each.

(*c*) is a similar list; a number of metretae are sold for 3791 dr. $1\frac{1}{2}$ obols, which is in silver 3399 dr. $4\frac{1}{2}$ obols. Total $574\frac{3}{4}$ metretae for 4462 dr. 3 obols, i. e. a little over $7\frac{3}{4}$ drachmae each.

In (*d*) the metretae are sold προς αργυριον, the average being about 8 drachmae, since far the greatest number is sold at that price.

To return to (*a*), in col. 1 lines 10 and 11 obviously refer to metretae sold for 6 drachmae each, the totals being 209 and 160 drachmae, and we should expect line 12 to be the sum of these two lines, cf. lines 7–9. But in place of 369 drachmae, we have 332 dr. 4 obols. Probably the prices in 10 and 11 were προς χαλκου, and the writer has given the equivalent amount in silver without writing down the amount προς χαλκου. The proportion between silver and copper is then very nearly the same as in (*c*).

APPENDIX III.

THE SILVER AND COPPER COINAGE OF THE PTOLEMIES.

§ 1. *Introduction.*

I PROPOSE in this Appendix to discuss the evidence available for the solution of three questions; (1) what was the normal ratio of exchange between a_silver_and a copper drachma; (2) under what circumstances was copper at a discount, and what was the discount; (3) what was the ratio of weight between a silver coin and an equivalent amount of copper coins, or what was the ratio between silver and copper regarded as coins, and was this the same as the ratio between silver and copper regarded as metals? The generally accepted authority for the monetary standards and ratios of value in Ptolemaic coinage is M. Eugène Revillout, whose famous *Lettres à M. Lenormant* in the Rev. Égypt. for 1882-3 have been thought to offer a satisfactory solution of the difficult problems. The evidence on which he there relied consisted partly of demotic papyri, partly of coins. Since then however much new evidence has come to light. In 1883 appeared Mr. Poole's monumental Catalogue of the Ptolemaic coins in the British Museum, in which we have a classification of the copper coins by a numismatist of the first rank. The discovery of the Petrie papyri and now of the Revenue Papyrus has revolutionized our knowledge of the earlier Ptolemaic period. Lastly Prof. Wilcken has collected much valuable information connected with the coinage in his forthcoming Corpus Ostracorum, information which he has most generously placed at my disposal. To these, I am told, will shortly be added M. Revillout's long promised *Mélanges sur la métrologie et l'économie politique*, &c. Whether he has changed his views in any respects I do not know, though from the fact that he has just republished his *Lettres à*

M. Lenormant with only a few unimportant alterations, I conjecture
that he has not. The uncertainty is perhaps regrettable, for the contention of this essay is that of the conclusions first enunciated by
M. Revillout in the Revue Égyptologique, re-asserted in his *Papyrus
Bilingue du temps de Philopator* (Proc. Soc. Bibl. Arch. 1891–2), and
now once more asserted in his re-issue of the Lettres, the greater part
is altogether invalid, and the remainder requires in several cases
much modification. Side by side with my criticism of M. Revillout's
theory, I propose to develop my own theory on the whole problem,
so far as the available evidence can as yet carry us. And here let
me say that however much I may have occasion to disagree with
M. Revillout, no one recognizes more fully than myself that it was
his elucidation of the signs for the fractions of the drachma in Greek
papyri, and the evidence from demotic papyri brought by him to
bear upon the question, which have made any satisfactory solution
possible.

The history of Ptolemaic coinage has been divided by M. Revillout
into three periods; (1) the period of the silver standard from Soter
to Euergetes; (2) the period of transition, when copper first comes
into general use in the reigns of Philopator and Epiphanes; (3) the
period of the copper standard from Philometor onwards. It will be
convenient to follow this classification, and for the present I pass
over the evidence of the copper coins, and confine myself to the
documentary evidence, which, supplemented by the evidence of the
silver coins, must be the first guide towards forming a satisfactory theory
concerning the copper coinage, although the ultimate solution of the
chief problems connected with the standard and ratio must be looked
for more from the numismatist than from the scholar.

§ 2. *Documentary Evidence for the period of the Silver Standard.*

First then as to the copper coinage of the three earliest Ptolemies,
what was a copper drachma, and in what relation did it stand to the
silver drachma? Here we are met at the outset by M. Revillout,
who arguing from the silence of the demotic papyri on the subject
of copper maintains that copper was only money of account, used
merely for paying the fractions of the silver drachma, and that silver

was the practically universal coinage. But how little reliance can be placed on the silence of the demotic documents was shown both by the Petrie papyri, which contain mentions of comparatively large sums paid in copper drachmae as far back as the thirty-first year of Philadelphus, and by the Revenue Papyrus, which proves that in the twenty-seventh year of the same king all the accounts of one of the principal revenues in the country, the oil monopoly, were kept in copper, the contractors paying the government in copper, [60] 13–15, and receiving payments in copper, [40] 9–11 note.

Copper therefore was largely used in Philadelphus' time not merely in private transactions, but even in official payments to the government. In what relation did it stand to silver? The Rev. Pap. shows that in the case of the oil monopoly copper was accepted by the government from the tax-farmers at its full value. This is the only possible interpretation of [60] 13–15 πωλουμεν την ωνην προς χαλκον και ληψομεθα εις τον στατηρα οβολους κδ. From the context either the stater or the obols must be copper coins, cf. [76] 4. The silver stater is by far the commonest silver coin of the Ptolemaic period, and there is no evidence, documentary or numismatic, that there were copper staters. The phrase in the pap. C of Leyden, χαλκους στατηρειηους, which has been sometimes thought to prove the existence of copper staters, is, as M. Revillout has excellently pointed out, quite different from χαλκου στατηρας, and means 'copper coins representing staters.' Therefore in [60] 13 as the staters cannot be copper, and gold staters were worth 20 silver drachmae, which is clearly unsuitable, they must be silver and the obols must be copper. The formula by which the equality between silver and copper is here expressed, not '6 obols = 1 drachma,' or '48 chalci = 1 drachma,' or anything else, but '24 obols = 1 stater,' is extremely important, because it shows that just as the typical unit of silver both here and in [76] 4 is the stater or tetradrachm, by far the commonest coin, so the typical unit of copper in both cases is the obol, which therefore was probably also a common coin. The far-reaching consequences of this formula will appear when I come to discuss the demotic papyri of the next period.

In the case of certain taxes then copper obols were accepted in payment of large sums without discount. But there is no mention in the Rev. Pap. of the 'copper drachmae' which are found in con-

temporary documents from the Petrie collection. Wherever payments
in copper are mentioned in the Rev. Pap., the payments are uniformly
προς χαλκον, i.e. in drachmae on the silver standard paid in copper,
about which phrase there is no difficulty; but the phrase χαλκου δραχμαι
does not appear. With regard to the instances of the last phrase in
the Petrie papyri, is the theory provisionally proposed by Mr. Mahaffy
to be accepted, that they are 'copper drachmae' in the same sense
as the copper drachmae of the next century which, whatever may
be their precise ratio of exchange, were worth but a small fraction of
a silver drachma?

There are nine instances of copper drachmae among papyri which,
whether dated or not, can safely be attributed to the period before
the great change from a silver to a copper standard took place. These
are (1) part II. xiii (17), dated the thirty-first year of Philadelphus;
(2) xxvi (7), dated the thirty-third year of Philadelphus, where in line 7
Wilcken reads the original τα χαλκου [δρ]ραχμ[ων καθ]ηκοντα; (3) xxvi
(6), dated the eighth year of Euergetes, which has χαλκ[ου ⊢.]; (4)
xxvi (4), dated the eighth year of Euergetes, where in line 8 I read
χαλκου ⊢ λ; (5) xliv, written in the reign of Euergetes; (6) xiv (1 c); (7)
xxviii; (8) xxxix (d); (9) xxiv (b)[1]. Of these (2), (3), (4), (8), and (9)
are too fragmentary to prove anything. With regard to the rest the
most noticeable fact is that nowhere among them are found the enormous
sums in copper drachmae which are found in the next century, when
e g. the price of an ox is 21,000 drachme (L. P. 58, ll. 4–5); and the
house of Nephoris and the twins is valued at 120 talents of copper
(L. P. 22, ll. 18–19).   In (1) 231½ dr. of copper are paid together
with 617½ dr. of silver; while in (5) the rent of a farm is 65 dr. of
copper, apparently for a year. These facts alone would make us suspect that χαλκου δραχμαι at this period are equivalent to the drachmae
in payments προς χαλκου of the Rev. Pap. For though it may seem
at first sight that χαλκου δραχμαι ought to mean in the third century B. C.
what they mean in the second, to a Greek of the third century B. C. the
drachma was essentially a silver coin, and in reality there is much
less difficulty in speaking of a drachma of copper as a silver drachma's
worth in copper than in using it for a 'copper drachma.' The question

---

[1] In P. P. part I, xxiii the large numbers refer not to copper drachmae, but to ναυβια.

is however definitely settled by (6), where in lines 3–5 the correct reading

is πλινθουλκοι οι εξειληφοτες ελκυσαι [πλινθου] $\overset{\beta}{M}$ ωστε εις την συντελουμενην

εν Πτολεμαιδι βασι[λικην] καταλυσιν, εκαστης $\overset{a}{M}$ ├ ι, χαλκου ├ κ. Mr.
Mahaffy, reading the last letter χ, was led to suggest that in this passage
600 copper drachmae were equivalent to 10 silver. But the κ is certain,
and therefore the price for dragging 20,000 bricks (including the value
of the bricks themselves, cf. 1 *b*) was 10 dr. χαλκου for each 10,000.
Now in xii (4) the price of 10,000 bricks is 12 dr., which, as the metal
is not stated, we should expect to be silver drachmae, and in xiv (1 *b*)
the price of 10,000 bricks is 15 dr., χαλκου being erased. The difference
in the prices depends, as Mr. Petrie suggests, on the distance which
they have to be carried. But it is absolutely impossible that the price
of bricks could ever have been 10 copper drachmae per 10,000, if these
copper drachmae are the copper drachmae of the next century; and if
any doubt can still rest on the identity of χαλκου δραχμαι at this period
with payments προς χαλκον, it is removed by (7). That papyrus contains
a long list of names with sums of money opposite to them; that these
sums are copper drachmae is proved by the totals χα(λκου) which occur
e.g. in [1] 2, and the payments are clearly concerned with oil, which is
probably sesame oil since cici is only specified in a few instances.
The whole process of the manufacture and sale of oil is known from
part C of the Rev. Pap., and there can be little doubt as to the correctness of Mr. Mahaffy's suggestion in P. P. App. p. 5, that this papyrus
is a list of ελαιοκαπηλοι for the Fayoum together with the sums paid
by them to the contractors, cf. [47] and [48]. Mr. Mahaffy remarked
that all the sums were multiples of 7, but he might have gone a
step further, for they are nearly all multiples of 42. If Mr. Mahaffy's
explanation of this papyrus is correct, the meaning of this number in
the light of the Revenue Papyrus is clear. The retail price of a metretes
of sesame oil and cici was προς χαλκον 48 dr., [40], 9, therefore the
ελαιοκαπηλοι must have received the oil from the contractors at a re-
duction, cf. [48] 13. And, though the retail price may of course have
altered considerably between the date of the Rev. Pap. and that of
the P. P. xxix, the correspondence between the number which
would be expected and the number which is found is strong enough

to make it extremely probable that the 42 drachmae χαλκου are the price of a metretes paid to the contractors by the καπηλοι, and that 7 drachmae, of which the remaining numbers are multiples, was the price of 2 choes. In any case it is hardly possible to suppose that the 42 drachmae χαλκου are calculated on a standard different from the 48 drachmae paid προς χαλκου.

To sum up the results reached so far, while M. Revillout's contention that in the reigns of the first three Ptolemies there was only one standard has been vindicated from objections which might be brought from the Petrie papyri, his theory that copper was at this time merely money of account, used for the fractions of the drachma, and that as late as the time of Philopator all the taxes were paid in silver (*Pap. Biling.* Proc. Soc. Bibl. Arch. Jan. 1892, p. 128), has been shown to be erroneous. As far back as the Greek papyri carry us, we find large payments being made in copper at its full value, even in payments to the government. Moreover the excessive rarity of all Ptolemaic silver coins of a smaller denomination than the tetradrachm shows that payments of sums less than 4 drachmae must habitually have been made in copper. In order to obtain the ratio between silver and copper at par, it only remains to discover the normal weight of the obol. But as on this point M. Revillout and I are not agreed, I postpone the question for the present, and pass to the consideration of the second question—under what circumstances was copper at a discount, and what was the normal rate of the discount at this period?

The all-important authority for this would have been [76] 4–5, but the passage is mutilated and the decisive number is lost. Nevertheless several conclusions may be drawn from that passage. First the regulation concerns all banks throughout the country, therefore the rate of discount on the copper in question was the same everywhere. Secondly, as in [60] 13, the stater and the obol are used as the typical silver and copper coins. Thirdly, this copper which was at a discount must have been paid into the banks either as payment of a tax προς χαλκου, or of a tax which ought to have been paid in silver. But as the copper paid into the banks by the contractors for the oil monopoly was accepted by the government from them at par, [60] 13–15, it is very unlikely that, when the government came to reckon with the contractors for the banks, the bankers had to pay on the copper a discount which the contractors for the oil monopoly had escaped. Moreover the analogy of the next century, when copper was accepted at par (χαλκος ισονομος) in the case of certain taxes and at a discount as payment of taxes which ought to have been paid in silver (χαλκος ου αλλαγη), makes it practically certain that even in the time of Philadelphus copper was accepted at a discount by the banks on behalf of the government in payment of taxes which ought to have been paid in silver.

What has been lost through the mutilation of [76] 4, can however to some extent be recovered from other sources. In App. ii. no. 5 there are three examples of the conversion of sums paid προς χαλκον into silver drachmae. In (a) [2] 7-8 1157½ dr. in copper are equivalent to 1043½ in silver, in (b) 6-7 3429 dr. ½ obol in copper to 3091 dr. 1½ ob. in silver, and in (c) 14-15 3791 dr. 1¼ obols in copper to 3399 dr. 4½ ob. in silver. The discount on copper is in the first two cases approximately 10⅛ per cent., in the third 9¾ per cent. It is noticeable that in the case of these sums which refer to wine, probably received by the oeconomus as payment of the απομοιρα and sold by him in the open market, cf. [33] 5, [34] 10, the rate of discount varies slightly, so that the official rate for the banks did not altogether control the rate of exchange in commercial transactions, although it is not likely that there was ever a considerable difference between the official and the private rate of discount.

Besides this papyrus there is an instance of the rate of discount in ostracon 331 of Prof. Wilcken's Corpus, which records the payment of χα(λκου) εις κϛν π, i. e. '80 drachmae of copper at the rate of 26¼ obols.' The ostracon is dated in the twenty-second year of a Ptolemy who for palaeographical reasons must be one of the earlier kings, and as the drachmae in question must from the smallness of their number be calculated on the silver not on the copper standard, it is far more likely that the ostracon belongs to the reign of Euergetes than to that of Epiphanes, when copper drachmae usually, perhaps universally, meant copper drachmae on the copper standard. The meaning of the 26¼ obols was in the light of [60] 13 and [76] 4 at once obvious to Mr. Mahaffy and myself. This copper 'at the rate of 26¼ obols' means copper obols of which 26¼ would be counted as the equivalent of a stater, as opposed to the 24 copper obols of the Rev. Pap. accepted at par. This explanation is completely corroborated by a hitherto unexplained passage in Pap. Zois I line 33, in which χα εις κϛν (or possibly c, i. e. ½ obol) is prefixed to the sum which is elsewhere in the papyrus called χαλκος ου αλλαγη, and these two passages confirm the view expressed above, that the obol is the typical copper coin just as the stater is the typical silver coin. According to the ostracon therefore 26¼ obols in copper are equivalent to a stater or 24 obols in silver, and the rate of discount is 11⅜ per cent., a little higher than the rates found in App. ii no. 5.

Ostr. 329, which belongs to the same reign as Ostr. 331, mentions προς αργυρι(ο)ν εξηκοντα sc. drachmae. These must be different from 60 dr. αργυριον, and probably χαλκου is to be supplied, since χαλκος προς αργυριον occurs in the next century, and, as I shall show, means copper accepted at par.

To sum up the slender evidence available for the rate of discount at this period, the most remarkable point is the excessive smallness of the premium on silver. For it is possible that from the 10 per cent., which seems to have been the normal rate, something ought to be subtracted for the carriage and other expenses of the heavier metal, cf. L. P. 62 [5] 17, so that the real rate of discount may have been even less than 10 per cent. In any case it is probable that in many private transactions copper passed at its full value, and there is no evidence from the papyri that copper was in the time of Philadelphus and Euergetes a token coinage, nor, as I shall show, is there any from the coins. The reign of Soter, of whose copper coinage there is no literary and hardly any numismatic evidence, will be discussed later.

§ 3. *Documentary Evidence for the period of Transition.*

The demotic papyri of this period show, according to M. Revillout, that Philopator was the first Ptolemy who introduced the copper standard of 120 : 1, by which 24 copper 'argenteus-outens' or, to give the demotic names of the coins their Greek equivalents which have been perfectly established by M. Revillout, 480 copper drachmae, were equal to $\frac{2}{10}$ of a silver argenteus-outen, or 4 silver drachmae. Silver, he thinks however, still remained in Philopator's reign the principal standard (*Pap. Biling.* l. c. Dec. 1891, p. 80) for all Egypt, and in the next reign for the Thebaid, so long as it was governed by the insurgent kings, the discovery of whom is one of M. Revillout's most valuable contributions to Ptolemaic

history. But for the rest of Egypt at the beginning of Epiphanes'
reign, and for the Thebaid when it was reconquered at the end of his
reign, the copper standard implying payment in copper became universal in private transactions and appears even in payments to the
government.

Before discussing the demotic papyri of this period, I will consider
the Greek. Two alone can be certainly assigned to the reign of Philopator, P. P. xlvii (see Wilck. G. G. A., Jan. 1895) in which the drachmae
are silver, and the bilingual papyrus in the British Museum commented
on (l. c.) at great length by M. Revillout. M. Revillout claims that the
Greek docket of this papyrus confirms his previous theory about the
standard at this period, and in order to explain certain 'anomalies' in
it builds up what is certainly a most elaborate and ingenious theory.
Unfortunately, in all the points essential for the question of the coinage,
M. Revillout has misread the papyrus, of which the correct transcription
with an autotype is given by the Palaeographical Society, series ii, 143.
The papyrus has not οκτω διοβολους, i.e. 8 diobols, but οκτω δυοβολους
i. e. 8 (drachmae) 2 obols, the sign for drachma being omitted as so often
happens on the ostraca ; not χαλκ(ου) η α(λλαγης) τεσσαρας οβολους, but
χαλκιαιαν τεσσαρας οβολον i.e. 'for χαλκιαια 4 drachmae 1 obol.' If it
is worth while to hazard conjectures about an unknown word like χαλκιαιαν, possibly it refers to the discount on copper, though on what sum
is not clear, since the sum for χαλκιαια is half the 8 dr. 2 obols, which
was the tax of $\frac{1}{10}$ levied on the sale of the farm in question. But in the
absence of any parallel passage it is useless to found an argument upon it.

Thirdly, there is P. P. xxxii (1), dated in the eighth year of a Ptolemy
who on palaeographical grounds was almost certainly neither Philadelphus nor Euergetes, and who, as there is no reason for assigning any
papyrus in the Petrie collection to the reign of Philometor, was therefore
Philopator or Epiphanes, with a slight balance of probability, palaeo-
graphically, for Epiphanes. The question is of some importance since
the copper drachmae mentioned in the papyrus are unquestionably on
the copper standard, but cannot be decided unless it should appear that
the copper drachmae on the copper standard were not instituted before
Epiphanes' reign. Fourthly, there is P. P. xxvii. 5, undated, but written
in a very peculiar hand quite different from the ordinary hands of the
third century. The papyrus mentions enormous sums in χαλκος ισο-

νομος and χαλκος ου αλλαγη which are unquestionably copper drachmae on the copper standard, and it is therefore on every ground to be assigned to the end of the third century or the beginning of the second. Fifth, and most important of all, is P. P. xlvi, dated the second and fourth years of Epiphanes, where is found the mention of 2 talents and of 1 talent 516⅓ dr. in χαλκος προς α(ργυριον), for so Prof. Wilcken rightly explains the abbreviation comparing the known use of χαλκος προς αργυριον elsewhere. It is quite certain that these sums were calculated on the copper standard ; and this will be a convenient place for considering the meaning of the three difficult phrases χαλκος ισονομος, ου αλλαγη and προς αργυριον. The fourth technical term, χαλκος εις κϛν, has already been explained.

It is to Prof. Lumbroso that the credit of elucidating the first two terms is due, see Rec. pp. 43–6. He there suggests that the distinction between them is purely financial and has nothing to do with two kinds of coinage. χαλκος ισονομος is copper paid in the case of taxes in which payment was required in copper and therefore no discount was charged, while χαλκος ου αλλαγη, copper on which there was a discount, is copper paid in the case of taxes which ought to have been paid in silver. This perfectly explains the passage in L. P. 62 [5] 16–21, and is confirmed by the interchange of χαλκος ου αλλαγη with χαλκος εις κϛν, since the one explanation suits both terms. M. Revillout however, when he was issuing his first edition of the *Lettres*, was not content with this view (see Rev. ég. iii. 117). He there suggests that χαλκος ισονομος is the new copper coinage of Philopator and Epiphanes at the ratio of 120 : 1, while χαλκος ου αλλαγη was the pre-existing copper of Philadelphus and Euergetes, which as it was not on a ratio of 120 : 1 was at a discount. That I am not misrepresenting M. Revillout's meaning is shown by the fact that this view of χαλκος ισονομος as a coin is mentioned as his by Mr. Head in his *Historia Nummorum*, p. 713 note, and by Mr. Mahaffy in P. P. part ii. Introd. p. 12. This explanation suits excellently, and indeed would, if correct, be a strong argument for the position which M. Revillout there and elsewhere, as in *Pap. Biling.* l. c. Dec. 1891, p. 96, takes up, that a drachma χαλκου ισονομου, or copper drachma weighing the same as a silver drachma of which it was worth $\frac{1}{120}$, was the invention of Philopator ; but it is quite incompatible with the position which he adopts in his discussion of the weights of the copper

coins, when he speaks of 'la proportion préexistante' of 120 to 1 set up
by Philopator, and makes the identity of weight and value between the
obol on the silver standard and the 20 drachmae on the copper standard
the whole basis of his system. The confusion is made worse by the fact
that in his explanation of ισονομος in *Pap. Biling.* l.c. Jan. 1892 he
returned to the view expressed by Prof. Lumbroso and yet speaks of
the 'nouvelle isonomie' in the time of Philopator. The fact is that
M. Revillout has tried to stand alternately upon two contradictory pro-
positions. Either copper at 120 : 1 was instituted by Philopator, or it
was not. If it was (as M. Revillout says in Rev. ég. iii. 117 and *Pap.
Biling.* l. c. p. 96), and the previously existing obols of Philadelphus did
not weigh the same as the new 20 drachmae pieces of Philopator, then
M. Revillout has successfully demolished his own theory of the weights
and the identity of the obol with the 20 drachma piece, which is the basis
of his theory of 120 to 1 as the ratio between both the value of a silver
and a copper drachma, and the weight of 120 copper drachmae and
one silver drachma. On the other hand if M. Revillout elects to stand
by his weights, he must, to be consistent, renounce his first explanation
of ισονομος as having anything to do with coins, and cease therefore
to speak of 'cuivre isonome' as if it were a special coinage at all.
Which horn of the dilemma M. Revillout is prepared to choose I do not
know, for in his recent re-issue of the *Lettres* he speaks of ισονομος as
he spoke of it in the first edition of the *Lettres* when, to judge by his
article which appeared contemporaneously in the Rev. ég., he believed
his own explanation of that term. But as that explanation was fatal to
his theory of the coinage and is on his own showing contradicted by
the coins, I shall assume that he now adopts Prof. Lumbroso's explanation which is less disastrous to him, and for the present content myself
with pointing out that the only support from the papyri which might be
given to his theory that the copper drachma and silver drachma after
Philopator's time weighed the same, must be withdrawn. How far the
theory will stand without this support will be discussed later.

It is noticeable that ισονομος and ου αλλαγη have not yet been
found with drachmae on the silver standard, while χαλκος εις κϛν and
perhaps χαλκος προς αργυριον are found applied to copper drachmae on
both standards. Just as χαλκος εις κϛν seems to be the forerunner of
χαλκος ου αλλαγη, which usually, though not always, as the papyrus of

Zois shows, superseded it, so χαλκος προς αργυριον seems to be the fore-runner of χαλκος ισονομος, which after the adoption of the copper standard became the commoner term. First a term is required in the period of the silver standard to be contrasted with χαλκος εις κϛν and to mean copper which was accepted at par. Secondly the literal meaning of χαλκος προς αργυριον, 'copper against silver' (cf. [60] 13 πωλουμεν προς χαλκου), suits the view that it is identical with χαλκος ισονομος, while it is very difficult to see what third class of copper could exist in addition to copper at par and copper at a discount (cf. L. P. [5] 16–21). My explanation is somewhat confirmed by a comparison of P. P. xlvi with a second century B. C. ostracon, cf. note on [37] 19. In the papyrus a surety has to pay 1 talent 516⅓ dr. χαλκου προς αργυριον on behalf of a taxfarmer who was unable to pay the goverment the two talents which he had agreed to collect as the απομοιρα from two villages. It is by no means certain that because the surety had to pay in χαλκος προς αργυριον, therefore the two talents originally promised were also in χαλκος προς αργυριον. But the analogy of the Zois papyri, in which the original debt and the sum paid by the surety are both in χαλκος ου αλλαγη, at any rate makes that view tenable. If this assumption be correct, the identity of χαλκος προς αργυριον with χαλκος ισονομος is practically certain, for the ostracon shows that the απομοιρα in the second century B. C. was no longer an ωνη προς γενηματα or προς αργυριον, as it had been in the time of Philadelphus [24] 4, 10, 12, but had become an ωνη προς χαλκον ισονομον, since the payment recorded by the ostracon is in χαλκος ισονομος and there is no reason to suppose that χαλκος προς αργυριον represents a third stage intermediate between the other two. The phrase χαλκος προς αργυριον is found as late as the fortieth year of Euergetes II, see Wilck. Akt. i. 19; and the meaning which I have proposed is quite consistent with its use there, where it is interchanged with χαλκος alone.

So far as the slender evidence of the Greek papyri from this period carries us, it confirms M. Revillout's theory that the general change from the silver to the copper standard took place at the beginning of Epiphanes' reign, but it is indecisive on the question whether the copper drachmae were instituted side by side with the silver by Philopator, and on the question what their exchange value was. These problems there-fore must be discussed on the evidence of the demotic papyri. The equivalence of the demotic names of coins in Greek drachmae has, as

I have said, been perfectly established by M. Revillout, whose theory, based at first only on demotic, has been since confirmed by numerous bilingual papyri and ostraca. The demotic system is founded on the 'argenteus-outen' or 20 drachmae, divided into 5 shekels or tetradrachms and 10 kati or didrachms; and as the 'argenteus-outen,' shekels, and kati may be either of silver or copper, the drachmae may equally be silver or copper. The numbers found in the period of the silver standard are very small compared with the numbers in the period of the copper standard, when thousands of 'argenteus-outens' not infrequently occur, and there is, as a rule, no difficulty in determining which standard is meant. The same cannot however always be said of the formula $24 = \frac{2}{10}$, from which M. Revillout arrives at the ratio of $120 : 1$ between the value of a silver and copper drachma. As M. Revillout bases on two papyri his theory that Philopator gave the name of 'argenteus-outens' and drachmae to the previously existing copper coins called obols and chalci in Greek (since no mention of copper has yet occurred in a demotic papyrus earlier than Philopator, I leave their demotic names to M. Revillout), I give his latest translation of the passages in the two papyri relating to the coinage, together with an example from the later period, when there is no question as to the standard meant. But first, for the sake of clearness, it is necessary to point out that in discussing the ratio of exchange between silver and copper drachmae, I am not discussing the ratio between silver and copper as such, that is to say the ratio of value between a silver and copper coin of equal weight, which is another and distinct question, to be decided by different evidence. We cannot find out the last question until we have a more or less probable hypothesis on the question how many copper drachmae were worth one silver drachma. But even if we solve the first question and find out how many copper drachmae were worth one silver, we still cannot discover the answer to the second unless we know how much a copper drachma normally weighed, and this is just the disputed point. I do not of course mean by this to imply that we are not much nearer to the ultimate ratio when we have found out the ratio of value between a silver and a copper uten and drachma. Both the Greek and the demotic names for the copper coins imply certain weights, but unfortunately there are at least two possible utens and drachmae of different weights. The choice of one or the other of these alternatives must depend on which suits the general classification of the coins best, and that can be decided only by an expert in the coins themselves. In fact no theory of the ratio of exchange between a silver and a copper drachma can, in the absence of direct evidence, be accepted unless it explains the coins; and on the other hand, a theory based on probabilities will be raised to a much higher level of certainty, if it explains the coins. The two questions therefore have these points in connexion, and as on M. Revillout's theory the answer to each is the same, he naturally does not keep them distinct; but, as I have said, the solution to each really comes from a different quarter. No papyrus can tell us the normal weight of the copper drachma, on which the ultimate ratio between silver and copper depends. The scholar may with the help of the numismatist lead us to the edge of the stream which separates us from the ultimate ratio, but it is only the numismatist who can conduct us across the ford. It is because M. Revillout, at any rate in the latest exposition of his theory, has attempted to dispense with the numismatist, that his system, as a whole, breaks down. But in the meantime I return to the question of his demotic formula.

The formula $24 = \frac{2}{10}$ first occurs in a papyrus dated the fifth year of Philopator. In Rev. ég. i. 121 M. Revillout translates the passage 'Tu as $5\frac{2}{10}$ argenteus dont le change à me reclamer.' In Lettres p. 238 he expands this into 'Le débiteur doit payer 5 argenteus et $\frac{2}{10}$ en tout (en monnaie d'argent) ou en monnaie d'airain au taux 24 unités d'airain pour $\frac{2}{10}$ d'unité d'argent.'

The second instance occurs in a Theban papyrus dated the fifth year of Harmachis, one of the insurgent kings, and M. Revillout translates (Rev. ég. i. p. 121) 'Tu as $2\frac{1}{10}$ argenteus . . . dont le change en airain est 24 pour $\frac{2}{10}$ à me reclamer.' In Lettres p. 238 he translates it 'Tu as $2\frac{1}{10}$ argenteus à me faire ou en équivalence de 24 pour $\frac{2}{10}$.'

A third instance, which I select from the period when there is no question as to the standard, is in a papyrus at Dublin, dated the fifth year of Philometor (Lettres p. 239), 'contenant une amende de 1000 argenteus ou 5000 sekels en airain dont l'équivalence est de 24 pour $\frac{2}{10}$.' The same formula is found in numerous demotic papyri of the second century. I shall lay no stress on the uncertainty still attaching to all translation of demotic when there is not the Greek to compare it with, but shall frankly admit the following points about the formula :—

(1) That the word which M. Revillout translates variously ' mélange,' 'équivalence,' 'change,' and ' taux ' has to do with the exchange between silver and copper.

(2) That the 24 refers to unities of copper.

(3) That the $\frac{2}{10}$ refers to a ' unity of silver' and means $\frac{2}{10}$ of an 'argenteus-outen,' i. e. 2 kati or 4 drachmae.

(4) That the 24 and the $\frac{2}{10}$ are equated. More than this M. Revillout himself cannot desire. Then does M. Revillout's theory of the ratio of 120 : 1 between the value of a silver and copper drachma follow, (a) for the reigns of Philopator and the insurgent kings in the Thebaid, (b) for Epiphanes and his successors?

The question turns on what is meant by the ' unities of copper ' in the three cases. M. Revillout's explanation is that the 24 in all cases refer to the copper 'argenteus-outens,' and that, translated into drachmae, the formula means, ' 480 copper drachmae = 4 silver drachmae.' There is however this great difference between the first two papyri and the third. In the first two the only argentei mentioned in the papyrus are on the silver standard, in the third the argentei are on the copper standard. The first papyrus does not say ' $5\frac{2}{10}$ argentei or in copper 624 argentei at the rate of 24 for $\frac{2}{10}$,' but simply ' $5\frac{2}{10}$ argenteus dont le change (en airain est 24 pour $\frac{2}{10}$).' It was natural that M. Revillout, who denied the use of copper, except for the smallest payments, in the reigns of Philadelphus and Euergetes and thought that its extensive use began with Philopator, should, ignoring this difference, explain the first two papyri in the light of the third. Since however it has been shown that copper was largely used even in the reign of Philadelphus, and M. Revillout admits that in the other papyri of Philopator's reign and those of the insurgent kings there are no instances of any argentei other than those on the silver standard, and since it is obviously better to explain a formula in the light of something which is known to have existed previously, than in the light of something which did not, it is necessary to ask—is there anything in the first period, when it is certain that no copper argentei on the copper standard existed, with which the formula $24 = \frac{2}{10}$ can be connected ? If so, the necessity for attributing to Philopator at any rate the institution of copper argentei at the ratio of 120 : 1 will disappear.

The answer is— what the reader has doubtless himself anticipated—

that the formula of [60] 15 ληψομεθα εις τον στατηρα οβολους κδ, is the original of which the demotic formula 'at the rate of 24 of copper for 2 kati (i. e. 4 drachmae) of silver' is the translation. I say advisedly that the Greek is the original. The coinage of the Ptolemies was issued by Greek kings from Greek mints at Greek cities, and under Greek names. These names the Egyptians refused to adopt into their own language, preferring to equate as far as possible the coinage of their conquerors to their own time-honoured system. But it must not be forgotten that the Egyptian names of coins and all the formulae connected with them are translations from the Greek, and that the ultimate explanation must come from the Greek, not from the demotic. I have insisted somewhat strongly on this point, because it is my answer to the objection which may be levelled against this part of the present essay that it is presumptuous for me to criticize the interpretations of demotic scholars. If the formula 24 copper $= \frac{2}{10}$ silver has no analogy to the passage in the Revenue Papyrus, M. Revillout's translation of it must be far from the truth, for the correspondence between the formula and [ᶜ0] 15 is exact. In both there is an equation between unities of silver and unities of copper, in both the number of the copper unities is 24, and in both the meaning and number of the silver unities comes to the same, 4 drachmae. The only difference is that in the demotic the name of the 24 copper unities is uncertain, in the Greek it is given and is the obol; and therefore in the demotic it is the demotic equivalent of the copper obol, whatever that may be.

At last firm ground has been reached. There is no longer any reason for separating the monetary system of Philopator from that of his predecessors, or in fact to suppose a transitional period at all. The dividing line, so far as the evidence goes, is the adoption of the copper standard at the beginning of Epiphanes' reign for Egypt without the Thebaid, at the end of his reign for the Thebaid as well.

Another question, which arises out of the occurrence of the formula $24 = \frac{2}{10}$ in the 2 papyri of Philopator and Harmachis, is—why was the formula inserted, with what was it contrasted? On M. Revillout's theory the object of the formula was to show that the payment might be made not in silver argentei, but in argentei on the copper standard of 120:1. But as it has been shown first that the 24 unities of copper in question are probably obols, not copper argentei, secondly that copper was largely used as far back as Philadelphus, some other explanation is necessary. Here again, if the Greek be taken as the guide, the solution is easily found. In [60] 15, the 24 obols at par were clearly contrasted with obols at a discount as in [76] 4, and the ostracon which mentions χαλκος εις κςν gives an example of what the discount was. Since the formula $24 = \frac{2}{10}$ was the demotic equivalent of the Greek, it too was contrasted with copper of which $26\frac{1}{4}$ or any other number of obols were paid for a stater   M. Revillout will perhaps object, as he once objected when criticizing Droysen, Rev. ég. ii p. 279, that the demotic papyri give no examples of copper at any other ratio than $24 = \frac{2}{10}$, but as another ratio is found in Greek papyri and ostraca, the objection is disposed of; moreover in denying the existence of an extensive copper currency in the time of Philadelphus and Euergetes, the unsoundness of arguing from the silence of the demotic documents has already shown itself.

So far therefore as the documents of Philopator's reign are concerned, M. Revillout has not yet come to the ratio of value between a silver and a copper drachma, for he has not yet come to the period of copper argentei and drachmae, but is still in the period of copper obols. Does the demotic formula however give the ratio for the reign of Epiphanes and his successors? The fact that in the papyri of this period the argentei mentioned are on the copper standard makes it much more intelligible that the 24 should refer to them in these papyri than in the two papyri where the only argentei mentioned were on the silver standard. On the other hand, since it appeared that in the case of the two papyri of Philopator and Harmachis the 24 referred to obols, it is a perfectly tenable position to hold that the 24 throughout means obols, not copper argentei. In the first ·place it is now known that the formula $24 = \frac{2}{10}$ in any case belongs to the period when there were as yet no copper argentei ; and, since the Greek original of the formula dates back to Philadelphus, it is far more probable that the demotic formula goes back to the same reign than that it was first used in the reign of Philopator. And if the formula $24 = \frac{2}{10}$ was well established at the time when the change was made to copper argentei, it is perfectly possible that the formula ' 24 unities of copper (i. e. obols) for $\frac{2}{10}$ silver ' should be continued after obols had given place to copper drachmae on

E e

a copper standard.   This argument will be much strengthened if it can
be shown that a parallel case exists of a term properly belonging to
obols alone, but continued in the period of the copper standard.   Such
a parallel is afforded by the converse phrase χαλκος εις κϛν.   That
phrase was first found in the period when the copper coins were called
obols, and it is strictly applicable only to that period.   Nevertheless it
is used in the Zois papyri with a sum of copper drachmae on the copper
standard.   But why, if the ratio of exchange between silver and copper
was 120 : 1 and the old copper obol was now 20 drachmae, did not the
writer say 'copper at the rate of 525 copper drachmae for a stater'?
Obviously the answer is that in equating silver and copper the obol
had been and continued to be the typical copper unity.

Applying this to the demotic formula—we are on the firm ground
of the Greek so long as we maintain that the 24 refer to obols, but we
are on the treacherous path of assumption, if we maintain that the 24
refer to the copper argentei ; while to argue that the obol was the copper
argenteus is obviously to beg the whole question at issue.   If it can be
shown on other grounds that the ratio of exchange was 120 : 1, and
therefore the obol and the copper argenteus were identical, the demotic
formula may be taken as confirming that view.   But to attempt to prove
the ratio from the formula is to argue in a circle.   We should indeed find
the ratio of 120 : 1, but only because we had already put it there.

The conclusion therefore is that if the demotic formula is the only
evidence for the exchange ratio of 120 : 1, the verdict must be 'not
proven.'   But the other evidence leads to the consideration of the
third and last period.

§ 4. *Documentary evidence for the period of the copper standard.*

With Epiphanes the monetary changes of the Ptolemies came to an
end.   The Greek papyri mention almost universally copper drachmae
on the copper standard, with occasional mentions of silver, chiefly in
payments of fines or taxes.   In the demotic, from the reign of
Euergetes II M. Revillout distinguishes two kinds of silver coins,
first, the 'argenteus fondu du temple de Ptah' accompanied by the
same division into fractions which he says that he has found in the
demotic papyri of Darius, Philip, and Euergetes I, and secondly, the

'argenteus en pièces d'argent gravé.' The last he connects with the
Greek phrase found in pap. O of Leyden, αργυριου επισημου Πτολεμαικου
νομισματος, and explains it as the normal coinage struck by Euergetes II
and his successors, while he explains the other as the 'vieil argenteus,'
(*Lettres*, p. 244), though whether he means by this the silver coins
of the Persians, as contrasted with the silver of the Ptolemies, or the
heavier silver of Soter compared with the lighter coinage of his successors,
or the purer coinage of the earlier Ptolemies with the more or less
debased silver of the later kings, or all three, is not clear. But, at any
rate, if the argenteus 'en pièces d'argent gravé' is equivalent to αργυριου
επισημον κ.τ.λ., then αργυριον επισημον according to M. Revillout, is not
silver of the best quality. How does this view suit the papyrus O of
Leyden?

No papyrus has been more discussed than this one, which has been
the standing difficulty with regard to the rate of exchange between
silver and copper drachmae, and the rate of interest, for the last half
century. The papyrus is dated the twenty-sixth year of Ptolemy
Alexander and records the loan of αργυριου επισημου Πτολεμαικου νομισματος δραχμας δεκαδυο. The debtor binds himself if he does not repay
the sum at the stipulated time to pay the ημιολιον, i. e. 18 drachmae,
and interest from the stipulated time of repayment at the rate of
60 copper drachmae a month for each stater.

In the discussion of this papyrus M. Lumbroso, as usual, is the best
guide. In pp. 171–2 of his *Recherches*, he states the theories of his
predecessors: (1) Letronne, who arguing that the stater was a gold
coin worth 100 silver drachmae and that 60 copper drachmae were
worth 1 silver, arrived at the interest of 12 per cent. a year: (2) Reuvens,
who postulating a stater of gold worth 20 silver drachmae and an exchange
ratio of 1 : 30 between silver and copper drachmae, arrived at the interest
of 120 per cent.: (3) Leemans, who assuming the same gold coin, but
an exchange ratio of 1 : 120 between silver and copper, reached the
interest of 30 per cent. Against all these theories M. Lumbroso brings
two weighty objections; in the first place, there is absolutely nothing
to show that the stater in question was anything but a silver stater,
especially as the loan in question was in silver and the normal stater
of the Ptolemaic period without further definition is the silver stater,
a statement which is entirely confirmed by [60] 15 and [76] 4; secondly,

that the rate of interest in the papyrus is clearly exceptional, being the interest on a fine, and therefore it is difficult to apply to it more or less parallel cases of the rate of interest under normal circumstances. M. Lumbroso tentatively suggested a theory of his own that the stater in question was a silver octodrachm, based on the erroneous supposition of Letronne that the gold stater was an octodrachm. But as M. Revillout has shown, the only staters in Egypt were the gold didrachm and the silver tetradrachm, and the choice therefore is narrowed down to these two alternatives.

M. Revillout (*Lettres*, p. 153) adopts M. Leemans' theory that the stater in question was the gold didrachm, worth 20 silver drachmae, which on the exchange ratio of 120 : 1 between silver and copper drachmae gives 30 per cent. interest, and tries to support it by adducing instances of interest at 30 per cent., though the fallacy of the argument from analogy in this case had already been pointed out by M. Lumbroso. The supposition that the stater could be a silver tetradrachm was dismissed by M. Revillout on the ground that this would result in a rate of interest of 120 per cent. M. Revillout has here by an oversight understated his case, for if the stater in question was an ordinary silver one and the rate of exchange 120 : 1, the rate of interest is 150 per cent. The difficulty however of supposing that the rate of interest was, in the case of a fine, as high as 150 per cent. is much less than that of supposing the stater to be a gold stater, seeing that the papyrus records a loan of silver and the stater is the commonest silver coin. But was the stater in question an ordinary, i. e. as the silver coins of this period show, a debased stater? The phrase αργυριου επισημου Πτολεμαικου νομισματος seems to me to point to the silver coins lent being unusual, though as Wilcken in a recent letter pointed out to me the 12 drachmae αργ. επισ. κ.τ.λ. are in the summary at the beginning of the document called 12 dr. αργ(υριου) νο(μισματος) simply, and αργυριου νομισματος does not differ from αργυριου alone. But in any case the possibility that these 12 dr. were staters coined by one of the earlier Ptolemies cannot be eliminated, and there is no means of discovering what the premium on pure silver coins at this period was. It is perfectly possible that in the first century B.C. the staters of Soter on the Attic standard passed at 100 per cent. premium or more. But if the stater in question refers to one of these staters at a premium, the interest was very much less than 150 per cent., and as the argument from the analogy of the rate of 30 per cent. found in other papyri is not only irrelevant but misleading, since the rate in the case of a fine would probably be higher than the normal rate, the theory that the stater in question was a silver stater, whether of pure or of debased metal, provides an adequate solution without rendering it necessary to complicate the question by the irrelevant introduction of gold into a papyrus which records a loan of silver and therefore implies interest on that silver. But as the rate of interest perhaps depends on the unknown premium on pure silver, and is ·under any circumstances exceptional, the papyrus cannot help towards finding out the normal rate of interest, nor can it even be used to confirm, much less to prove, any theory concerning the ratio of exchange between the normal or debased silver drachmae of this period and the copper drachmae.

To return to the question of M. Revillout's identification of ' pièces d'argent gravé' with αργυριον επισημον and his explanation of both as the ordinary silver coins of the late Ptolemies, the interpretation of the papyrus O of Leyden is so complicated by the exceptional circumstances of the case, that it is very doubtful whether it can serve as a basis for generalization. The staters of Soter and Philadelphus which remained in circulation must have commanded a large premium. But the description in Greek of the staters of pure silver, as contrasted with the more or less debased staters of the later Ptolemies, is quite uncertain.

Since the arguments in favour of the exchange ratio of 120 : 1 have been found inadequate, and as the arguments adduced by Prof. Lumbroso in his *Recherches* rest on passages where the original editors of the papyri in question had misread the text, while the evidence of the ratio of exchange in the Roman period, as Mommsen has pointed out, cannot be admitted as evidence for the Ptolemaic, there remains the argument of M. Bernardino Peyron, the original founder of the theory. Comparing two passages in papyri nearly contemporaneous in which the price of an artaba of ολυρα is given, first as 2 silver drachmae, secondly as 300 copper drachmae, the price in the latter case being in a period of great scarcity, he suggested that the normal price was probably about 240 copper drachmae, and so proposed the exchange ratio of 120 : 1. This argument, though far too weak to serve as a sole basis for the exchange ratio of 120 : 1, is nevertheless fairly conclusive

evidence against supposing that the ratio was more than 150 : 1, or so
low as 30 : 1, as was once proposed, and it is a strong though hardly
conclusive argument against the theory of Letronne that the exchange
ratio was 60 : 1.

But though the documentary evidence on which these distinguished
scholars based the theory of 120 : 1 is very far from being conclusive,
their verdict is not therefore lightly to be set aside. Their general
conclusion, which is on the whole supported by recent discoveries,
is in favour of 120 : 1 as the exchange ratio between silver and copper
drachmae, on the ground that it suits the comparative prices better than
any other theory, and if that ratio can by the numismatic evidence be
made practically certain or even only probable, no difficulty is likely
to be raised on account of the papyri.

For the rate of discount on copper at this period the evidence consists
of, first, the Zois papyri of Philometor's reign in which χαλκος εις κςν is
interchanged with χαλκος ου αλλαγη, secondly, L. P. 62 [5] 17, probably
belonging to the later part of the second century B. C., in which in the
case of ωναι προς χαλκον ισονομον (vid. sup.), just as in the case of the
oil-monopoly during the third century, copper was accepted at par, but
the discount on copper paid in the case of προς αργυριον ωναι, or ωναι
which ought to be paid in silver, is 10 dr. 2½ obols for every mina ; in
other words 110 dr. 2½ in copper were worth 100 in silver. The rate
therefore was approximately 10 per cent. at this period, as it had been in
the third century. The explanation of this fact which, since silver was
much scarcer in the second century, is at first sight remarkable is
afforded by the silver coins. In a country like Egypt with a double
currency, silver and copper, exchanging at practically the market value,
—for it is incredible that Philadelphus would have permitted large
payments of taxes in copper at its nominal value unless that nominal
value approximately represented the real value of copper—there were,
when silver tended, as it did soon after Philadelphus' time, to become
scarce, three alternatives before the Ptolemies. Either they might
alter the rate of exchange between silver and copper, or they might
diminish the weight of the silver coins to meet the appreciation of silver,
or they might meet it by debasing the silver coinage. That the
Ptolemies did not adopt the first course, is shown by the fact that
copper still in the second century exchanged at the same rate, either

at par or at a small discount, with silver, and that there is no alteration
of normal weights in the copper coins.   Possibly their policy in not
adopting that course was sound ; for the constant alterations of the rate
of exchange, which would have been necessary to keep the two metals at
their market value, might have been more fatal to all business transactions
than either of the other two courses.   Nor did they choose, as the
Rhodians under similar circumstances chose, to diminish the weight
of the silver coins, keeping the metal pure ; but, as the silver of the
later Ptolemies shows, they preferred to debase their silver, probably
to an extent which, while nominally keeping the same rate of exchange
as before, would alter the real ratio between silver and copper to the
level of the ratio of the two metals in the open market.   Therefore,
any particular weight of copper coins nominally continued in the second
century to exchange against the same amount of silver as that against
which it had exchanged in the third century.   But the real silver
in the 'silver' coins of the later Ptolemies continued to diminish,
until by the reign of Auletes the metal had become for the most part
alloy.

To sum up the results which have been reached by the aid of
the documentary evidence, the dividing line in the history of Ptolemaic
coinage is the adoption of the copper standard at the very beginning of
Epiphanes' reign, perhaps at the end of Philopator's, side by side with
the silver standard which it never altogether superseded.   In fact the
debased silver of the later Ptolemies is so common that it must have
played a much larger part than can be concluded from the papyri, and
it may well be doubted not only how far the recorded payments on the
silver standard in the third century were actually made in silver, but
also how far the recorded payments in copper drachmae during the
second were actually made in copper.   In many respects however the
change to a copper standard seems to have made little difference.   As
far back as Philadelphus' reign copper was used in the payment of large
sums in official as well as in private transactions, sometimes at par,
sometimes at a discount of about 10 per cent.   In the second century,
as the history of the απομοιρα proves (see [37] 19 note), payments were
made more frequently in copper, but the rate of discount was apparently
still about the same and there is nothing to show that the rate of
exchange had altered.

Of the three questions propounded at the beginning of this essay, the papyri and ostraca have given an answer to the second, and this answer has been verified by the silver coins ; with regard to the first, the normal ratio between silver and copper drachmae in the third century B.C. is known, and there is a certain presumption, though not yet a strong one, in favour of the exchange ratio of 120:1 between silver and copper drachmae in the second century. The third question has necessarily been left unsolved, except in so far that there is no longer any reason for separating the two parts of it, since the large payments of copper made to the government show that the ratio between silver and copper as metals must have closely approximated to their ratio as coins.

§ 5. *The evidence of the copper coins.*

The copper coins are discussed by M. Revillout in *Lettres*, pp. 112–124, where he makes a classification and table of weights, both of which are, as I shall show, disfigured by the most astonishing blunders. These pages are reprinted practically without alteration from his articles in the Rev. égypt., though the subject had in the meantime been revolutionized by the appearance of Mr. Poole's Catalogue of Ptolemaic coins in the British Museum.

As I have already said, it is necessary to have some theory of the rate of exchange between silver and copper drachmae before we attempt to argue from the weights. If it were possible to say at once that any particular coin was the copper obol, since the normal rate of exchange in the third century between drachmae paid in silver and drachmae paid in copper was par, it would be equally possible to obtain the ultimate ratio between an equal weight of silver and copper in the third century, and the knowledge of this would of course be of great service in deciding both the ratio of exchange and the ultimate ratio between silver and copper in the second century. But it is impossible to tell so easily what coin the copper obol was. On the other hand, if it can be discovered with how many copper drachmae the obol was identical, and how much the copper drachma weighed, the question of the ultimate ratio can be solved for both centuries at once. It is therefore necessary in order to reach the ultimate ratio between silver and copper even in the third century, to overcome the old difficulty of the rate of exchange between silver and copper drachmae in the second, and if that can be done, it will also be possible to explain the ultimate ratio in the second century B.C.

But at this point there are some general considerations to be taken into account. First, to quote Mr. Poole (Catal. Intr. p. xiii), 'No series of coins struck by the successors of Alexander is more difficult to class than that of the Ptolemies.' And if the difficulty of classifying the gold and silver coins is great, that of classifying the copper is far greater owing to the increased rarity of dated copper coins, the uncertainty attaching to the name of each denomination, and the frequent deviations, whatever theory be adopted, from the normal standard of weights. The time is never likely to come when every issue of copper coins can be assigned to its correct reign, or when at any rate the smaller copper coins can be assigned with certainty to their correct denominations. Under these circumstances, since finality is unattainable, the best theory will be that to which there are fewest objections.

Secondly, since the only numismatist of the first rank who has undertaken to weigh and systematize the copper coins is Mr. Poole, it is absolutely necessary for any one who is not a numismatist to base his explanations upon the facts as Mr. Poole records them, nor are conclusions likely to be of much value, if they are irreconcilable with Mr. Poole's.

If the classification of the coinage according to weights is a task of extreme difficulty, the copper coinage of the Ptolemies has nevertheless two great advantages. It was at any rate from the time of Philadelphus, as I have pointed out, in no sense a token coinage. The smallness of the discount and the fact that the government even in the time when silver was plentiful sometimes accepted copper at par are conclusive evidence that the nominal ratio of copper to silver approximately coincided with the market ratio of the two metals. It would obviously be a vain task to attempt from a consideration of the weight and exchange value of a shilling to deduce the ratio of value between silver and gold as metals at the present day. But with the coinage of the Ptolemies it is certain that the ultimate ratio is somehow expressed by the coins if they can be looked at in the right way; and there is no question of searching after a chimera. Secondly, a general consideration

F f

of the copper coins without adopting any particular theory of the normal
standard shows, as Mr. Poole remarks, that the change from the silver to
a copper standard in the reign of Epiphanes does not seem to have been
accompanied by an alteration of the normal standard of weights. The
names of the different denominations altered, but the normal weights
did not. There are great irregularities after the reign of Epiphanes as
there were before, but they are confined within the same limits, and
therefore an explanation of the normal weights and the names of the
denominations for one period will equally serve as an explanation for
the other. At the same time the normal weights primarily represent
the obol and its subdivisions to which the copper drachmae of the later
period were equated, and a theory of the normal weights can only be
accepted if it explains the origin of the subdivisions of the obol; on the
other hand the ratio of exchange adopted in the reign of Epiphanes is
likely to have been such that the new copper drachmae would accommo-
date themselves to the fractions of the obol.

With regard to the copper obol, though nothing can be deduced
from its name concerning its weight, there are two important points to
be considered. The fact that the obol is spoken of as the typical copper
coin, and still more the absence of any silver coin, at any rate after the
reign of Soter, which represented an obol, make it certain that one
denomination of the coins in Mr. Poole's table is the obol of which the
lower denominations are subdivisions. Secondly, it is known that the
Greek subdivisions of the obol in Egypt were chalci or eighths, as at
Athens, cf. *Pap. Biling.* l. c. line 9, διχαλκον, &c. Therefore any satisfactory theory of the normal weights of the obol must show that the
coin which is assumed to be the obol, was divided into eighths at any
rate approximately; and similarly no theory of the equivalence of
the obol in copper drachmae can be accepted, if the fractions which
result are unintelligible. The exchange ratio must be such that the
coins representing the fractions of the obol can be converted conveniently
into copper drachmae.

Next, as to the names of the copper coins in the second century; in
Greek they are called drachmae, in demotic 'argentei,' subdivided into
5 shekels and 10 kati or didrachms, the kati being also $\frac{1}{10}$ of the
uten, with which M. Revillout naturally identifies the argenteus, speaking
frequently of the 'argenteus-outen.' The names therefore of the copper

coins are the same as the names of the silver coins, and as the names 'drachma' and 'kati' connote weights, there is good reason for assuming that the coins which approximately weighed a drachma or a kati were the copper drachmae and the copper kati.

But what were the weights connoted by the terms 'drachma' and 'kati' in Egypt? For this it is necessary to consider the history of the silver coinage about which there is no doubt. Soter at first issued silver on the Attic standard, according to which the drachma weighed 67·5 grains, then adopted the Rhodian with a normal drachma of 60 grains, and finally adopted the Phoenician with a normal drachma of 56 grains, which standard was maintained by all his successors. Leaving the Rhodian drachma which is intermediate out of account, the approximate limits at each end are 67·5 and 56 as the weight of the copper drachma. Turning to the demotic, in so far as a kati is the translation of a Greek didrachm, it gives no new information, but it must be remembered that being the tenth of an 'argenteus-outen,' and the uten being an ancient Egyptian weight of very nearly 1400 grains, the kati also had a definite weight of its own, 140 grains, which, as it was equated to the didrachm, would give a copper drachma of 70 grains. On the other hand, it will be objected, have I any right to invent a fictitious copper drachma of which there is no instance in Greek? Is not this to explain the Greek coinage in the light of the demotic, a course which I have already frequently condemned? My answer is that in the first place 67·5 was but the approximate limit, and that no less an authority than Mr. Poole (Catal. Intr. p. xci) remarks that the difference between the Attic and the Egyptian standard 'is too small to be of consequence in the comparison (of the coins), considering the irregularity with which the copper money was struck.' Any series of coins which points to a normal weight of 67·5 can also be explained by a normal weight of 70. Therefore the Attic and Egyptian standards are for the present purpose identical, and the 'fictitious drachma' is nothing else than the Attic.

But still it may be objected that, as the Greek and the Egyptian standards practically coincided, it was the Egyptian system which was equated to the Greek, not vice versa, and that in speaking of the normal weights I ought to keep to the Greek. Here however a distinction must be drawn. There is all the difference in the world between explaining technical phrases or names of coins by the demotic instead of by the

Greek, and on the other hand arguing that the copper coins made in Greek mints by Greeks and with Greek names may nevertheless have been issued on an Egyptian standard to which the Greek was equated. That it would be as inconsistent as it would be absurd to explain the silver coins on any theory of an Egyptian standard, is obvious, for the silver coins were clearly issued on Greek standards, to which the Egyptian standard was equated.   But though a conquering race naturally imposes its own silver standard on the conquered, there are numerous cases, as in South Italy and Sicily, in which the conquerors have adopted the copper standard of the conquered and equated it with their own money.   Moreover the elaborate system of copper coinage of the Ptolemies is peculiar to Egypt and quite foreign to the rest of the Hellenistic world, while on the other hand copper had long been used in Egypt as a standard of value.   In fact, if the question had to be decided only on *a priori* grounds, the balance of probability would be rather in favour of an Egyptian origin.   But it is sufficient for my present purpose to have vindicated the consistency of holding that besides the kati which are equivalents of Greek weights, account must be taken of the true Egyptian weight of the kati, although, as I have said, for practical purposes a coin of 70 grains is not to be distinguished from the Attic drachma.

How does this bear on the ratio of exchange between silver and copper drachmae?   In the first place, if it is granted that the copper drachma weighs approximately the same as the Phoenician or the Attic drachma, it can be shown that any ratio of exchange higher than 120 : 1 is unsatisfactory if not impossible ; e. g. if it were 180 to 1, 30 copper drachmae would be equal to the obol ; but thirty times the weight even of the Phoenician drachma would result in a coin much heavier than any quoted in Mr. Poole's table, and, as has been shown, the obol is represented somewhere in the extant copper coins ; therefore this ratio will not do.   In fact, as the heaviest copper coin is a little over 1400 grains, any ratio of exchange over 150 is quite impossible on the same grounds.   This ratio however, which assigns 25 copper drachmae to the obol, may be dismissed on the ground that it involves a very inconvenient number, $3\frac{1}{8}$ copper drachmae for the chalcus, which will cause infinite confusion.   But it is unnecessary to go through all the unsatisfactory ratios in detail.   The number of copper drachmae in an obol cannot exceed twenty-four; on the other hand it cannot be less than ten, which would give a ratio of sixty, for under any circumstances a ratio below 60 : 1 is too low to account for the high figures in copper drachmae in the papyri; twenty-four and ten are therefore the two possible extremes. Of the intermediate numbers all the odd ones may be struck out, as they would lead at once to impossible fractions in copper drachmae as the equivalents of chalci, nor will twenty-two, eighteen, or fourteen suit for the same reason. There remain twenty-four, twenty, sixteen, twelve, and ten.

I have proceeded so far on general grounds without assuming even the normal weights of any particular coins, much less the relation of any one supposed denomination to any other, but merely showing that a number of ratios failed at the outset to fulfil the requirements which any satisfactory solution must have fulfilled, before it is worth while to apply the consequences of the ratio to the coins themselves; but it is hardly necessary to point out that a theory which starts with difficulties at the outset, cannot possibly overcome the obstacles which any theory, however simple or easy at the beginning, is bound eventually to encounter. In order to reduce the possible ratios of exchange on numismatical grounds to a still smaller number, it would be necessary to come to an understanding, if not about the supposed approximate normal weights, at any rate about the relation which a higher series bears to a lower one. But without prejudging the answers to these questions, there is one fact which is certain about the subdivisions of the Ptolemaic coins, and indeed it is the explanation of it which is the key to the whole problem.

Whatever theory be adopted as to the number of copper drachmae in an obol, and whatever coin be therefore selected as the obol, the subdivisions of it are not only in the series $\frac{1}{2}$, $\frac{1}{4}$, $\frac{1}{8}$, which fractions it is absolutely necessary to find in the coins, as the obol is known to have been divided into these fractions. Intermediate between these fractions comes another series, and it is chiefly by its answer to the questions, first what was this series both in terms of fractions of the obol and of copper drachmae, and secondly, why was there this second series, that a theory of Ptolemaic coinage stands or falls. On Mr. Poole's theory that the normal weight of the highest copper coins was 20 Attic drachmae, he obtains as subdivisions 10, 8, 5, 4, 2$\frac{1}{2}$, 2, 1$\frac{1}{4}$, 1,

(I leave out of account the smaller denominations which cannot be fixed independently of the larger), or, regarded as fractions of unity, $\frac{1}{2}$, $\frac{2}{3}$, $\frac{1}{4}$, $\frac{1}{5}$, $\frac{1}{8}$, $\frac{1}{10}$, $\frac{3}{10}$, $\frac{1}{20}$. It is obvious that by identifying 20 Attic drachmae with the copper obol, which gives an exchange ratio of 1 : 120, the fractions of the obol which are wanted will be obtained, and equally, if 10 Attic drachmae be identified with the obol; for the difference between the denomination of the small coin, which Mr. Poole supposes to be $1\frac{1}{2}$, i. e. $\frac{3}{20}$, and the denomination of $1\frac{1}{4}$, i. e. on a theory of 60 : 1, $\frac{1}{8}$ obol, is so trifling that it can be neglected. But there will also be a series $\frac{2}{3}$, $\frac{1}{3}$, $\frac{1}{10}$, $\frac{1}{20}$, which, though they cannot be finally proved until the explanation of them is found, are at any rate convenient fractions of the obol and can at once be converted into copper drachmae without any difficulty. But these advantages, which are shared equally by the exchange ratio of 120 : 1 or 60 : 1, the copper drachma being in both cases on the Attic standard, are not obtained by any of the ratios, according to which 24, 16, or 12 copper drachmae are equal to the obol, whatever normal weight of the copper drachma be assumed within the limits of 70–56 grains mentioned above. These three ratios of exchange all lead to inconvenient fractions both as divisions of the obol and as copper drachmae. Practically the question is ultimately narrowed down to the choice between 120 : 1 and 60 : 1. Further than that the evidence of the Ptolemaic coins cannot go, for if the coins can be explained on the theory of the one ratio, they can equally well be explained by the other, since the normal weights would remain the same, and the only difference would be that the denominations of the various fractions would on the theory of 60 : 1 be twice what they are on the theory of 120 : 1. But the theory of 120 : 1 is, Mr Gardner tells me, on general grounds of numismatics, preferable to the other theory, because the exchange ratio of 120 : 1 leads, if the copper drachma is on the Attic standard, as Mr. Poole supposes, and his classification of the coinage is satisfactory, to a ratio of $143\frac{1}{3}$: 1 between the normal weights of an equivalent amount of silver and copper, and even on M. Revillout's theory of the Phoenician standard of the copper coinage to a ratio of 120 : 1, and the analogy of other countries, e. g. Sicily and Rome, is in favour of a ratio over 100 in preference to one below.

Like the papyri therefore the coins on the whole point to the exchange ratio of 120 : 1, and as they practically narrow the question down to a ratio of 120 or 60, while the former ratio suits the prices found in the papyri much the better of the two, there is not much doubt that the exchange ratio is 120:1; and if so the continuation of the demotic formula $24 = \frac{2}{10}$ in the period when obols had given way to pieces of 20 copper drachmae or 'argenteus-outens' is easily explained.

That all these arguments for the exchange ratio of 120:1 leave much to be desired is recognized by no one more fully than myself; but it would be worse than useless to blind oneself to the fact that conclusive evidence for that ratio does not yet exist, though the question will probably some day be solved by an instance of the conversion of copper drachmae in the second century B.C. into silver, similar to the instances in App. ii (5) for the third.

It has hitherto been argued that the exchange ratio of 120:1, according to which the obol was equivalent to 20 copper drachmae on the Attic standard, produces a satisfactory solution for the initial difficulties which were fatal to the other ratios. But in order to place on an approximately firm basis the ratio of exchange, together with the ratio of weights between an equivalent amount of silver and copper, which follows from the other ratio provided that the weight of a copper drachma be discoverable, it is necessary both to show that, on the assumption that the ratio of exchange was 120:1 and the normal weight of the drachma was the Attic, the coins can be classified into suitable subdivisions both of the obol and of 20 copper drachmae, and to provide an explanation for the double series of fractions. Here if I wished I could stop, and, ignoring the table of weights proposed by M. Revillout, whose classification and theory of normal weights are quite different from Mr. Poole's, settle the questions at issue by an appeal to the authority of the first numismatist on the subject. Seeing that Mr. Poole has adopted the theory that the normal weights of the copper coins were on the Attic standard, and that the normal weight of the largest copper coins was 20 drachmae, which are on the theory of an exchange ratio of 120:1 the obol, it will naturally be asked, 'What is the use of going further? Is not Mr. Poole's verdict sufficient? and even if it is not, how can you who are not a numismatist expect to strengthen it?' The fact that Mr. Poole, having for a short time accepted M. Revillout's theory of the Phoenician standard of the weights, deliberately rejected it in favour of another explanation before publishing his Catalogue is a sufficiently strong condemnation of M. Revillout's theory, and had M. Revillout in his recent re-issue of the *Lettres* renounced his classification, there would have been no necessity for my discussing a superseded system. But as M. Revillout, who has committed in his classification, as I shall show, blunders which would have been incredible if he had not made them, has made no alterations in his theory of the weights, and dismisses the condemnation of his theory by the first authority on the subject with the remark, 'Maintenant M. Poole en est revenu à son ancienne erreur qu'il a encore essayé de défendre dans son catalogue,' it is necessary to put an end to possible misconceptions, and to show on the one hand how and why Mr. Poole's conclusions based on recorded facts solve the numerous difficulties, and on the other how and why the generalizations of M. Revillout break down. I therefore proceed to a more or less detailed examination of M. Revillout's theory and that of Mr. Poole, into which I wish, though with considerable hesitation, to introduce a few unimportant modifications; and will only preface my remarks by repeating that until a greater authority on Ptolemaic coins than Mr. Poole shall arise, the question has been long ago settled, at any rate for those who are not numismatists, and that if I have to spend my readers' time in criticizing the revival of an obsolete theory, it is not I who am to blame.

§ 6. *M. Revillout's theory of the Phoenician standard of the copper coinage.*

M. Revillout, starting with the exchange ratio of 120 : 1, supposes that the 20 copper drachmae, or a copper 'argenteus-outen,' or an obol on the silver standard, weighed the same as 20 silver drachmae on the Phoenician standard which was in use for gold and silver from the end of Soter's reign onwards.

Having obtained the weights of a large number of copper coins, he arranges them according to the following table of 'principales séries,' in which, as the differences between the coins are clearer when the weights are expressed in grains than when expressed in grammes and in Mr. Poole's table the weights are given in grains, I have converted

M. Revillout's weights into their nearest English equivalents. It may first be stated that M. Revillout takes 207–223 grs. as the average weight of the actual silver tetradrachms, but it is the higher extreme which is the normal weight, according to Mr. Poole.

Denomination in silver.	Denomination in copper dr.	Actual weight.	Supposed highest normal weight.
1½ obol	30	1580 grains	1668 grains
1¼ obol	25	1280–1390	1390
obol	20	1032–1112	1112
¾ obol	15	774–834	834
⅝ obol	(12½)	635–695	695
½ obol	10	516–556	556
(⅖ obol)	8	414–445	445
⅜ obol	(7½)	387–417	417
¼ obol	5	258–278	278
(⅕ obol)	4	207–223	223
⅛ obol	(2½)	129–139	139
(1/10 obol)	2	104–111	111
1/16 obol	(1¼)	64–70	70
(1/20 obol)	1	52–56	56
(1/40 obol)	½	26–28	28
(1/80 obol)	¼	13–14	14

The advantages of this classification, provided that it represents the facts, are obvious. In the first place it will be observed that the actual weights of all the coins have an obliging method of stopping short at the precise point where, on M. Revillout's theory of their highest normal weights, they ought to stop. Secondly, the symmetry of the classification is perfect. On the one hand the coins representing fractions of the obol which are enclosed in brackets occur only in the period after copper drachmae were instituted, and those representing copper drachmae enclosed in brackets occur only before the period of copper drachmae. The only fractions of the obol are therefore the coins divided according to eighths or chalci, the ordinary Greek fractions of the obol, and the subdivisions of the 20 drachmae piece give only round numbers. There are no fractions which ought to be there and are not, still less any that ought not to be there but are. Could there be a more convincing proof of M. Revillout's theory that until the reign of Philopator copper was ' only for the Greeks,' and that the coins represent only the obol and its normal fractions, and on the other hand that the copper drachmae, implying the extensive use of copper, were the invention of Philopator?

But what are the facts? On this point M. Revillout does not afford any help. The only approach towards a fact in his discussion of the weights (*Lettres*, pp. 113-117) is the statement that an indefinite number of coins weigh 102 grammes, unless it be a quotation from Mommsen about the weight of coin mentioned by Pindar. In all the other cases he gives generalizations about the 'limits' within which the coins fell; sometimes he states how many coins fell within those 'limits,' though generally he does not do even that. But on the actual weights of actual coins, from which alone his theory could be tested, he is silent. Nothing is said of their condition, a knowledge of which is the first essential before any reliance can be placed on their weights; nothing of their provenance, though, as Mr. Poole shows, the copper coinage of the Cyrenaica and Cyprus had distinct features of its own, which differentiate it from the coinage of Egypt and Phoenicia and make it at least questionable how far the weights of coins from the Cyrenaica and Cyprus can afford a solution of Egyptian coinage; and with regard to the dates he gives only the crude division between coins belonging to the period before Philopator and coins belonging to the period after. Lastly, M. Revillout's theory is confessedly incomplete, for he gives us only generalizations about ' les principales séries' (*Lettres*, p. 113).

His generalizations must therefore be tested by the recorded weights of the coins as they are found in Mr. Poole's table. Here of course reference is always made to the particular coins, whether the weight given represents the average of a particular number, or whether it is based on single coins. The coins whose weights are given were selected on account of their excellent condition (Catal. Introd., p. xci), and every available information about their dates and provenances is placed before the reader. Lastly, Mr. Poole gives not only the principal series but the exceptional weights which he finds, however difficult they may be to reconcile with the classification which he proposes. And if it be objected that this contrast is unfair to M. Revillout and that it is unreasonable to expect a precise classification from any one who is not a trained numismatist, my answer is that M. Revillout, by the republication of his classification unaltered in spite of Mr. Poole's Catalogue, has still chosen to appeal in support of his theory to the coins, and to the coins he must go.

On comparing the facts recorded by Mr. Poole with the generalizations of M. Revillout four inconsistencies attract attention : (1) that the coins which, according to M. Revillout, not only ought to occur but do occur only in the first period, nevertheless occur in the second, and vice versa ; (2) that some series of coins which M. Revillout includes in his 'principales séries' do not occur in Mr. Poole's table at all ; (3) that other coins which are extremely common do not occur in M. Revillout's table ; (4) that the actual coins by no means stop short at the exact point where, on M. Revillout's theory, their normal weights stop short. I will first take the chief instances of each inconsistency and then discuss their combined effect upon M. Revillout's theory.

The 1½ obol of M. Revillout does not occur in Mr. Poole's table. How many examples M. Revillout had before him he does not say, but the coin must be extremely rare, since it is not represented in the collection of the British Museum. The actual weights of the 1½ obol are, according to M. Revillout, 1280–1390. There are however coins of 1445 and 1413, the first being the average weight of seven Egyptian coins assigned by Mr. Poole to Ptolemy Philadelphus. M. Revillout's ¾ obol does not appear in the British Museum collection, the only coin approaching it being a Phoenician coin of 752 grains belonging to Euergetes I ; but it is very difficult to suppose that this is an example of a series whose normal weight rises to 834 grains. The ⅝ obol is not, as M. Revillout supposes, confined to the first three Ptolemies. Egyptian coins of 684 and 656 grains occur in the reigns of Epiphanes and Philometor. Therefore, on M. Revillout's theory of its denomination in silver, it must have then been equivalent to 12½ copper drachmae. Next, the coin whose actual weight, according to M. Revillout, is 414–445 grains and denomination 8 copper drachmae is not found in Mr. Poole's table, any more than his supposed coin of 387–417 or ½ obol. On the other hand, there is an Egyptian coin belonging to Philopator which weighs 486, and there is a very large series of coins of somewhat varying weights (325, 368, 332, 323, 330, 316, 354, 316, 354, 370), enjoying the sole distinction in Mr. Poole's list of being assigned to

every reign from Soter I to Soter II, not one of which is found in
M. Revillout's list.   M. Revillout's brilliant imagination has at this
point soared so completely out of the region of facts that it is difficult
to bring him back to earth at all.

First as to the supposed coins representing 8 copper drachmae and
⅔ obol; even admitting their existence, it will be noticed that their actual
weights, according to M. Revillout, overlap each other, and as numerous
examples show that M. Revillout's assignment of certain coins to the
period before Philopator and certain coins to the period after is quite
invalid, he has clearly made two series out of one.   M. Revillout may
adopt whichever denomination suits him best ; both he cannot have.
But it is worth while to point out that the one denomination will give
him an inconvenient fraction of the obol, the other an inconvenient
fraction of the copper drachma, and that whichever denomination he
adopts the weights of the other one will be a strong argument against
his theory of the normal weight of the denomination which he has
adopted being correct ; and that if his theory of the normal weights will
not suit the coins, it is not the coins which can be ignored.   Secondly,
to extricate M. Revillout from the inevitable consequences of his remarkable blunder in omitting from his list of 'principales séries' the very
commonest series of Ptolemaic coins is not my affair.   Nevertheless, the
least havoc is wrought in his system by supposing—what is from the
weights the most probable solution – that this series which he has
omitted represents a normal weight which is half of that series which
on M. Revillout's theory is ¾ obol.   The omitted series then is
$\frac{3}{10}$ obol or 6¾ copper drachmae.   That both these fractions are highly
unsatisfactory, and in fact unintelligible, is of course obvious, but some
denomination has to be found for these coins between the denominations
which on M. Revillout's theory are ⅔ obol and ¼ obol, and I have been
unable to find any better explanation than that which I have suggested.

M. Revillout's ¼ obol may perhaps pass, although the coins do not
suit it by any means so much as from his statement of their actual weight
would be supposed, as the majority of those coins which can be
assigned to this denomination have lower weights than 258 grains.   The
next two denominations present insuperable difficulties..   The coins
whose actual weight is from 207–223 grains are represented in Mr.
Poole's table by one series whose average weight is 214, but they all

come from Cyprus, and are therefore a very slender foundation for founding a theory of the normal weight of Egyptian coins; and it is far more probable that these coins are an exceptionally light issue of the series which M. Revillout makes his $\frac{1}{4}$ obol. Between this doubtful denomination of 4 copper drachmae weighing 207–223 and his next denomination of $\frac{1}{8}$ obol weighing 129–139 grains, M. Revillout has again committed the extraordinary mistake of omitting from his 'principales séries' a whole series of extremely common coins. From Euergetes I's reign five coins from Phoenicia and four from Egypt have an average weight of 168 grains, while there are two examples of 180 and 157; 171 is the average weight of three coins from Egypt belonging to Philopator's reign, 170 the average of six from Cyprus belonging to Epiphanes, and coins ranging from 145–170 are common in the reigns of Philometor, Euergetes II, and Soter II with various provenances. The extreme commonness of this series was apparently sufficient to secure its rejection from M. Revillout's list of 'principales séries,' amongst which are frequently found coins whose very existence may be doubted, and which must in any case, since they are not found in the magnificent collection of the British Museum, be extremely rare. But as this series exists in great abundance, a place has somehow to be found for it in M. Revillout's system, though the stability of that ingenious fabric has already become so questionable that a fresh shock is likely to prove fatal to it altogether. But the easiest, which is also the most probable, theory is to suppose a coin whose denomination is half that coin equivalent to $\frac{1}{16}$ obol or $6\frac{1}{4}$ copper drachmae of which the insertion in M. Revillout's system was found to be necessary. This series therefore will be $\frac{5}{32}$ obol or $3\frac{1}{8}$ copper drachmae, which is a more inconvenient fraction than ever.

Next to his $\frac{1}{8}$ obol, which, it may be noticed, is much commoner in the period after Philopator than before and therefore must be also $2\frac{1}{2}$ copper drachmae, M. Revillout places his copper didrachm of 104–111 grains. As this coin occurs in Ptolemy III's reign it must then have been $\frac{1}{10}$ obol. Next comes his $\frac{1}{16}$ obol, which may pass, though whether it can be assigned only to the period before Philopator rests on the admissibility or the reverse of coins weighing 67 grains from Cyprus in the reign of Philometor, and a similar kind of difficulty exists concerning the occurrence of his copper drachma before Philopator's reign, when it would be $\frac{1}{20}$ obol. M. Revillout has by this time so effectually led his readers to expect the omission of a more than usually common series in his table, that it is not surprising to find no mention in it of a number of very common coins weighing 40, 45, 39, 40, 46, 40, 38, 32, 35, 33, 30 grains of various dates and provenances. The simplest explanation of them on his theory is to suppose that most, if not all, are half of either his copper didrachm or his $\frac{1}{16}$ obol, though either course is practically fatal to supposing that his theory of their normal weights can be correct, and either course involves him in a still more inconvenient fraction, both of the obol and of the copper drachma, than those which have already been found to be necessary.

The denominations of the smaller coins are, on any theory, so doubtful that it is not worth while to discuss them, beyond pointing out the fact that the weight which, on M. Revillout's theory, represents the $\frac{1}{4}$ copper drachma has not yet been found in coins which can certainly be ascribed to Egypt or Phoenicia, and that the period in which the coin occurs is precisely that period in which M. Revillout says that it does not.

To sum up the leading objections to M. Revillout's classification, in the first place the only chronological determination which he gives is not only misleading but incorrect, and he has therefore found himself involved in a number of fractions both of the obol and of copper drachmae which are more or less inconvenient and improbable. If M. Revillout can show on numismatical grounds why the coins, which Mr. Poole assigned both to the period before Philopator and to the period after, in reality belong to either one period or the other, I am ready to accept his division. But if, as seems more probable, his chief, perhaps his only, reason for assigning the coins to one period or the other was that such a division was necessary for his theory, while giving ready credence to this necessity, I cannot treat seriously a division that so palpably assumes the whole point which it was required to prove. Secondly, the weights of the actual coins are, to postpone other objections, very much more irregular than M. Revillout allows. So far from the actual weights of most coins corresponding with M. Revillout's supposed normal weights, there are considerable variations both above and below. If M. Revillout should argue that these irregular coins are the exception, my answer is that by suppressing their weights and their numbers compared with those which he says are the 'principales séries,' he begs the whole question at issue, and moreover, though the precise condition of admission into M. Revillout's 'principales séries' must remain a matter of conjecture, it at any rate had little to do with the commonness of the series.

Thirdly, in order to obtain any approach to a satisfactory classification which will give the ordinary fractions of the obol and the intelligible fractions of 20 copper drachmae, M. Revillout's theory rests on several series of coins which are not found in Mr. Poole's table. I do not intend here to discuss the question whether any coin so rare that it is not represented in the table of copper coins in the British Museum can be made to serve as one of M. Revillout's 'principales séries.' When it is known where these coins are, what is their number, what their condition, what their precise weight, what their probable date, and what their probable provenance, it will be time to discuss them as evidence for or against M. Revillout's and Mr. Poole's theories. But M. Revillout has by the astonishing omissions from his classification completely given away his case, and forfeited any right to expect the world to accept his generalizations about the weights of coins, whose very existence he has not yet proved.

All the faults of M. Revillout's system however, amply sufficient though they are to show its powerlessness to overcome the difficulties with which every system has to contend, pale into insignificance beside his extraordinary mistake, in still ignoring in his classification of 'les principales séries' three series of coins, which were not only three of the very commonest series, but were absolutely fatal to the symmetry, and therefore to the correctness, of his system.

Further comment on M. Revillout's classification is needless, since the internal evidence, which is by far the most important, has sufficiently condemned it. But for the sake of completeness I will add what appears to be a strong external argument against it.

M. Revillout's theory supposes the identity of weight between 20 copper drachmae or one copper 'argenteus-outen,' and 20 silver drachmae or one silver 'argenteus-outen,' both on the Phoenician standard. At first sight there would seem to be no difficulty in supposing that, as the silver 'argenteus-outen' on the Phoenician standard was called an argenteus, although it only weighed ½ of the real uten, so the copper 'argenteus-outen' might weigh only ⅔ of the real uten. There is however an essential difference between the two cases, which becomes apparent as soon as the origin of the term 'argenteus,' i. e. uten, as the equivalent of 20 silver drachmae is considered. When Soter began to coin silver, his first tetradrachms were, as has been stated, on the Attic standard and their normal weight 270 grs. The difference between 20 silver drachmae and the argenteus-outen of about 1400 grs. is, as M. Revillout himself has occasion to point out, too trifling to be considered. When the weight of the silver coins was reduced to the Phoenician standard, it was natural that the demotic names continued to be used, although the divergence in weight between the real uten and the coins called argentei had become serious.

But this analogy does not hold good for the copper argentei. Here there is no question of a coin which once approximately weighed an uten and, though diminished in weight, still represented the same denomination, but rather of the adoption of new terms to express coins whose normal weights, as Mr. Poole remarks, had not diminished. Moreover there is this difference that while in silver there never were two denominations issued simultaneously, one approximately weighing the uten the other not, in copper there were, according to M. Revillout's own theory, two series, one corresponding almost exactly to the real uten, and another weighing on the average 280 grains less. Yet on M. Revillout's theory it is the latter coin, not the former coin approximating to the real uten, which in copper received the name 'argenteus' or uten. It may be objected that the 'nouvel outen monétaire' representing ⅛ of the old uten had been for a hundred years in existence; but this hardly alters the difficulty of supposing that one of the most conservative nations in the world, a nation whose conservatism is shown by nothing clearer than the fact of their preferring with regard to the silver coinage an approximately equivalent term in their own language to the official term used by their rulers, had in one hundred years so far forgotten their ancient and historic weights, that they applied the names of argenteus and kati not to classes of coins which were almost, perhaps actually, identical with them, but to another series of classes approximating in weight much less closely to the real and historic weights.

At any rate it will hardly be denied that a theory of the copper drachma which will make the normal weights of the various denominations correspond closely, if not actually, to the literal meaning of the demotic names will possess a great advantage; and it is in fact such a theory of the copper drachma which Mr. Poole has adopted, though on the evidence of the coins themselves.

§. 7. *The theory of the Egyptian standard of the copper coinage.*

Mr. Poole in his Catalogue hesitates between the Egyptian and the Attic standard for the copper coins. On p. xxxvii he thinks it is probably Egyptian, on p. xci he adopts the Attic in preference on the ground that 'the subdivisions would rather suggest the Attic system, and it is unlikely that an Egyptian one would have been forced on the inhabitants of Cyprus and the Cyrenaïca.' But he proceeds to say 'The difference is too small to be of consequence in the comparison, considering the irregularity with which the copper money was struck,' and concludes by referring the reader to M. Revillout's researches in the demotic papyri. In the light of the new information afforded by the Greek papyri discovered since 1883, the examination of M. Revillout's speculations based on the demotic papyri has shown that Mr. Poole's estimate of their value was far too high ; and M. Revillout's classification of weights, to which I have been unable to find any reference in Mr. Poole's work except on p. xxxvii where he remarks that 'since M. Revillout's researches doubt has been cast on this hypothesis' (that the copper coinage was on the Egyptian standard), has already been disposed of. The theory of the Egyptian standard has therefore to be decided by reference to the coins in accordance with the facts given in Mr. Poole's table and by general considerations, but without reference to M. Revillout's theories which cannot now affect it either for good or for evil.

As Mr. Poole concedes that the difference in the normal weights of the denominations on the Attic and Egyptian standard is of practically no consequence, so that, as far as the coins are concerned, they will suit either theory, and as the latter standard is the one which I wish to propose as the theoretical standard of normal weights, I will first give a table of supposed normal weights, and then explain and, if I can, justify the slight modifications which I have ventured to introduce into Mr. Poole's system. It is not necessary here to give the actual weights,

H h

which the reader will find stated at length in Mr. Poole's table (Catal. p. xcii).

Denomination in silver.	Denomination in copper.	Supposed normal weight.
obol	20 dr. = 1 uten	1400 grains
$\frac{4}{5}$	16	1120
$\frac{1}{2}$	10	700
$\frac{2}{5}$	8	560
$\frac{1}{4}$	5	350
$\frac{1}{5}$	4 = 1 shekel	280
$\frac{1}{8}$	$2\frac{1}{2}$	175
$\frac{1}{10}$	2 = 1 kati	140
$\frac{1}{16}$	$1\frac{1}{4}$	87.5
$\frac{1}{20}$	1	70
$\frac{1}{32}$	$\frac{5}{8}$	43.75
$\frac{1}{40}$	$\frac{1}{2}$	35
$\frac{1}{64}$	$\frac{5}{16}$	21.87
$\frac{1}{80}$	$\frac{1}{4}$	17.5

In so far as the denominations which I propose are taken direct from Mr. Poole's table, it is not necessary for me to justify them in detail. Mr. Poole considered them on the whole the most suitable, and that is sufficient. Difficulties and exceptions are of course numerous, as the reader will see by referring to Mr. Poole's table, and difficulties and exceptions there must be to every theory of a coinage so irregular. The question is—which theory will explain the greatest number of coins with the greatest symmetry; and it was because M. Revillout could only obtain any approach towards symmetry by ignoring the commonest coins, that his theory breaks down. Moreover, exceptions are of two kinds, those above a supposed normal weight and those below it, and of the two the first class is much the harder to explain. Impoverishment of the Exchequer or frauds on the part of the Mint supply an explanation for the frequent issue of coins even far below the normal weights, and it is perhaps to causes which are the converse of these, to a stop in the appreciation of silver, coinciding with the appointment of a liberal director of the Mint, that issues of coins rising above the normal weights may be assigned. It must also be taken into account that coins often gain weight by oxidization as well as lose it. But the existence of coins above the supposed normal weight remains a permanent difficulty. It is therefore to some extent an advantage to place the normal weights as high as possible, since in that case there are fewer coins above them and more below; and this advantage, whatever it be worth, is gained by raising the supposed normal weights from the Attic to the Egyptian standard, and substituting a 20 drachma piece or uten of 1400 grains for Mr. Poole's 20 Attic drachmae of 1340. Moreover, if it is supposed that 20 Attic drachmae were equated to the uten, this hypothesis perhaps helps to explain the variations in the weights of the coins which may have been issued now according to one system, now according to the other, in the different countries.

Mr. Poole considers the coins whose weights are 1023, 1082, and 1128 grains to be exceptionally light issues of the 20 drachma piece or obol. But though there are great irregularities in the weights of other denominations there are none so great as these, and I prefer therefore to suppose the existence of another denomination between the obol and the $\frac{1}{2}$ obol. As the copper coins have to be explained primarily as fractions of the obol, not as fractions of 20 copper drachmae, which were afterwards equated to the fractions of the obol the choice lies between $\frac{4}{5}$ and $\frac{3}{4}$. The second fraction is in some respects simpler, but its normal weight, 1050 grains, does not suit the coins so well as the normal weight of the other fraction. Moreover, between the coin whose denomination is $\frac{1}{2}$ obol or 10 drachmae and the coin whose denomination is $\frac{1}{10}$ obol or a copper didrachm, Mr. Poole sees two series alternating with each other, one $\frac{1}{2}$, $\frac{1}{4}$, $\frac{1}{8}$, the other $\frac{2}{3}$, $\frac{1}{5}$, $\frac{1}{10}$. For the sake of symmetry therefore it is convenient to suppose a $\frac{4}{5}$ obol between the obol and the $\frac{1}{2}$ obol, and the difficulty of the fraction $\frac{4}{5}$ is not any greater than that of $\frac{2}{3}$, $\frac{1}{5}$, or $\frac{1}{10}$. I have already pointed out that this second series, $\frac{2}{3}$, $\frac{1}{5}$, $\frac{1}{10}$, which is found alternating with the easily explicable series of $\frac{1}{2}$, $\frac{1}{4}$, $\frac{1}{8}$, $\frac{1}{16}$, causes the principal difficulty in Ptolemaic copper coins, and on this point the theory of the Egyptian standard seems to offer a solution. For since, as I have said, there are historical analogies for the case of a conquering race imposing its own silver coinage on the conquered, but retaining the pre-existing system of copper coinage, there is not much difficulty, if the theory of the Egyptian standard is correct, in supposing that these fractions of the obol, $\frac{4}{5}$, $\frac{2}{3}$, $\frac{1}{5}$, $\frac{1}{10}$, were issued because they were the fractions of the copper uten to which the Egyptians had from time immemorial been accustomed. But the advantage of this explanation, the value of which I leave to the consideration of numismatists, is of course shared by Mr. Poole's theory to practically the same degree, since whether the normal standard was Egyptian or Attic or both, the obol was at least as approximately identical in weight with the uten as was the silver 'argenteus outen' with the 20 Attic drachmae of which in Soter's reign it was the equivalent.

The fact seems to have been that there were two series of fractions, one for Greeks representing the normal fractions of the Attic obol, the other for Egyptians representing fractions of the uten. The Greek papyri naturally mention only chalci or the Greek fractions of the obol. With regard to the demotic names of the copper coins, it is for demotic scholars to decide whether the copper coins representing in weight the uten and its subdivisions, shekels and kati, were in the third century ever *called* utens, shekels and kati of copper, as they were called in the second, or whether they were treated only as fractions of the silver kati. In the latter case, it is probable that mentions of the Egyptian series of fractions $\frac{2}{5}$, $\frac{1}{5}$, $\frac{1}{10}$ of the obol or $\frac{1}{30}$, $\frac{1}{60}$, $\frac{1}{120}$ of the kati will be found in demotic accounts of the third century corresponding to 2 shekels, 1 shekel, and 1 kati, which are found in demotic papyri of the second.

Between his didrachm of 135 grains and his drachma of 67.5 Mr. Poole places a supposed $1\frac{1}{2}$ drachma weighing 101.25, which would be 105 on the Egyptian standard. Both these normal weights are somewhat high, for the actual coins weigh 100, 92.5, 85 Phoenicia: 80, 75 Egypt: 85 Cyrenaïca: 96 Phoen.: 79 Cyprus: 80 Eg.: 91 Cyren: 70, 87 Cyr. I have therefore preferred to make the supposed normal weight of this series 87.5, i. e. half the coin weighing 175, and double the coin of which Mr. Poole considers the normal weight to be 45, while on my theory its normal weight is 43.75. These modifications which I have suggested have perhaps an advantage in making the denominations descend more regularly, and, provided that they will suit the coins, the fractions $\frac{1}{16}$ and $\frac{1}{32}$ obol are more convenient than $\frac{1}{10}$ and $\frac{1}{30}$.

The next coin is on Mr. Poole's Attic standard $\frac{1}{8}$ drachma or $\frac{1}{10}$ obol, and on mine $\frac{1}{64}$ obol or $\frac{1}{8}$ copper drachma, the difference between our supposed normal weights for it being just over $\frac{1}{2}$ grain. But the fixing of all these small denominations below the drachma must remain largely a matter of conjecture, as even a slight irregularity of weight in the coins is sufficient to make it uncertain to what series it should be assigned. The important thing is to fix the larger denominations, and on all the essential points the theory of the Egyptian standard is perfectly consistent not only with Mr. Poole's facts, but with the conclusions which he draws from them. Whether the few slight modifications in his system suggested by an amateur like myself have any value is a question which I leave to the consideration of numismatists, who alone can decide it. But if my suggested improvements are found unsatisfactory, their rejection will only bring out into still clearer relief the authority attaching to the illustrious numismatist's own system and to his condemnation of M. Revillout's.

There is one point which although already stated, will bear repetition, that the Ptolemaic copper coins must, if not in the order of time yet in the order of thought, be explained as fractions of the obol before they are explained as copper drachmae. My reason for insisting on this is that Mr. Poole in his list of supposed denominations was clearly to some extent influenced by M. Revillout's erroneous but generally accepted theory that copper played a very unimportant part in Egypt before Philopator and the period of copper drachmae. As Mr. Poole does not in his Catalogue commit himself to any theory of the exchange ratio, it was natural that he should look at the copper coins as multiples of the Attic drachma, since he makes no statement about the weight of a copper obol. But the coins were obols and fractions of obols long before they were copper drachmae, and though it is necessary for purposes of argument to begin with them as copper drachmae, it is as far back as the reign of Philadelphus that the true meaning of the weights is found in that equation of the obol with the uten of copper, which, following equally from Mr. Poole's theory of the Attic standard or mine of the Egyptian, appears to offer the least difficult, the most symmetrical, and the most satisfactory classification of the coins.

This brings me to the last question to be considered, the origin of the copper coinage. For the reign of Soter there are only a few demotic papyri containing no mention of copper, and a certain number of copper coins, which, so far as their provenances can be ascertained, are assigned by Mr. Poole with a few exceptions to the Cyrenaïca or Cyprus. How far therefore these coins can be accepted as evidence for the Egyptian coinage may well be doubted, for, if there is any appreciable difference between Egyptian or Phoenician coins and those from the Cyrenaïca or Cyprus, it is that the Egyptian and Phoenician coins tend to be somewhat heavier on the average, so that the Attic rather than the Egyptian standard is the more suitable for Cyprus and the Cyrenaïca, in addition to the argument brought by Mr. Poole of the improbability that an Egyptian standard would be forced on the outlying Greek dependencies. But a comparison of these copper coins assigned to Soter's reign with the coins from the Cyrenaïca and Cyprus of a later date shows that the normal weights did not materially alter after Soter's reign, and it may therefore be conjectured that copper in Egypt, so far as it was used in Soter's reign, was on the same standard as it was afterwards.

The circumstances of that reign were of course exceptional. The conquests of Alexander had poured on the Hellenistic world the vast treasures of the East, of which Soter had secured his full share. Necessarily for a time silver was much cheapened, and as Soter could afford at first to issue his tetradrachms on the Attic standard, the copper coins which were actually or approximately on the Attic standard, stood during that period at the ratio of 120 : 1. But the period of cheap silver during which even the obol seems to have been coined in silver, since the large copper coins representing the obol are not assigned by Mr. Poole to an earlier date than Philadelphus' reign and there are a few very small silver coins which may be assigned to that of Soter, soon passed away. Soter first reduced his silver coins to the Rhodian standard, bringing the ratio between silver and copper up to 140 : 1, and finally reached the Phoenician standard for silver with a ratio of 150 : 1, maintained in reality by Philadelphus and Euergetes, but only in name by their successors, who, as has been explained, adopted the alternative of debasing the silver down to the market ratio in preference to that of reflecting the market ratio in a pure coinage of diminished weight.

§ 8. *Conclusion.*

Of M. Revillout's two brilliant and elaborate fabrics, based on his interpretation of the demotic papyri and his classification of the coins, by the glamour of which he has stood forth in the eyes of Europe since

1882 as the chief authority on the subject, what remains? The first has in the light of the new information afforded by the Greek papyri assumed an aspect so changed as to be hardly recognizable; while of the second a comparison with the recorded facts has left hardly one stone standing. In bidding farewell to M. Revillout's ingenious but unsound speculations, the conclusion of the whole matter is this: that the science of numismatics is concerned with actual, not with imaginary coins, and that if M. Revillout had been anxious not to risk his high place in the long roll of the illustrious successors of Champollion, he would have left questions of coinage to the numismatist, or, when he had to discuss them, he would at any rate have listened, and listened humbly, to what the numismatist has to say.

The evidence for the solution of the three problems which I proposed at the beginning of this essay has now been reviewed. With regard to the discount on copper and the standard metal in use at various periods the papyri have provided the material for an approximate generalization, which was both confirmed and explained by the history of the silver and copper coinage. Both papyri and coins were found to converge towards the exchange ratio of 120 : 1; though they have not yet finally reached the goal. Lastly the two divisions of the third question, the ratio between silver and copper as metals and their ratio as coins, were found to be practically one question, the answer to which is that from the time of Philadelphus the rate was either in reality or name approximately 150 : 1; and the answer to this problem is sufficient to convert, at least provisionally, the whole system of Ptolemaic coinage, of which the outline as complete as the evidence will allow has been given in these pages, into a consistent whole.

Much still remains to be done. The publication of detailed and accurate catalogues of the Ptolemaic copper coins in other European collections on the lines of Mr. Poole's great work will probably go far to solve many of the difficulties of classification which have yet to be overcome. The demotic papyri may be expected to give some new and much confirmatory evidence for the extensive use of copper before Philopator and the problems connected with it. But it is from Greek papyri, especially of the reigns of Philopator and Epiphanes, when taken in conjunction with the coins, that most will probably some day be learnt, since it is there, if anywhere, that an instance of the conversion of silver drachmae into copper drachmae is most likely to be found.

It is even possible that the final solution of some of the problems may be within reach. Prof. Flinders Petrie has handed over to me for publication the remainder of the vast Petrie collection, which exceeds in bulk, though it falls short in importance, the selections already published by Prof. Mahaffy. Many of these papyri, it has now appeared from the occurrence in the collection of documents dated as late as P. P. xlvi, might belong to the reigns of Philopator and Epiphanes, and the cursory examination which I have made of them has shown me that many of them probably belong to the end rather than the middle of the third century, and has resulted in my publishing those printed in App. ii, of which the last is of the utmost importance for the history of the coinage. To the further examination of this collection, supplemented by the papyrus mummy cases of the same period, which I found at Gurob last spring but have not yet had time to open, I propose, with the aid of Mr. A. S. Hunt, to devote myself in the course of the next few years, in the hope of making more complete the answer here given in outline to the questions of the coinage, the solution of which must always, as Lumbroso has observed, form the basis of a correct understanding of Ptolemaic political economy.

I conclude by thanking Profs. Wilcken, Gardner, and Mahaffy who have kindly revised the proofs of this Appendix, and who, I may add, have expressed their agreement with the general theory which I have proposed.

INDEX.

I. PROPER NAMES AND PLACE NAMES.

(The figures in heavier type refer to columns.)

I i

II. SYMBOLS AND ABBREVIATIONS.

III. GENERAL INDEX.

59. 10; 61-72 *sacp.*; 74. 5; 76. 5;
98. 2, 3; 103. 2, 8; Fr. 6 (e) 10.
αλλως 30. 6.
αμγαιος 97. 7.
αμπελος 36. 5.
αμπελων 25. 2; 26. 17; 33. 11, 13,
19; 36. 12, 15; 37. 10.
αναγειν 12. 3; 44. 16; 52. 8, 10, 17.
αναγραφειν 27. 18; 47. 11.
αναμετρησις 27. 2.
αναφερειν 11. 1, 7; 18. 15; 19. 5;
75. 2, 3.
αναφορα 16. 10; 34. 8; 53. 24; 56.
17; Fr. 1 (c) 1.
ανευ 10. 11, 18.
ανηλισκειν 50. 9; 51. 17, 18; 54. 19.
ανηλωμα 48. 11; 51. 20; 53. 25;
55. 4.
αντι 41. 19.
αντιγραφευς 3. 2; 10. 6, 11, 14, 18;
11. 2, 4, 8, 12; 12. 1; 13. 3; 16. 2;
20. 14; 25. 6, 11; 28. 6, 12; 29.
4; 30. 11, 17; 32. 6; 33. 4; 34.
12; 37. 4; 40. 1, 20; 41. 2, 4, 8;
43. 22; 44. 13; 45. 16, 19; 46.
8, 9; 47. 10; 48. 1, 5; 49. 12,
16, 23; 50. 3, 23; 51. 15, 20;
54. 16, 20, 22; 55. 21, 22; 81. 6;
82. 3; 84. 3; 87. 13; 88. 14;
96. 4; 97. 1; 104. 1; Fr. 4 (i) 1;
Fr. 5 (a) 1, (c) 5.
αντιγραφον 18. 1, 4, 7; 27. 4, 18;
37. 1, 6.
αντιλεγειν 28. 5; 29. 12; 89. 2.
απαιτειν 19. 14; 35. 3.
απας 18. 9.
απειθειν 43. 10.
απεχειν 17. 2.
απογραφειν 14. 3; 26. 1, 6, 15; 27.
9, 16; 29. 2; 33. 9, 15; 36. 4, 17;
49. 10; 50. 21; 51. 7, 17; 52. 14;
78. 4; 85. 10; 86. 12; Fr. 2 (d)
1, 2; Fr. 6 (d) 10.
απογραφη 14. 2; 86. 11, 13.

αποδεικνυειν 26. 4, 8; 27. 15; 41. 3;
54. 8; 57. 8; 59. 9; 75. 2; 87. 9.
αποδειξις 30. 15.
αποδιδοναι 19. 12, 13, 14; 25. 13;
29. 14, 17; 32. 17; 33. 21; 35.
2, 4; 41. 25; 45. 8; 46. 18; 50.
18; 84. 7; 91. 9; 103. 9.
αποδοχιον 31. 1, 19; 32. 2; 54. 18.
αποκαθαρσις 39. 10.
αποκαθισταναι 17. 5.
αποκομιζειν 30. 20.
απολειπειν 47. 5, 7.
απομοιρα 25. 12, 15; 27. 3, 17; 28.
14; 30. 18, 20, 21; 31. 1, 3; 32.
9, 17, 20.
αποπραμα 18. 16.
αποστελλειν 18. 6; 37. 6; 51. 22;
54. 17.
αποσφραγισμα 31. 17, 19; 40. 2, 5;
84. 5.
αποτιθεται 50. 17; 53. 5; 56. 21.
αποτινειν 11. 2, 5, 9; 13. 12; 15. 1,
9, 14; 19. 14; 20. 3; 21. 5; 25.
16; 26. 9; 31. 2; 33. 16; 40. 6;
41. 6; 43. 8; 44. 16; 45. 9, 15;
46. 6; 47. 7; 49. 8, 20; 50. 18;
51. 8; 55. 23; 56. 11; 75. 3;
84. 8; Fr. 2 (c) 5; Fr. 6 (d) 5.
απρακτος 49. 23.
αργος 46. 12; 47. 4.
αργυριον 24. 12; 37. 18; 39. 17;
46. 6; 47. 8; 75. 6; 77. 2.
αριστος 32. 15.
αρουρα 32. 12; 36. 5; 41. 6, 18 *bis*;
42. 9; 43. 4; 57. 7; 59. 6, 8;
61-72 *sacp.*; 87. 6. See also
Index of Symbols.
αρταβη 39. 2, 6 *bis*; 46. 16; 59. 14;
61-72 *sacp.* See also Index of
Symbols.
αρχιφυλακιτης 37. 5.
αρχωνειν 14. 3.
αρχωνης 10. 10; 11. 14; 13. 4, 7;
14. 2, 9; 34. 15, 18.

εργασια 40. 6.
εργαστηριον 44. 1, 5; 45. 20; 46.
11; 47. 4; 50. 24; 51. 1.
ερικος 103. 2.
ερρωσθε 36. 2; 37. 9.
ετερος 7. 1; 16. 10, 11; 27. 11.
ετος 24. 2; 57. 5; Fr. 6 (h) 7. See
also Index of Symbols.
ευδοκειν 29. 8.
ευρισκειν 41. 5; 48. 16; 49. 16;
56. 7.
εφεικοστος 34. 3; 56. 15.
εφισταται 48. 6, 14.
εφοδος 10. 1, 16; 12. 17.
εφοραν 25. 1.
εχειν 4. 3; 16. 3; 27. 12; 31. 3;
36. 12; 37. 10; 39. 19; 43. 12;
53. 27; 54. 7; 85. 3; 88. 6;
96. 1. εχομενος 16. 15; 18. 11;
34. 20; 56. 17. εχ. την ωνην or
τας ωνας 10. 13; 16. 3; 18. 1, 10;
20. 1; 25. 1, 16; 26. 9; 27. 1;
28. 3, 15; 29. 13, 16, 20; 34. 13;
41. 9; 42. 7, 14; 46. 8; 49. 14,
19, 20; 50. 15; 51. 19; 52. 4;
53. 4, 23; 54. 21; 55. 25; 57.
23; 60. 1; 84. 1, 2, 6, 9; 85. 8;
107. 9; Fr. 2 (f) 1.
εως 10. 14; 13. 13; 34. 5; 37. 14;
55. 22.

ζητειν 55. 19, 20; 56. 1, 7, 8.
ζητησις 55. 17, 23; 56. 4, 9, 13.

η μην 56. 8.
ηγεμων 37. 3.
ημερα 4. 1, 2; 6. 3; 9. 1, 5; 15. 16;
19. 13; 29. 15; 32. 7; 33. 10,
11; 34. 3, 4; 35. 4; 43. 5; 46.
13, 15; 47. 15; 48. 10, 15, 16;
49. 12; 50. 10, 14, 19; 53. 6, 7;
56. 1, 16; 75. 3, 4; 81. 4; 86.
1, 2; 93. 10.
ημερολεγδον 4. 1.

ημιολιος 54. 3.

θυσια 36. 19.

ιδιος 16. 14; 19. 3; 32. 10; 52. 13,
23; Fr. 2 (h) 2.
ιερευς 37. 17; 106. 3; 107. 4.
ιερον 33. 14, 20; 37. 15; 50. 20, 24;
51. 9, 12, 21, 25; 56. 8.
ιερος 36. 8.
ικανος 32. 4; 40. 17; 43. 16; 44.
6; 45. 14.
ιππαρχος 37. 2.
ιπωτηριον 49. 6, 13; 51. 1, 2.
ισος 39. 12; 57. 17, 21; 59. 19, 24.
ισταναι 16. 4; 18. 12.
ιστος 90. 4; 94. 2, 5.

καθαιρειν 39. 9.
καθαπερ 29. 9; 52. 27.
καθαρος 39. 3, 4, 5, 8.
καθηκειν 41. 14.
καθισταναι 3. 2; 13. 1; 21. 4, 6, 8;
29. 5; 31. 18; 34. 2; 44. 4; 45.
7, 13; 46. 8; 47. 10; 48. 1; 51.
19; 52. 27; 54. 20; 56. 14; Fr.
6 (a) 12.
καθοτι 28. 7; 45. 13; 55. 16; 74.
3; Fr. 4 (m) 2.
καθως 21. 3.
καλειν 8. 3; 21. 12, 16; 35. 3.
καπηλος 47. 11; 48. 3, 7.
καρπιμος 55. 20.
καρπος 29. 13, 18; 34. 10; 43. 5.
καταβαλλειν 48. 10; 52. 15, 18, 23;
74. 2; 75. 5.
καταβλαπτειν 40. 8; 45. 11, 15.
καταγραφη 34. 4.
καταδικαζεσθαι 5. 2.
καταλαμβανειν 46. 5.
καταπροιεναι 27. 11.
κατασκευη 45. 20; 46. 11.
κατασπειρειν 41. 6; 42. 16; 57. 8;
59. 9.

K k

www.ingramcontent.com/pod-product-compliance
Lightning Source LLC
Chambersburg PA
CBHW031401270326
41929CB00010BA/1271